PACIFIC
GRILLING

PACIFIC
GRILLING

Recipes

for the

Fire from

Baja to the

Pacific Northwest

DENIS KELLY

SASQUATCH BOOKS
SEATTLE

Printed in Canada
Distributed in Canada by Raincoast Books, Ltd.
04 03 02 01 00   5 4 3 2 1

Cover photograph: Susan Marie Anderson
Food stylist: Patty Wittman
Vintage dinnerware: Laguna (Historic Pioneer Square, Seattle)
Cover and interior design: Karen Schober
Interior illustrations: Kurt D. Hollomon
Copy editor: Barbara Fuller

Library of Congress Cataloging in Publication Data
Kelly, Denis, 1939–
    Pacific grilling : recipes for the fire from Baja to the
Pacific Northwest / by Denis Kelly.
        p.   cm.
    Includes index.
    ISBN 1-57061-175-0
    1. Barbecue cookery. II. Title.
    TX840.B3 K44 2000
    641.5'784—dc21   00-021749

Sasquatch Books
615 Second Avenue
Seattle, Washington 98104
(206) 467-4300
www.SasquatchBooks.com
books@SasquatchBooks.com

To my daughter, Meghan Kelly.

Fays ce que voudras.

—Rabelais

For Kent Liz —

Friendship is the best

Spice!

Denis Kelly

Christmas 2000

Contents

Recipe List

LAMB

DESSERTS

Essay List

ACKNOWLEDGMENTS

My hearty thanks to my daughter, Meghan Kelly, who aided me in virtually every phase of this book, from creating and testing recipes to keeping track of files and recipes to editing and proofing and making sure we met deadlines. My editor at Sasquatch Books, Gary Luke, gave constant support and encouragement and good advice throughout the project. Martha Casselman, my agent, as always was a source of help, good humor, and common sense. Justine Matthies of Sasquatch and Barbara Fuller provided clear and intelligent editorial support.

I would also like to thank those friends and fellow grillers who provided recipes, advice, tips, and inspiration: Chester Aaron, Bruce Aidells, D Alexander, Jim Bangert, Gene Cattolica, John Clark, Jeffery Clark, Ron DiGiorgio, Tom Douglas, Joel Herman, my wife, Kathy Kelly, Alan Kuehn, Mike Lopez, Alice McNeil, Tom Moran, John Neudecker, Jane O'Riordan, Ponnarong Nimearm-on, Luke Putnam, Polly Rose, Tony Salinas, Margaret Smith, Michael Wild, and, of course, Old Bill.

PACIFIC COAST: GRILL COUNTRY

Out here on the edge of the continent, with our temperate weather and outdoor way of life, it seems that just about everybody grills just about anything anytime. Grilling, or barbecuing (as West Coast folks call it, to the chagrin of Southern 'cue fanatics) is a way of life from the sunny beaches of Baja and Southern California to the rocky coasts of the Pacific Northwest. And we don't just put steak on the grill for the weekend ritual where Dad presides over the barbecue wearing a funny apron and sucking down a couple of cold ones with the neighbors. Many West Coast grillers use their hibachi or kettle barbecue or gas grill or built-in patio barbecue on a daily basis to grill everything from scallops and shark steaks from the Pacific to zucchini and tomatoes plucked from the garden to whole turkeys and loins of pork and even pizzas, grilled fruits, and berry cobblers.

Cooking food on the grill is a West Coast tradition that dates back a long way. Grilling itself is perhaps the oldest way of cooking meat and poultry (see Grilling: An Ancient Art, page 6). Native Americans all along the Pacific Coast cooked deer and rabbit and quail, seafood and fish and ground acorn dough over open fires or on flat stones heated on the coals. In the Northwest, local Indians smoke-cooked salmon and other fish on alder or cedar planks, a tradition that continues in Seattle and on the islands of Puget Sound.

The Californios who built ranchos and haciendas up and down the coast were famous for their grilled meat or carne asada. Travelers wrote of splendid feasts with seemingly unlimited amounts of beef served at fandangos and fiestas. Helen Evans Brown, in her *West Coast Cook Book* (Little, Brown, 1952), describes how "a huge fire was made, and freshly killed beef hung in the shade of a tree and vaqueros and their ladies cut off pieces every time that hunger called, and cooked it over the waiting fire. The *frazada,* which is the meat covering the ribs, was a favorite morsel. It was, according to one account, '. . . thrown on the coals and eaten half raw, with salt.' "

This West Coast grilling tradition continues from Californio times to the present day. Ms. Brown writes of a famous barbecue held every year by a sheriff of Los Angeles County, in which sixty thousand hungry voters consumed "over twelve tons of top-quality beef, hundreds of sacks of Mexican red beans, and fifty pounds of chile powder." Today grill masters in Santa Maria on California's Central Coast make a specialty of throwing huge barbecues where people come from all over the state to gorge on thick rib steaks and sirloin tri-tips grilled over native live oak coals (see Santa Maria Barbecue, page 175).

The built-in brick grill in the backyard was for a long time a standard fixture in West Coast houses and embodied a shared attitude toward entertaining and cooking. Hacienda architecture was the most popular Southern California house style in the early twentieth century, and the Californio's outdoor feasts continued on these patio barbecues. I grew up in a tract home on the outskirts of Los Angeles, and I remember the big rancho-style houses that some friends lived in. We envied the kids who lived in these old-fashioned stucco and tile-roofed houses with large patios in back and huge white-painted brick grills with tile chimneys. When we went to parties and get-togethers, their folks would fire up these brick behemoths and grill steaks and burgers and corn for crowds of people. Back home on Sundays, we made do with metal stand-up barbecues on smaller patios, but the idea was the same. Cooking outdoors on the fire was what you did when you wanted to celebrate the good life the West Coast way.

Sunset magazine and boosters of the idyllic, orange-grove-and-endless-summer way of life in the West emphasized outdoor cooking as a defining feature of the Pacific Coast style. *Sunset*'s vastly popular series Chefs of the West featured barbecue recipes from exclusively male cooks for many years until it was overcome by political correctness awhile back.

The backyard barbecue spread all over the country after World War II when the American Dream of a freestanding house with a lawn in front and a yard out back became available for the first time to large numbers of returning servicemen and -women. With the revolution of Levittown's inexpensive housing and the expansion of suburbia throughout the country, the dream included a barbecue grill where Dad could exercise his culinary talents on Sunday afternoons. And he did indeed, often in clouds of black smoke generated by those charred burgers or steaks smothered in sweet barbecue sauce that we all remember.

The invention of the kettle barbecue and easy-to-use charcoal briquettes made backyard grilling a part of our way of life, and the summer Sunday dinner of char-broiled burgers and steaks and chicken was as American as apple pie. But on the West Coast, people started to use

their grills in a different way. The kettle grill enabled us to roast turkey and chickens and hunks of savory beef on the grill. Black Southern cooks who slow-roasted pork to succulent perfection came west to work and cook in Oakland and San Francisco. And the discovery (or rediscovery) of traditional charcoals such as oak and mesquite, coupled with the availability of hardwood chips, brought new flavors and ways to cook fish and seafood and meats of all kinds.

A new attitude toward grilling came into being among West Coast chefs. Many talented cooks, amateur and professional, realized that the barbecue was not only for steaks or burgers slathered in sweet sauce, but also could be used to grill highly flavored seafood, fish, poultry, and vegetables over coals scented with the smoke from aromatic hardwoods. At creative restaurants such as Chez Panisse in Berkeley and trendy grills in Beverly Hills, at barbecue pits along the beach in San Diego and seafood houses in Seattle, in luxury hotels on Maui and on beach cookouts on Kauai, grilling became the basis of an exciting and distinctively regional Pacific Coast cuisine.

The Mexican influence on West Coast cooking is paramount. Latino cooks in Baja, in Southern California, and all along the coast created a style of grilling that is based on spicy rubs and marinades of chiles, herbs, limes and lemons, salsas, and other fresh ingredients. All along the beaches of Baja California you can find handmade grills shaded by palm frond *palapas* that turn out some of the most flavorful grilled fish and seafood you'll ever eat. There's even a little town called Puerto Nuevo, south of Tijuana, that is composed of family restaurants serving lobster and little else (see Baja Lobster or Prawns with Lime Ancho Chile Butter and Salsa Roja, page 107). Fish tacos, based on grilled white fish flavored with chiles and limes, and carne asada—highly seasoned, thin-cut steaks—are beach city favorites from Ensenada to Santa Barbara. Fajitas—lime- and chile-marinated skirt steaks—and boneless chicken thighs are popular up and down the coast.

Cooking on the Pacific Coast has always been eclectic and everchanging. Our ports open to Asia, and much of our restaurant cooking since the 1850s has been performed by Asian cooks. Chinese and Japanese—and more recently Korean, Thai, and Vietnamese—flavors and techniques have been incorporated into our West Coast cuisine. Soy, ginger, star anise, black beans, wasabi, lemongrass, and Asian sauces such as hoisin sauce and hot chile oil are all familiar tastes. Marinades and sauces based on Asian ingredients give food on the grill a spicy and luscious character, especially fish and seafood. Japan has a great tradition of grilling that ranges from elegant and elaborate (and very expensive) robata grill restaurants to roadside yakitori parlors. Chicken, beef, seafood, and vegetables are flavored with soy, ginger, sake, miso, and other Japanese favorites and grilled to perfection in even the most humble establishment. Korean tableside barbecue is very popular with West Coast diners—beef, chicken, and vegetables are marinated in spicy, garlicky, and often sweet sauces before being grilled over charcoal or gas fires. Thai and other Southeast Asian chefs are especially skilled at grilling—street grills in Bangkok serve some of the most delicious food in the world—with fiery chiles, aromatic basil and lemongrass, and pungent fish sauce providing intense and unforgettable flavors.

Hawaiian cooks love to grill over kiawe wood, mesquite brought to the islands by *panaiolos,* the early cowboys who came over to herd cattle. Hawaii's creative chefs were among the first to blend Asian flavors and ingredients into the Pacific style of cooking. Marinades and crusts based on miso, sesame, ginger, and other Asian ingredients enliven grilled fish, seafood, meat, and poultry all over the islands. While Hawaii, strictly speaking, is not on the Pacific Coast, cooks there share the coast's outdoor cooking tradition and imaginative approach to grilling. Hawaii's exciting East-West flavors and ingredients are a constant influence on grillers from San Diego to Seattle.

Vegetarian cooking is popular along the West Coast, especially in California. After all, this is where the New Age began, with thinkers like Krishnamurti, Swami Vivekanda, and Aldous Huxley in Southern California in the 1930s and 1940s and Zen masters such as Suzuki Roshi and writers like Alan Watts and Baba Ram Dass in the San Francisco Bay Area in the 1950s and 1960s. Often for religious and health reasons, many along the coast prefer not to eat meat, and grilled vegetables of every kind have become popular. Grilling brings out the innate sweetness in vegetables, and the browning provides a "meaty" flavor that is satisfying and much enjoyed. Certain grilled vegetables, such as mushrooms and eggplants, are thought of as meat substitutes for their rich textures and hearty flavors. Tofu, a soybean curd much loved in Japan and China, is delicious on the grill. Polenta, French bread, focaccia, pizza, and other grain-based foods are also delightful when grilled and can be topped with a great range of flavorful vegetables and sauces. Greens, the wildly successful vegetarian restaurant in San Francisco, is an inspiration to vegetarian chefs and grillers everywhere.

The Northwest has a long tradition of grilling fish and seafood that lives on in its restaurants, in backyard barbecues, and in the thriving Native American communities that continue to harvest and preserve salmon and other local fish and seafood. Cooked on the grill in aromatic wood smoke, salmon is especially luscious. Its high oil content stands up to high heat and the fish stays juicy and succulent. Aromatic spice rubs and salt-based cures and brines lend salmon even richer flavors and a luscious texture. The rich products of the Pacific Northwest's forests and meadows—berries, fruits, fresh vegetables of all kinds—are often incorporated into grill cooking by the region's cooks. Berry cobblers (see Alaskan Campfire Berry Cobbler, page 214), grilled fruits (see Grilled Fruit Pizza, page 220), and grilled vegetables (see Out-of-the Garden Grilled Salad, page 71) all have a place in the Northwest grill cook's repertory. Seattle's International District is home to thriving Asian restaurants and markets that have done much to enliven local grilling traditions. Rubs and marinades based on ginger, soy, wasabi, and other Asian ingredients are used creatively by local chefs and home cooks on local seafood and fish with exciting results.

Most of the flavorings from these varied cuisines—chiles and Mexican seasonings, Asian sauces, produce, and other ingredients—are widely available in West Coast supermarkets and in Latino and Asian groceries and specialty stores. For those who can't find them in their locality, I've provided mail-order sources (see Sources, page 225).

GRILLING: AN ANCIENT ART

Fire came from the sky, the place of gods and lightning, and transformed us. Early people worshiped fire, and for good reason. The first evidence of real humanity, increased brain size and the ability to walk upright, is found in the fossils of our direct ancestor, *Homo erectus.* These first men and women hunted game and gathered roots and vegetables on the African veldt, in Java, and near Peking, over a million years ago. And with the remains of *Homo erectus* we also find the earliest signs of communal hearths, the first evidence of the use of fire.

Fire changed us from being subject to nature as other animals are to being able to control our environment for the first time. Fire warmed us and protected us from predators. And fire gave new humans the ability to cook meat, to tenderize and preserve it. Cooking made animal flesh more succulent and appealing and made it easier for our bodies to absorb its rich proteins and nutrients. And how did our ancestors cook meat? They grilled their antelope steaks or mastodon cutlets or fillets of pony on a spit or a grid of green branches over the coals of their campfires. Grilling is our most ancient culinary art.

Greeks and Romans loved to grill meat, especially pork. Homer writes about heroes cutting up sacrificial animals, putting the meat onto skewers, seasoning the pieces well, and laying them on a grill over a fire in a bronze tripod, which looks surprisingly like today's kettle barbecue. The heroes offered the smoke to the gods with prayers and supplications. Then they took the cooked meat off the fire and fell to. In the epics, we hear again and again of cooks grilling choice cuts of meat—with the best cuts, the pork loin or beef fillet, going to poets and singers at the feasts. One of the first cookbooks in history, *De Re Coquinaria,* by the Roman author Apicius, features grilled and spit-roasted pork in a mind-boggling variety of ways. One of the most mouth-watering recipes describes cooking suckling pig over coals on a spit with a basting sauce of pepper, herbs, oil, onion, and spiced wine. You could put this dish on the menu at a trendy Hollywood restaurant today and sell it out in an hour or two.

In the Middle Ages, the manor house centered on a huge fireplace in which whole deer or wild boar were cooked on spits over the fire. Grilled meat, with all its luscious flavors and health-giving protein, was a luxury that only the nobility and higher clergy had access to. Peasants had to make do with bread and gruel made from the grain they grew and the occasional rabbit poached from the lord's forest or chicken or pig raised in back of the hut.

With the coming of the Industrial Age and the ensuing Agricultural Revolution in America's Midwest, meat became available to just about everyone. Vast fields of grain fed huge herds of cattle, sheep, and pigs, and by the mid-twentieth century, most Americans of all classes were able to put steaks or hamburgers, lamb chops or pork chops on the table every day. And the way we've come to love our daily meat is crisp and browned from the grill. Today hamburger joints boast that their burgers are flame-broiled, and steak houses, where tender beef is grilled directly over the fire, are the most popular type of restaurant in America.

It's no wonder that today we love meat or poultry or fish cooked over the fire. The glow from the coals and the taste of the wood smoke, the brown, crisp surface of the meat and the luscious flesh within, bring us back to our roots. Sophisticated though we are, living in a world of instant worldwide communication, in high-rises and overpopulated cities, we yearn for that taste of the wild life and dream of wood fires and chants of the hunt in swirling smoke, under a huge moon, red at the edge of the grassland.

BARBECUE: WHAT'S IT MEAN?

If you want to get an argument started, just ask any group of cooks what they mean by *barbecue.* Those with a twang in their voice that suggests the South will most likely tell you, firmly and at some length, that folk down Dixie way have the lock on barbecue and that any flat-land furriners that use the term are misguided at best, and most likely ignorant damn Yankees to boot. To most Southerners, barbecue means pork (or beef if they're from Texas) slow-cooked in a smoky fire until it is almost falling off the bone. Or it actually is falling off the bone, as in Tennessee pulled pork. Tough cuts such as pork ribs are cooked for many hours and then brushed with a spicy sweet sauce. Southern-style barbecue is popular in the big city also, and barbecue cooks from Oakland to Chicago to Kansas City vie for the honor of being called the King of 'Cue.

Well, that's one meaning of the word. Those who insist that this is the only meaning of the word *barbecue* are strict constructionists, linguistic puritans much like that columnist in the *New York Times* who's always telling us poor dummies how we ain't got a chance of using the King's English right. But there are others who say that language is determined by usage, that is, whatever we say is—if enough of us say it—right.

Where I grew up, in Los Angeles at the height of the backyard barbecue craze, when my dad said, "I think I'll barbecue this weekend," he wasn't thinking of pit-smoking a passel of shoats using Bubba Jim's prime hickory gnarls and Uncle Billy Joe's Kick-Ass Gunpowder and Molasses Sauce. He was suggesting to us eager suburban kids that he was going to put some charcoal briquettes in that thing we called the barbecue out back, let them burn down to white coals, and put a steak or some burgers on the grill. To many Americans, East and West, North and South, a barbecue is a charcoal or gas grill. The verb *to barbecue* means to grill a steak or pork chop or chicken or what you will on that thing, and barbecue sauce is what we put on the food. *Barbecue* as a freestanding noun, however, seems generally to mean what the strict constructionists want it to mean: slow-cooked pork ribs or beef in a hot, tomato-based sauce. Most of us usually don't cook this barbecue ourselves, but get it as takeout on Friday nights and end up with a greasy steering wheel from nibbling on those good ribs all the way home.

So who's right? Well, if you go along with the usage school, everybody's right. I remember getting into a long argument with a friend from Indiana who insisted that what I called a green or bell pepper was a mango. That's what his folks called this green (and sometimes red) thing he held in the hand while we stood over the gumbo. I argued that it might be a mango to him, but to many others in the world a mango was a sweet tropical fruit and the capsicum he had there was a bell pepper, on the green side. He wouldn't go for all that Commie weirdo stuff about how words didn't mean what they meant: a mango was a mango, and that was that. I shrugged and poured some more home brew into our mugs. "What the hell," I said, "go ahead and put the mango in the gumbo. We'll make culinary history."

There's some discussion about where the word *barbecue* comes from. Some argue that it's from the French *barbe à queue,* "from the beard to the tail," meaning, I guess, that when you grilled a goat you stretched it out over the fire from the head to the other end. Others link it to *barbacoa,* a Taino Indian word for a grill of green sticks built over an open fire, a usage that is common today in Mexico (although the green sticks have been replaced by 55-gallon drums). Some even find a connection between *barbecue* and *boucanier,* a French word meaning to smoke meat on a wooden frame—and thus to buccaneers and pirates grilling meat on the beach.

So I don't think anybody has the exclusive right to the word. Like so many words, *barbecue* has a number of meanings, ranging from the grill we cook on to the sauce we put on our food to the act of grilling meat or fish or poultry to slow-cooked, Southern-style pork or beef. To avoid bringing down the wrath of the 'Cue Mafia, I'll use grilling to refer to the act of cooking itself, but we'll refer to kettle barbecues and barbecue sauce whenever we damn well please.

GRILLING TECHNIQUES

The Charcoal Grill

When we talk about barbecuing or grilling, it's most likely the charcoal grill that we are referring to. Cooking outdoors over a charcoal fire has long been popular in the West, and with the expansion of suburban living after World War II, the backyard barbecue became an emblem of success and the good life for American families. The grill could be as elaborate as the ornate brick grills with decorative tiles and a wet bar found in designer magazines or as simple as a hibachi on a picnic table. Most of the time, the backyard barbecue was a simple, freestanding metal grill that Dad cooked steaks or burgers or cut-up chicken on, putting out flare-ups with a squirt bottle or a splash of beer.

A big impetus to the spread of the backyard barbecue was the invention, by Henry Ford of all people, of the charcoal briquette. Ever the innovator and alert entrepreneur, Ford turned the sawdust from a factory that built wooden frames for his Model Ts into the compressed briquettes that fuel most of America's barbecue fires today. They were originally sold through Ford Motor Company outlets but soon became available in the new supermarkets that enabled Americans to buy all the ingredients (charcoal, steak, sauce, beer) for the backyard barbecue in one place. Briquettes, conveniently packaged and easy to light, made backyard and patio grilling simple and available to virtually all Americans. All you needed was a barbecue grill or hibachi, a bag of briquettes, and some lighter fluid; then, with the obligatory apron saying "Kiss the Cook" and some long-handled tongs, you were a backyard chef.

In recent years, traditional charcoal has made a comeback—especially mesquite charcoal, which is widely used by West Coast grill cooks. Mesquite and other hardwood charcoals retain the form of the wood they were made from and do not burn with the even heat and consistent pattern of briquettes. Free-form mesquite charcoal provides a much hotter fire than briquettes, which makes it my preference for quick-grilling fish or seafood. Whenever I want a really hot fire, I choose mesquite charcoal. The heat can be a disadvantage, though, when you are cooking really thick steaks or a whole turkey or beef roast by the indirect method. High heat can char the surface before the center is done. Here you might prefer the less intense, more manageable heat of briquettes. Briquettes are now available with mesquite and oak and other hardwoods compressed with the sawdust, and these provide manageable heat with some of the characteristics of the hardwood charcoals.

Some feel that the flavor imparted by free-form hardwood charcoals is superior to the flavors given off by briquettes, which include kerosene-based products in their manufacture. I'm not a purist here: mesquite charcoal gives a pleasant, lightly smoky character to food on the grill, but a similar effect can be easily achieved by adding mesquite (or other hardwood chips) to a briquette charcoal fire or a gas grill. Some grill cooks prefer to burn down hardwoods such as oak or hickory to create a bed of coals to cook over. This is a more complicated method that can yield excellent results (see Hardwood Coals, page 1?).

In 1952, George Stephens, an employee of Weber Metal Company, got an idea. He'd seen the covered grills made by serious barbecue cooks from 55-gallon drums cut in half lengthwise. The bottom acted as the fire box and supported the grill; the hinged top could be closed to smoke and roast the food on the grill. Stephens thought he could create a more efficient covered grill by cutting in half one of the company's round metal buoys. The result, of course, was the Weber kettle grill, which revolutionized backyard grilling in America. Now amateur cooks could do what only big-time grillers had been able to do: slow-cook large cuts of meat and cook whole chickens or turkeys in aromatic smoke for hours. The kettle barbecue also gave home barbecuers the ability to regulate heat and put out flare-ups by using the lid and the vents in both halves of the cooker. The kettle grill pioneered by Weber and now widely imitated by other companies gave us the ability to cook over indirect heat, in effect roasting the meat or poultry or fish, and opened up a whole new range of possibilities for outdoor cooking.

The kettle barbecue is by far the most popular grill today, and it's the type of grill I have in mind for most of our recipes. You can use an open grill for anything cooked over direct heat, of course, but a top of some sort, round or rectangular or square, gives the grill cook the ability to damp down flare-ups quickly and also to roast or smoke any type of food.

There is some discussion about whether or not to cover the grill when cooking directly on the fire. Some feel that the food gets an unpleasantly smoky taste from fat dripping on the coals and turning into smoke that is then trapped by the lid. My feeling is that, in most cases, the food is improved by covering the grill, whether you are grilling directly or indirectly. I find the smoked taste of grilled food attractive and like to emphasize it even more by using hardwood chips or chunks (see Smoke on the Grill, page 21). If you prefer a less smoky taste, then don't cover the grill and don't use hardwood chips. If this is your preference and you don't want to cook by indirect heat, a hibachi or other open grill is all you need. If you prefer smoke and all the options, purchase a grill that has a cover of some sort.

Charcoal is an ancient cooking medium that is made by heating and charring wood at low temperatures in an oxygen-deprived environment. It burns more slowly than wood and provides an even and easy-to-regulate fire on which to grill. Traditional charcoal is widely available, often made from mesquite wood, and provides a hot fire and a clean, lightly smoky taste. Since it is created directly from wood, pieces of traditional charcoal are irregular in size and shape. Building a good fire can take a little getting used to, but with practice, traditional charcoal can yield good results. It's best to use uniformly sized pieces or to break large pieces up into a manageable size when setting up your fire. And remember, mesquite and other traditional charcoals often burn much hotter than briquettes. I prefer to use mesquite charcoal when grilling fish, because then I want a very hot fire for quick direct grilling. Mesquite and other traditional hardwoods can be purchased by mail order (see Sources, page 225).

Charcoal briquettes are a relatively recent invention; they are the charcoal of choice for most backyard barbecuers. Briquettes are formed from sawdust and other wood by-products mixed with a kerosene-based liquid and compressed into the familiar rounded shape. They burn easily and are simple to ignite. The uniform shape of the briquettes makes them convenient for layering and building a fire under the grill. Some object to the kerosene components, but I feel briquettes work well for most grilled foods. The addition of hardwood chips adds a pleasantly smoky flavor to food cooked over briquettes, which I recommend in most cases (see Smoke on the Grill, page 21).

Briquettes are now available with mesquite, oak, and other hardwoods pressed into them. These give a little more smoky taste to the food, and they can add to the overall flavor of the finished product. I think hardwood chips give a richer smoked taste, but it's easier to use the hardwood briquettes, and they give good results.

Hardwood coals, burned down from such woods as oak and hickory, are becoming increasingly polular with backyard grillers and restaurants as a heat source. French cooks, especially in Provence and Languedoc, love to grill lamb, beef, or poultry *à la feu du bois.* In California, the town of Santa Maria on the Central Coast boasts that it is the Barbecue Capital of the World (see Santa Maria Barbecue, page 175). Cooks there grill chunks of beef tri-tip and thick rib steaks over the coals of local red oak, with wonderful results. Cooking with hardwood coals takes a little more time in preparation than charcoal but can give very good results. The smoke from the wood flavors the food, and the coals, when properly arranged, provide clean and even heat. Several companies specialize in providing hardwoods suitable for grilling (see Sources, page 225). A warning note: never use wood from conifers such as pine or fir for grilling. These softwoods are too resinous, burn far too quickly, and will give the food an unpleasant piney taste. See Smoke on the Grill (page 21) for information about various hardwoods and their flavors.

Building a Charcoal or Hardwood Fire

The key to successful charcoal grilling (or any type of grilling, for that matter) is controlling the heat levels so that food can be seared and browned on the outside, not charred or burned, and cooked to perfection on the inside. Creating the right kind of fire for the food you want to cook is essential.

For direct grilling, you want to end up with three distinct areas on the grill: one with high to medium-high heat, one with low to medium-low heat, and one with no heat at all. Pile your charcoal briquettes or pieces in the middle of the grate beneath the grill and ignite. You can use a charcoal chimney, an electric starter, a small wood fire, or liquid fire starter.

I prefer to start the fire using a charcoal chimney. It's basically a metal cylinder with a little grate in the bottom and a wooden handle. Its origin, I expect, is simply a coffee can with the lid removed and holes punched in the bottom (this still works, as I found out one summer night in Sonoma County). You stuff the cylinder with newspaper, pile charcoal on top, put it on the grate, and light the paper. When the coals are going, empty them onto the grate and pile more coals on top.

An electric starter is clean and easy to use. Just plug it into an extension cord and stick the metal coil into a pile of coals until they ignite. Remove it and let them burn until they are covered with white ash. Some prefer to make a small fire of kindling and pile coals on top. This works but seems to be more trouble than it's worth. Most people use commercial charcoal starter, which is basically kerosene (a component of the briquettes themselves) and burns away quickly. Some object to starter because, they say, it imparts an unpleasant, kerosene flavor to the food. I've never found any problems with it if I let the starter burn away completely.

When the coals are uniformly white, move two-thirds of them under one-third of the grill, making a couple of layers of coals. This will be your hot spot. Move one-third of them under another one-third of the grill. This will be your medium- to low-heat area. Leave one-third of the grill without any coals underneath. You can move food that is cooking too fast or is almost done to this unheated region of the grill.

For indirect grilling, arrange the coals into two equal piles on either side of the middle of the grill. Set up the two piles so that they are under the holes made by the grill handles so you can add more charcoal to each pile as needed (follow the manufacturer's directions). Leave enough room for a drip pan in the middle to put under the food.

For hardwood coals, start a small fire with kindling in the center of the grate and add pieces of hardwood once it is going well. Let the hardwood cook down to coals and arrange as above for direct or indirect grilling.

The Gas Grill

In recent years, covered grills fueled by propane or natural gas have become popular. Gas grills are very easy to use and don't involve either the preparation or the cleanup that charcoal or wood grilling requires. Purists object, saying that you need a live fire for successful grilling, but I feel that gas grills can provide excellent results, if used correctly.

One of the big advantages of gas grills is the ease of controlling and regulating heat levels on them. The better models have two or three sets of burners, and it is easy to keep one part of the grill at high heat and others at lower levels. Indirect cooking is also simple on a gas grill, because one area of the grill can be kept without a heat source while others provide heat.

Many gas grills come equipped with a built-in thermometer that can be used to regulate temperatures for indirect cooking. They are often furnished with racks and baskets that are useful for baking potatoes, roasting corn or garlic, or keeping foods warm. A handy accessory for a gas grill is a smoke box (sometimes with a well for water) that enables the cook to add hardwood chips, which provide plenty of smoky flavors to the food. The water well adds some steam that helps keep the food moist. If you don't have a smoke box, you can get all the smoke you need by placing a packet of wood chips in foil, punctured to form air vents, on the grill or near the burners (see Smoke on the Grill, page 21).

Coals vs. Gas

For years, I did all my grilling over charcoal, mesquite, and briquettes, or occasionally over hardwood coals. I heard about gas grills from friends and ate what they cooked on them at parties, but I wasn't convinced that the gas grill could cook food the way I'd come to like it: smoky and juicy and tender. When the idea for this book came up, I went out and bought a three-burner gas grill with a built-in thermometer and a smoke box and rotisserie as add-on options. I tested many of the recipes in this book on my new gas grill. I must say that I was impressed with the ease of cooking and cleanup. And I loved the results.

The three gas burners gave me more control of heat levels than I was used to with the charcoal grill, and I found that I quickly learned how to adjust the burners and move food around the grill for maximum results. Chicken and pork seemed especially easy to cook on the gas grill. No longer was I concerned about charring the outside and leaving the inside undercooked. With a little practice and constant use of the meat thermometer, I learned how to sear the food quickly and then move it to a cooler spot to finish cooking. This was something I'd done for years on the charcoal grill, but the adjustable burners let me regulate heat precisely, which made the whole operation a lot easier and the results more consistent.

I was able to generate plenty of savory wood smoke by using the smoke box and water well that came as options with the gas grill. I just filled up the smoke box with unsoaked hardwood chips and topped up the water well before firing up the burners. After 5 to 10 minutes, the box would be smoking, and I would be ready to begin grilling. For most direct grilling, one load of chips was plenty, although in a few cases I added more chips when needed—simple enough to do. For indirect grilling or cooking on the spit, I would fill the smoke box with chips, and they would ignite during the preheating phase. After they were smoking, I would turn the burners down to medium to get the oven to a moderate 350°F. Again, the adjustable burners let me regulate the heat throughout the cooking process. Lower temperatures, though, can keep wood chips from igniting or from burning throughout the roasting period. In the few cases when chips wouldn't burn, I made up foil packets (see Smoke on the Grill, page 21) and placed them directly over the burners and got all the smoke I wanted.

One drawback to the gas grill is that it doesn't provide the intense heat you can get with mesquite charcoal piled high under the grill. The gas grill will provide a hot enough fire for most direct grilling, but if you want to sear quickly a fillet of escolar or a skewer of shrimp or to grill a block of ahi so that it's still raw inside, mesquite in a conventional grill or hibachi will do the job better.

Indoor or Stovetop Grilling

If you don't have access to the outdoors, you won't be able to grill over charcoal (see Safety Tips, page 30). If you have a built-in gas grill, just follow the directions from the manufacturer and use any of our recipes that involve direct grilling. And with a ridged grill pan on top of the stove, you can get great results with steaks, chops, fish, and seafood and with most vegetables.

Any number of stovetop grills will work well for most of our direct grill recipes. These range from old-fashioned black-iron ridged frying pans to large grill pans, often Teflon-coated, and ridged griddles that cover one or two burners. For adequate grilling, all of these should have raised ridges that enable the food to stand above the surface while the fat drains away. Pan-broiling with a flat skillet or griddle will give you a similar effect, but will cook the meat in its own fat and will not create the attractive grilled surface we look for.

An exhaust fan above the stove or some other means of venting the smoke caused by grilling is a necessity. Removing extra fat from meat or poultry, always a good idea, will cut down on smoke. Fish and seafood are especially successful when cooked on a stovetop grill. They cook quickly, and their low fat content cuts down on the amount of smoke produced.

Food can be cooked by direct heat only on a stovetop grill. If the pieces are thin, an inch or less, spray or brush the grill with oil, and get it quite hot over high heat. Put the food on the grill, and sear and mark it quickly on both sides. Grill for 6 to 10 minutes total, turning with tongs until done (see Quick Grilling, page 17). If the food is thicker, preheat the grill as directed, and sear and mark the food on both sides. Reduce the heat under the grill and cook until done, up to

15 minutes or more, as needed. Regulate the heat, and turn the food often to prevent burning (see Composite Grilling, page 18). I don't recommend stovetop grilling for thick (2 inches or more) steaks or chops or for poultry other than thin-cut boneless chicken breasts. These are more successfully cooked on top of the stove by pan-broiling or sautéing.

Fireplace Grilling

Small stand-alone grills and handheld basket grills are available for cooking over hardwood coals in your fireplace. Thick rib steaks and garlic-laced lamb chops grilled over oak coals in the hearth have been memorable dinners with friends in the Sonoma County ridgelands north of San Francisco. Friends with a cabin at Lake Tahoe in the Sierra have rigged up a spit in their large fireplace and roast boned leg of lamb and pork loin over the coals. For safety reasons, don't use charcoal in the hearth (see Safety Tips, page 30), and follow the directions for Building a Charcoal or Hardwood Fire (page 12).

Campfire Grilling

There's nothing like pulling a trout out of a mountain lake and grilling your catch that evening over a campfire under the stars. Campfire cooking is simple and can yield delicious results. Use hardwood for the fire, and let it burn down to coals (see Building a Charcoal or Hardwood Fire, page 12). Set up a grill over four stones at the desired height, or put the food into a grill basket. Grill baskets are especially handy for fish, which are delicate and can fall apart easily. Spray or oil the grill or basket. Put the food as close as needed to the coals; fish and most steaks or chops should be cooked quickly on a hot fire, chicken or other poultry more slowly and for a longer time. After dinner, don't forget to make that campfire favorite, Sierra S'mores (page 216).

COOKING METHODS

Direct Heat

Quick Grilling Grilling directly over high heat is an excellent way to cook tender cuts of meat such as steaks and chops and most fish and seafood. The surface sears and caramelizes through a process called the Maillard reaction, and the juices are sealed in. The heat source can be charcoal or wood coals under a grill, or it can be a gas flame or an electric element that heats a grill or stovetop grill pan.

The simplest method of direct grilling should be used only with pieces of meat or poultry, fish, seafood, or vegetables thin enough to cook through quickly. You build a hot fire or turn burners to high under the main portion of the grill. Leave another part of the grill unheated. Brush or spray the grill with oil. When the grill is hot (use the counting method: hot means that you can't get to 3 when your hand is held an inch from the grill), place the food directly on the hottest part. You may cover the grill or not, as you wish. I use the cover most of the time to prevent flare-ups and to get a bit more smoke flavor, but this is not necessary. Another way to control flare-ups is to move pieces out of the flame to the cool part of the grill briefly, and then return them to the fire when flare-ups die down. Food will cook quickly in the intense heat, so turn pieces with tongs quickly and often until done. You can cook just about anything in 6 to 10 minutes total using this high heat method. As pieces of food cook, remove them to the unheated portion of the grill until all the pieces are cooked to your liking.

Virtually any kind of grill can be used for high-heat direct cooking: a hibachi or open barbecue, a kettle-style barbecue using either charcoal or gas, or a stovetop grill.

Foods best grilled directly over high heat are:

- Seafood: shrimp, scallops, clams, oysters, and lobster
- Fish steaks and fillets
- Thin-cut beef steaks (1 inch or less)
- Thin-cut pork chops
- Small lamb chops
- Butterflied pork tenderloins
- Boneless, skinless chicken breasts

■ Meat, poultry, seafood, and vegetable skewers

■ Zucchini, summer squash, corn, and green beans

■ Peppers and chiles of all kinds

■ Mushrooms and asparagus

■ Tomatoes, cut or whole

■ Thick-sliced onions

■ Fruits such as peaches, nectarines, and figs

■ Bruschetta and grilled bread

■ Grilled polenta

■ Grilled corn tortillas

■ Grilled quesadillas

Composite Grilling Thicker cuts of meat and fish and most types of poultry are best seared over high heat as described in the previous section and then moved to a cooler or even unheated part of a covered grill to complete cooking. The idea is to create a tasty and attractive browned and grill-marked surface and then finish cooking the center of these thicker pieces of food over slower heat or by indirect cooking. After searing a thick steak, for example, you will have a nicely browned surface but an undercooked raw center.

Prepare your grill with one area of high heat, one with a lower level of heat, and one with no heat at all (see Building a Charcoal or Hardwood Fire, page 12, or The Gas Grill, page 13). Spray or rub the grill with oil. Place your food directly over high heat and sear and mark the piece as described in the previous section, turning often, for 6 to 10 minutes total. You may cover the grill or not at this stage; I usually do. After creating an appetizing, browned surface, move the food to the cooler part of the grill, cover the barbecue, and complete cooking. This will take anywhere from a few minutes to half an hour, or possibly even more, depending on what you are cooking. An instant-read digital meat thermometer will come in handy, or you can cut into the food to check for doneness. If you are cooking a number of pieces of meat or poultry (chicken, for example), pieces will be done at different times. As they are done, move them to the unheated part of the grill. They will continue cooking at a slower rate and will keep warm while the other pieces cook. If what you are cooking is very large (big country-style spareribs or butterflied leg of lamb, for example), you might want to move it to the unheated portion of the grill to complete cooking by the indirect method.

The best grill to use for either charcoal or gas is the kettle barbecue. You can also grill with a large hibachi or an open barbecue with good results, or regulate a stovetop grill simply by turning down the heat after initial searing. Heavy-duty aluminum foil can be used, if needed, to keep cooked pieces warm on cooler or unheated portions of the grill.

Foods best grilled by composite method are:

- Thick steaks (more than 1 inch)

- Thick pork and lamb chops

- Whole pork tenderloins

- Whole filet mignon

- Whole beef tri-tips

- Small birds

- Chicken pieces

- Baby back ribs and country-style spareribs

- Butterflied leg of lamb

- Pizza

- Garlic bread

Indirect Heat

Cooking by indirect heat is basically roasting in a covered grill. The food is placed on the grill between two heat sources with no heat directly underneath. A grill pan should be placed beneath the food to catch juices and fat. Virtually anything suitable for roasting in an oven can be cooked over indirect heat.

Prepare a fire with heat sources on either side of an unheated center (see Building a Charcoal or Hardwood Fire, page 12, or The Gas Grill, page 13). Use a premade aluminum-foil drip pan or roasting pan or make your own from heavy-duty foil. Place the drip pan underneath the unheated center of the grill. Spray or rub the unheated portion of the grill with oil, and place the food over the drip pan. Add hardwood chips if you want more smoke flavor (see Smoke on the Grill, page 21). Cover and roast at moderate temperature (350°F) or the temperature in the recipe until done. Use an instant-read meat thermometer or cut into food to check for doneness. Remove the food from the grill and let it sit, covered loosely with aluminum foil, for 10 to 15 minutes before serving. You may make a sauce or gravy from the drippings if you wish.

You will need a kettle-style or other covered barbecue for this type of cooking.

Foods suitable for cooking by indirect heat are:

- Whole chicken
- Whole turkey
- Beef loin or shoulder roast
- Pork loin, shoulder or ham roast
- Leg or shoulder of lamb
- Veal roast
- Whole salmon
- Spareribs
- Whole garlic heads
- Fruit or berry cobblers
- Baked potatoes

Spit-Roasting Any large and tender piece of meat or whole bird is delicious when cooked on a spit. It's best to use roasts that are roughly cylindrical in shape and to tie poultry wings and legs to make them more compact. Cooking is similar to using indirect heat (see previous section), except that the food is arranged on a spit that rotates between two heat sources. A drip pan is placed beneath to catch juices and fat.

After the meat or poultry is seasoned, skewer it with the spit and attach it, following the manufacturer's directions. Try to center the skewer in the meat or poultry to balance the weight when it rotates, so as not to strain the motor. Many rotisseries come with a counterweight to balance the spit. Place the spit in the rotisserie mechanism and arrange the food over a drip pan with heat sources on either side. You will have to remove the grill in many gas or charcoal kettle barbecues to arrange the rotisserie and drip pan. Start the motor, cover the barbecue, and cook until done. Use an instant-read meat thermometer or cut into food to check for doneness. Remove from the spit when done and cover loosely with aluminum foil for 10 to 15 minutes before carving. You can make a sauce or gravy from the pan drippings if you wish.

You will need a charcoal or gas covered barbecue with rotisserie attachment.

Foods best spit-roasted are:

■ Whole chicken

■ Whole turkey

■ Game hens or other small birds

■ Pork loin, boned or bone in

■ Beef roast, boned and rolled

■ Leg of lamb, boned and rolled

■ Racks of baby back ribs

SMOKE ON THE GRILL

The smell of wood smoke brings us back to the campfire and ancestral feasts. The special woodsy aroma and wild flavor of food cooked over and in smoke has an appeal that awakens ancient appetites. A thick steak grilled over smoky coals, the outside browned and crisp, fat sizzling and lightly charred, the meat inside bloodred and juicy, satisfies us like no other food.

So when I grill, I like to make sure that the food is bathed in flavorful smoke, either from the coals themselves or from hardwood chips or chunks added to the fire. If you use hardwood to create the fire (see Hardwood Coals, page 12), then you'll have plenty of smoke to flavor the food you grill. If you use charcoal or a gas grill, the addition of hardwood chips or chunks can add a wonderfully smoky taste. So far I haven't figured a way to add smoke to stovetop-grilled foods. I have enough trouble with my smoke alarms as it is and would hate to think of what would happen if I started playing around with this idea. You can brush the stovetop-grilled food with a smoky barbecue sauce just before removing it from the grill. Or you could rub the food prior to cooking with liquid smoke.

Chips and blocks of many types of hardwoods are widely available throughout the country. If you can't find what you want in your area, consult our list of mail-order sources (see Sources, page 225). Adding hardwoods to your grill is simple and gives great results with very little trouble.

The kettle charcoal grill is probably the easiest barbecue to use for flavor-smoking grilled foods (for a discussion of smoking techniques, see Smoking, page 26). If you use chips, you can soak them for an hour or so before adding to the fire, if you wish. I do this to make the wood burn longer when I am cooking something that requires long cooking by the indirect method, such as chicken or turkey or a pork roast. For a quick direct grill—steak or pork chops or butterflied tenderloins—I use chips without soaking. If I have thick steaks or pork tenderloins that work best with the composite method, I usually soak the chips to make them last a little longer. Chunks of hardwood should always be soaked before using.

For direct or composite grilling, prepare a charcoal fire (see Building a Charcoal or Hardwood Fire, page 12). When the coals are uniformly gray, remove or lift the grill (wear a mitt or use tongs). Sprinkle about 1 cup, or more if you wish, of hardwood chips of your choice over the coals, or place soaked hardwood chunks on the coals. Replace the grill, put the barbecue cover on, and open all vents, top and bottom. Within a few minutes, you will see smoke coming out of the top vents. Put your food on the grill and cook as directed in the recipe.

For indirect grilling, ignite two piles of coals (see Indirect Heat, page 19). Be sure the coals are positioned underneath the holes made by the handles so you can feed more charcoal to the two fires as needed. Lift the grill carefully and put ½ cup or more water-soaked wood chips or some hardwood chunks on each fire. Put a drip pan between the two piles of coals, and replace the grill. Open all vents, top and bottom. When smoke is issuing freely from the top vent, put the meat or poultry on the grill and cook as directed. If the chips are burned up before cooking is finished, use the holes by the handles to drop or push more chips or chunks onto the fire as needed. You can also lift the grill carefully and drop chips or chunks directly on the coals.

Some grill cooks prefer to put wood chips in a pouch of aluminum foil, punch holes in the top, and place this on the coals. This works well for both direct and indirect methods and conserves wood chips. It is especially good for foods that require long indirect cooking, such as ribs or turkey. The pouch method is especially useful for gas grills and is described in more detail following.

Hardwood chunks work well on the charcoal grill. Make sure the chunks are not too big; otherwise, you'll end up with a flaming fire rather than with smoking coals. I like to soak chunks in water for a couple of hours before putting them on the coals. Be careful with wood chunks, though; one or two will provide plenty of smoke, and too many will leave you with a mini-inferno.

A safety note: I don't recommend using pieces of wood left over from construction projects and picked up from building sites. First, you can't really be sure what type of wood you are getting. Softwoods such as pine or fir will end up blazing away and covering the food with greasy black pitch. Second, many woods used for construction are treated with preservatives that you would not want in or on your food. Get your hardwoods from a recognized and reputable source. You don't use all that much, and it pays to be safe.

Many gas grills come equipped with a smoke box or offer one as an add-on option. I think this is well worth the money, as the built-in box makes smoking with hardwood chips a simple operation. The smoke box I purchased with my gas barbecue fits right into one side of the grate. It consists of a large metal box fitted with a lid; inside is a smaller box for hardwood chips, perforated at the bottom for draft and for the ashes to drop through. It also contains a small rectangular pan for water. The chips ignite from the gas fire, and the smoke is drawn across the meat on the grill by vents on each side of the cover. The water turns to steam, which moistens the meat and helps to keep it juicy.

The technique for flavor-smoking with a smoke box is easy. Fill the smoke box with wood chips of your choice. Fill the water pan, if you have one. Start the gas grill with the spark ignition, or light it with a match or flame wand. Turn all burners to high. Close the cover and wait until the desired temperature is reached and the coals have ignited and are smoking well. Cook food as directed in the recipe. If in doubt, follow the manufacturer's directions for your gas grill and smoke box.

If you don't have a smoke box, you can make an aluminum-foil pouch for the wood chips and place it on the flavorizer bars or lava rocks above the burners. Heavy-duty aluminum foil is preferable: just spread out a good-size piece—say, 10 inches square. Put a good handful of hardwood chips into the center of the foil and fold the foil up around it. Seal and crimp the top to close tightly. With a skewer or carving fork, punch holes in the top of the foil pouch. Put the pouch into the grill and ignite the burners. After a few minutes, the chips will start to smoke. One pouch should provide plenty of smoke for a quick direct grill. For composite grilling or indirect grilling, you might need more wood chips. I think it's easier to make up new foil pouches than to try to retrieve the pouch from the fire and refill it after the chips have burned away. Just make up a new pouch, if needed, and place it on a different spot over heat. Be sure to remove and discard the pouches after the barbecue cools down.

With gas grills, I see no need to soak chips beforehand. In fact, one of the drawbacks of the smoke box is that chips will often go out at the lower temperatures sometimes required for indirect cooking. Soaked chips can be even more of a problem. What I do when I'm grilling indirectly or spit-roasting on my gas barbecue is to get a full smoke box going well with high heat before I add the meat or poultry. The already-burning smoke box should provide plenty of smoke for the first hour or so of cooking. If I'm going to cook for longer than that, I add more chips after the first half hour and usually get plenty of smoke throughout the cooking time. If I have a problem with getting enough smoke with a low temperature fire, I just make up an aluminum pouch with chips and place it right on the flavorizer bars over an active burner.

To use hardwood chunks with a gas grill, soak for an hour or so and then place chunks directly on the flavorizer bars or lava rocks under the grill and over an active burner. If the chunks are small and might fall through, use an aluminum pouch. Replenish hardwood chunks as needed.

Not everything you cook on the grill requires smoke. Seafood, fish, vegetables, poultry, and many meats have delicate flavors that can be overwhelmed by smoke, so don't feel you always have to stoke up the smoke box. I suggest you go lightly at first and experiment with types of wood and times and amounts of smoke. I've developed some favorite combinations over the years, and there are traditional pairings of different woods with various foods. So I'll make suggestions from time to time about what wood goes with what dish. But these are suggestions only: suit the use of smoke to your taste buds and to the foods you and your family prefer.

Following are some thoughts about the flavors and uses of some of the many hardwoods available. I've arranged woods in descending order of intensity.

Oak This is the most powerful and flavorful of all the woods. Perhaps it's because of my years in the wine business and all the wines I've aged in oak, but the flavor of this wood works for me, especially with pork and beef. Oak smoke is a great match for pork loin or ribs

or pork tenderloin. Or try a thick porterhouse rubbed with garlic and grilled over smoldering oak coals. Oak is easy to find, both chips and chunks, and makes a good base if you want to cook over hardwood coals. One of the best smoking materials I've ever used was charred oak sawdust scraped out of old bourbon whiskey barrels when they were reconditioned for use as wine barrels. I used to sell these barrels to wineries years ago, and I ended up with burlap sacks full of this savory stuff. I tossed it on just about every charcoal fire for years, with steak or pork chops or turkey, and loved everything I cooked in the whiskey-scented oak smoke. My burlap sacks are long empty, alas, although I have heard that some entrepreneur is marketing this by-product of the cooper's trade. If I ever find out who he is, I'll be first in line.

Hickory This is the favorite wood of many southern smokehouses and produces some of the finest country hams you'll ever eat. I love the flavor of hickory with pork of any kind, from quick-grilled chops to ham smoke-roasted on the grill. Hickory's intense, nutty flavor is also delicious with chicken or turkey rubbed with herbs and plenty of spice.

Mesquite The lightly resinous and pungent smoke of mesquite is wonderful with spicy, chile-accented chicken, turkey, or pork. It is my choice with anything with a Southwest touch, from fajitas made from chicken or beef to carne asada to Baja-style grilled fish or seafood. When I make fish tacos, I like to cook the fish quickly over mesquite charcoal with a touch of mesquite wood smoke and then grill corn tortillas over the coals right at the end. Hawaiian chefs cook fish, seafood, and marinated beef and chicken over kiawe wood coals—another name for mesquite. A good combination for a Hawaiian-style grill would be mesquite charcoal for a hot fire with just a bit of mesquite chip smoke for flavor. When using any kind of smoke with fish or seafood, use a light hand; you don't want to overpower the delicate flavors.

Apple Fruit woods provide mild, slightly sweet flavors that go well with chicken and pork. I often use apple wood when I cook with sweet glazes or brush fruit-based sauces on birds or pork tenderloins. It works well with small birds such as game hen or quail and can also be flavorful with fish such as salmon.

Cherry Similar to apple, cherry smoke is mild and sweet. It provides light smoke accents to chicken, turkey, or duck. I've also used it successfully with seafood such as prawns and scallops, although care must be taken to not oversmoke these.

Alder This is the preferred wood along the Northwest coast for smoking salmon. Its mild, lightly perfumed flavor is wonderful with fish of all kinds: salmon, black cod, halibut, swordfish, and shark. Northwest chefs often use alder as a base for hardwood coals for grilling salmon, and a specialty of the region is salmon roasted on an alder plank beside an open fire.

Rosemary If you have a rosemary bush, break off some of the woody stalks with leaves attached and soak them in water for an hour or so (hold them down with a rock or other weight). Toss the stalks right on the coals when you are direct-grilling steak, lamb chops, swordfish, or shark steaks. You can often find fresh rosemary at farmers markets or produce stands. Choose the woodiest you can find. Another use is to skewer small lamb chops or shish kebab pieces on the stalks before grilling (this time with leaves removed).

Grapevine Prunings If you live near the wine country, these can often be had for the asking (they're usually burned after pruning during the winter months). They can also be purchased in specialty markets and from mail-order sources (see Sources, page 225). Cut grapevine canes into 3- or 4-inch pieces and soak them for an hour or so. Put onto coals for direct grilling of chicken, beef, or lamb.

SMOKING

Many of our recipes call for adding hardwoods to create smoke that flavors food on the grill, but only two are, strictly speaking, smoking food. Smoking is an ancient technique that was used to preserve food over the ages, but now in the age of refrigeration, we add smoke more for flavor than for safety. Some foods, bacon for example, are cold smoked at temperatures too low to cook them through. The food must then be cooked after the smoking process. This technique is best left to professionals or to the group of dedicated amateurs willing to buy or build the equipment needed for cold smoking.

It is possible, however, to hot smoke food on the grill. Here meat, poultry, or fish is both smoked and cooked in a covered barbecue at a low temperature (usually 180°F to 200°F) for 2 or 3 hours. I use this technique in John's Cured Smoked Salmon (page 131) and Slow-Smoked Spareribs with Oakland Barbecue Sauce (page 165).

The technique is simple, but you need to pay attention to the temperature in the barbecue. A thermometer, built in or inserted into one of the top vents, is essential for success. Start the fire with half the coals you would usually use for indirect cooking, or turn gas burners to low. If you have a water smoker, follow the manufacturer's directions for indirect heat and fill the water buffer as instructed. Place soaked oak or hickory chunks or a packet of hardwood chips directly on the fire when it is going. Center the food over the unheated portion of the grill. Cook until done (see recipes for temperatures), keeping the inside temperature of the grill between 180°F and 200°F for fish, around 300°F for spareribs. To raise the temperature in a charcoal grill, add a few coals to the fire and open vents fully. To lower the temperature, close the lower and upper vents as needed. With a little practice, it's easy. Gas grills are simple: just turn the burners higher or lower to keep within the desired temperature range.

EQUIPMENT

First there's the grill. This can be as simple as an iron grid set up in the hearth, a wire fish basket over a driftwood fire on the beach, or a plain metal grill propped on stones over campfire coals. Or you can go for broke with an elaborate built-in brick and tile barbecue or a stainless steel gas grill with all the bells and whistles from a rotisserie to an extra burner to keep the barbecue sauce hot. Or anything in between.

Let's start with the simplest piece of equipment: a grill without a heat source. This can be a hinged basket for fish or seafood or a simple open metal grill or a ridged grill pan to go on the stove. You can get excellent results using the simplest grilling equipment. On the beach or at a campsite in the mountains, just burn down driftwood or hardwood to coals, set up your grill or fill your grill basket, and follow any of our recipes that call for direct grilling (see Quick Grilling, page 17). Some of the best food I've ever eaten has been grilled on the beach in Baja or Southern California (see Grilled Snapper on the Beach, page 121; L.A. Seafood Mixed Grill with Mango Vinaigrette, page 110) or over campfires on fishing and hiking trips (see Food on the Fire: A California Memoir, page 31). And you can achieve great things with a ridged grill pan on your home stove (see Indoor or Stovetop Grilling, page 15).

A step up is a hibachi or small open barbecue. These are inexpensive and easy to store and can be set up easily on a small deck or back porch. (For safety reasons, I don't suggest using charcoal inside; see Safety Tips, page 30.) Make a small charcoal fire with two heat levels (see Building a Charcoal or Hardwood Fire, page 12) and you can cook anything you want by direct grilling. Fish or seafood is especially easy to cook on a small open grill, because you can usually get the food very close to the coals for maximum heat. Small pieces of skewered foods are perfect for hibachi grilling, because they cook quickly over high heat (see Prawn-and-Scallop Skewers in Wasabi Dipping Sauce, page 105; Ahi Skewers with Miso-Sesame Crust, page 119; Chicken Yakitori, page 139). A trick of Asian chefs is to load up one end of a bamboo skewer with pieces of food, leaving 2 or 3 inches bare. Place the food end of the skewers over direct heat, and let the bare ends project out over the edge of the hibachi to keep cool. On a large barbecue, put the food over the heat and the ends of the skewers over an unheated portion of the grill. This way, you can take food right off the grill to eat without burning your fingers.

The most versatile and popular type of grill today is the kettle-style barbecue that comes equipped with a cover. Created by the Weber company in the 1950s and available today in many styles and types, the kettle grill enables home chefs to grill steaks and chops and pieces of poultry directly over the heat and also to roast large pieces of meat and whole birds by indirect heat. The cover also traps aromatic smoke from hardwood chips or chunks and serves as a damper to regulate heat levels. This is the best barbecue to purchase for backyard or deck cookery, and most recipes in this book are written with the kettle grill in mind. The gas grill is a version of the kettle barbecue using propane or natural gas as a heat source. All recipes can be cooked on either type of grill (see Coals vs. Gas, page 14).

Apart from the grill, the equipment needed for successful barbecuing is not very complicated. Here are some of the most common and useful grill tools:

Fireplace shovel or poker This is handy when it comes to moving the coals around for charcoal or hardwood fires, although, to tell the truth, I usually use a piece of tree branch and a garden trowel.

Chimney fire starter for igniting coals This is my preferred way of starting charcoal fires. Electric starters also work well.

Wire brush or cellulose pad for cleaning the grill Essential for getting bits of char and grease off the grill. I go through two or three a year.

Long, spring-loaded stainless steel tongs This is the most important piece of grilling equipment I own. I use tongs to turn steaks and chops, to move food around the grill, and for many other tasks. Get two or three tongs so that you'll always have one handy. Don't use forks on the grill, because they puncture the surface of the meat and let out flavorful juices.

Long-bladed and long-handled spatula I use a big restaurant spatula, but any large spatula will do. I generally don't buy fancy "barbecue" tongs and spatulas. I get most of my equipment at restaurant-supply houses; the tools there are generally cheaper and higher quality than the fancy stuff.

Baking mittens or pot holders Actually, I think leather-faced garden gloves are best for protecting your hands around the grill. White Mule are my favorites, in the garden and at the grill.

Mister or spray bottle I used to use one of these, but now I just damp down flare-ups using the barbecue cover with vents closed or move food away from flames to a cooler part of the grill. Use one if you want, or do what my dad used to do: splash some beer on the flames.

Premade aluminum foil drip pans There are two types, both sold by Weber and other barbecue manufacturers. The large type goes under roasts and birds as a drip pan for indirect cooking. Smaller pans fit under gas grills to catch grease. I use these drip pans all the time for these purposes and also for baking cobblers and other dishes on the grill. The pans can be put in the dishwasher and used again and again. Or you can make your own drip pans to order using heavy-duty aluminum foil.

Racks and fish baskets and grids Any number of racks can be fitted into kettle-style grills, both gas and charcoal. I find them handy for baked potatoes, for corn, and especially for roasting whole garlic heads when I am cooking something by indirect heat. Fish baskets and grids are great for cooking delicate fish, seafood, and vegetables. They keep fish from falling apart and prevent small pieces of food from falling through the grill.

Basting brush or mop I use a large pastry brush, but a small dish mop or brush will do as well. I clean mine by running it through the dishwasher after use. It has held up for many years.

Skewers I use small and large bamboo skewers that I buy in an Asian grocery. Some say you have to soak skewers before grilling, but I've never found the need; if they get a bit black, so be it. I also use large metal skewers to shape and stabilize large pieces of meat on the grill such as butterflied leg of lamb and very big boneless steaks.

Thermometer Other than the grill itself, the most important piece of equipment for successful barbecuing, in my opinion, is the instant-read meat thermometer. The thermometer takes the guesswork out of cooking meat or poultry; just take a reading, and you know exactly what the meat is like. Get the digital kind, because it's quicker to use and more accurate than older types.

Fire extinguisher Keep a filled and functioning fire extinguisher near the grill at all times. You never know. I remember seeing a bunch of bozos at a big cocktail party in the Hollywood Hills load up a rusty old kettle barbecue that lacked a bottom grid with so much mesquite charcoal that the outside started to glow after a while. Since it wasn't my party, I hesitated to say anything, and nobody else seemed to care much. Many martinis were being drunk, and I mean drunk.

So I went out to my car to get a fire extinguisher and stood by while the barbecue got hotter and hotter and redder and redder. I called my host's attention to the situation, and he laughed and told me that mesquite made a hot fire, just what we needed for the salmon steaks. I agreed that it made a hot fire all right and stood at the ready with the fire extinguisher. Which was a good idea, because the bottom fell out of the barbecue a couple of minutes later, dumping all those burning mesquite coals onto the wooden deck, which was poised over acres of dry brush. My host was pouring the martini pitcher over the coals when I swooshed it all with the extinguisher. We grilled the salmon on the stove that night and all agreed that it was almost as good as mesquite. The moral: don't try this at home, and always have a fire extinguisher at the ready. And watch out for martinis, good advice anytime.

SAFETY TIPS

To start with, take a look at the remarks on fire extinguishers (see Equipment, above). We're dealing with fire here, folks, and common sense and the need for survival should rule. So be careful. In California, especially out in the country, forest fires are an ever-present danger in the summer and fall, so we are extra careful with fires of any kind. Use your barbecue wisely, and protect yourself and the environment. Keep a working fire extinguisher on hand, and watch out for sparks and hot ashes.

If you are using charcoal, make sure you cook outdoors. Charcoal in an enclosed space can create deadly carbon monoxide, so don't take any chances. Gas or propane should be handled carefully, following the manufacturer's directions. Check for leaks at all valves and joints after installing a new tank and before igniting the barbecue. When grilling on the stove top, make sure you have plenty of ventilation or an exhaust fan to disperse smoke.

The rule here, as in most things in life, is to use your head. Most accidents occur because somebody has slugged down too many margaritas, is smoking the wrong herbs, or is demonstrating some new flambé technique for the girlfriend. Keep cool at the grill and enjoy it safely.

Food on the Fire: A California Memoir

I grew up on the southwestern edge of Los Angeles, just to the west of Watts. The city ended here: the limit then was Imperial Highway a couple of blocks from my house, and just south of that was open country. There were sagebrush and jackrabbits and quail and a wild landscape out there. Oil wells pumped constantly next to pools of tar and the occasional bunch of hard guys in hard hats drilling. Bikers roamed the wastes, gouging out bike climbs in the dirt and roaring up and down Devil's Dip. (These were real bikers, like the mean ratty guy played by Lee Marvin and not wimpy Marlon Brando in *The Wild One,* and definitely not one of those plump guys with beards you see these days on cushioned Harleys with two-way radios in their helmets.) Hoboes and wild kids like us rode the rails, slow oil trains that rattled under bridges covered with graffiti and inhabited by troll-like figures who gestured to us, mouthing dangerous invitations.

Amid this urban wilderness were pockets of green. Irrigation canals and ponds fed the truck farmers' fields of lettuce and tomatoes and

peas and beans and spinach and squash that dotted the landscape. We would escape to these watery oases amid the dry brush, with no shoes and no shirts on hot summer days, with our fishing rods and cans of worms or jars of salmon eggs. We'd pull crappies and bluegills and tiny sunfish, along with the occasional catfish or bass, from the lilypad-covered ponds all morning long.

Then came lunch. We'd take matches and a packet of salt out of our pockets along with a jar of really hot Mexican chiles; the yellow kind called güeros was most common, but sometime it would be jalapeños or serranos. We'd build a fire from broken-up produce crates and sage-brush along with fallen branches of cottonwoods and willow. Once the fire got going, we'd start the feast by roasting the smallest fish on willow sticks we pushed into their mouths and held over the fire. Sometimes we'd gut and scale the tiny fish, but if we were hungry (and we almost always were), we'd just grill them whole, right in the flames. These hot hors d'oeuvres were laid on pieces of produce box, and we picked the cooked meat out with our fingers, rolled it up with a chile, and chomped down. I don't remember fish ever tasting so good.

Large fish, especially any bass or catfish, got the deluxe treatment. In among the cottonwoods we'd stashed a blackened and bent iron grill that somebody had liberated from a backyard barbecue long ago. This was propped on four stones over the coals, and the bigger fish were gutted and scaled (or skinned if we'd caught any catfish). We'd season the fish with plenty of salt and pour on some of the juice from the jar of chiles. Then we'd lay whole fish on the hot grill over sagebrush and cottonwood coals, flip them over with our jackknives, and lay them on plank platters when they were done. We would feast on the burning hot fish with more salt and more chiles until we literally couldn't eat any more. Our moms always wondered why we never seemed to bring fish home from our daily expeditions. We'd save the biggest cat-fish or bass of the day once in a while for cover and to bring home as a trophy, but not many survived the lunch campfire.

As we grew older and achieved the highest level of teenage bliss, cars and the ability to roam, we extended our expeditions' range. We would head in either one of two directions: south and east to the Mojave Desert or up into the mountains near Big Bear, at the south-ern edge of the Sierra range. We'd equip ourselves with .22 rifles and a 4-10 shotgun if we headed for the desert, with fishing rods and nets if we set out for the high country.

In the desert, we'd find a dirt road leading off the main highway and drive along it as long as we could. We'd usually end up at a coulee or dry arroyo coming out of some mountains or hills; the Pinto Mountains south of Twentynine Palms were a favorite destination. At that point, we'd load up on water, shoulder our packs and guns, and hike in one direction for a day, using a compass to remember where the car was. Along the way, we'd stay on the alert for quail or doves or rabbits. Anything we shot went into the packs for dinner. We'd camp wherever we were at the end of the day and build a fire of mesquite and sagebrush and manzanita. If we had had luck hunting, we'd pluck the birds or skin the rabbits. We'd season them with salt, pepper, and wild sage leaves. For birds, we always carried long metal skewers, the kind you use for shish kebab. If we'd gotten a rabbit or two, we'd use the same beat-up metal grill from our lily pond days (this also served as support for a camp coffee pot and the one frying pan we brought along for anything fancy). When the coals burned down, we'd prop the skewers of birds on stones or put the rabbit on the grill. When they were done, we'd cut the birds or rabbits up on our army surplus metal mess kits and pour over juice from our ever-present jars of chiles. We'd chew on the smoky, sage-favored flesh and hot chiles, drink warm water from our big desert canteens, and listen to coyotes yip just up-canyon.

That was if we had had any luck hunting. If not, it was cans of Dinty Moore beef stew, opened and set on the fire. You'd be surprised how good canned beef stew tastes with four or five hot chiles tossed in for seasoning by a campfire at age 16 after a long day's walk across the Mojave.

Up in the mountains, we'd park and hike up-country to a string of lakes outside the main family camper zone. This is rugged country, and we'd try to keep weight down to a minimum, so no canned beef stew here. But there was plenty of water, so dried soups and dehydrated foods went into our packs. We'd figure on mountain trout as the main course for most of our meals and were hardly ever disappointed. Grilling rainbows or native brown trout is easy and gives the delicate fish a lovely light touch of wood smoke. We'd leave the old iron grill behind on mountain trips and rely on a lightweight, handheld fish grill to cook the fish. Once you gut and scale trout, a little oil, salt, and pepper and a squeeze of lemon on the skin is enough seasoning. Then we would prop the fish-basket grill on a couple of stones just a few inches from hot coals. Four or 5 minutes per side is enough time for grilling most fish. Poke the flesh along the backbone with the point of a knife or a fingernail to see if it's starting to flake.

Occasionally, as time went on, we would range farther afield in search of adventure and bigger fish. The Colorado River near the juncture of California, Arizona, and Mexico yielded some of the biggest largemouth bass any of us had ever seen. (If this is starting to sound like a fish story, it is.) It was so hot down there in summer that we would fish from dawn to about 10 A.M. and catch all the big bass we could eat in an hour or two. Then we'd spend the rest of the day in the river, in water up to our necks, with coolers full of ice and fish and beer floating on inner tubes nearby. When it cooled down a bit at dusk, we'd climb out of the water, skin puckered and white, and grill whole bass over mesquite coals. Side dishes were potatoes fried with bacon and onions and chopped green chiles, jars of jalapeños en escabeche, and many Coronas to wash it all down.

On beaches in Baja south of Ensenada, we'd surf fish, casting lines out into the breakers for sea bass and grouper and mackerel that we'd grill over open fires on the beach and eat with tortillas and salsa and beer we'd buy at *palapas* or beachfront huts. On days when we came up empty-handed fishing, we'd stow the rods and body surf all afternoon. Then we'd buy shark and albacore from small boats as they came into shore. We'd cut the big fish into steaks, rub them with limes and salsa, and grill them over driftwood coals on the wide, dark beach, listening to the mariachis playing their hearts out on the plaza back in town.

Dry Rubs and Marinades

Dry rubs make grilling easy and the end product delicious. These savory mixes of salt, various ground peppers, spices, dried herbs, and often sugar are used to flavor and lightly cure meat, poultry, fish, and seafood before grilling. Depending on what the mix is, you can point your grilled food in the direction of whatever cuisine or cooking style you want. Dried chile powder and oregano create a Southwestern flavor; garlic powder, oregano, and basil give an Italian taste; star anise and Chinese five-spice powder lend an Asian note.

I use dry rubs constantly. Whether it's a porterhouse on the charcoal barbecue or a boneless pork chop on the stovetop grill, I season the meat thoroughly with a dry rub that ties into the style of the meal and the other ingredients. I like to let the meat sit for an hour or two at room temperature or for up to 8 hours in the refrigerator. This allows the flavors of the rub to penetrate the meat, and the salt to draw a little moisture to the surface, where it mixes with the herbs and spices. Then when I grill, I get beautifully seasoned and juicy meat with a flavorful crust on the outside.

Many rubs, especially from Southern 'cue folk, are heavy on the salt, sugar, and cayenne. In fact, some commercial rubs are little more than that. I prefer flavor to saltiness and sweetness, so I cut back on the salt and sugar in most of my rubs. If you are sodium sensitive or on a restricted diet, you can leave the salt out all together and put as much salt (or as little) as you want on the food after it cooks.

Heat tolerances vary. I am not a fan of very hot food; I think all that heat tends to paralyze the tastebuds. So if you like things hotter, feel free to up the cayenne or other hot peppers in the rubs. The same goes for other ingredients; if you want more or less of a particular herb or spice, change the recipe to fit your taste.

When I make up batches of dry rubs, I usually double or triple the recipe. These rubs will keep for months in a closed jar, and you can just reach for whatever rub you want when you get ready to grill.

Marinating meat, poultry, and fish can add a lot to the flavor and texture of grilled food. It does not, however, do much for tenderness. Generally, food cooked on the grill should come from the tender cuts (spare ribs and brisket are exceptions), and steaks, chops, and most fish become mushy and unpleasant if left too long in an acidic marinade. So I don't recommend marinating fish more than a few hours, and most meat or poultry should be marinated for a couple of hours at room temperature or up to 8 hours in the refrigerator.

Marinades are great ways to emphasize tastes that can be continued in sauces, salsas, or other dishes served with the grilled food. Wine, fruit juices, vinegar, and citrus are all acids that liven the taste of food, while the oil in many marinades provides moistness. Herbs and spices penetrate marinated food for extra flavor, and the salt provides a firmer texture.

Brining is increasingly popular with Pacific Coast grill chefs. Here the intent is not to preserve food, as with ham or bacon or corned beef, but to draw moisture and flavor into pork, chicken, turkey, or fish. You'll be surprised at the extra juiciness and taste you get from brined pork chops or salmon.

Herb Rub for Pork or Chicken

This savory rub is great on pork chops, ribs of all sorts, and smoke-roasted pork loin. It is also tasty on chicken or duck.

. . . .

■ Mix all the ingredients in a jar or small bowl. The rub will keep, covered, for a few months.

MAKES 1½ CUPS

¼ cup paprika

2 tablespoons packed brown sugar

1 tablespoon dried thyme

1 tablespoon dried sage

½ teaspoon ground allspice

1 tablespoon chile powder

1 teaspoon ground fennel seeds (see Toasting and Grinding Spices, page 149)

1 tablespoon salt

1 teaspoon freshly ground black pepper

½ teaspoon cayenne

Herb Rub for Beef or Lamb

Use on steak or lamb chops, smoke-roasted beef, or lamb.

. . . .

■ Mix all the ingredients and store in a covered jar. The rub will keep, covered, for a few months.

MAKES 1 CUP

1 tablespoon dried thyme

1 teaspoon dried rosemary

1 tablespoon granulated garlic or garlic powder

1 teaspoon onion powder

1 tablespoon paprika

¼ teaspoon cayenne

2 teaspoons salt

½ teaspoon freshly ground black pepper

MAKES 2 CUPS

2 tablespoons paprika

2 tablespoons chile powder

1–2 teaspoons cayenne, or more or less to taste

2 tablespoons granulated garlic or garlic powder

2 tablespoons packed light or dark brown sugar

1 tablespoon ground cumin

1 tablespoon dry mustard (preferably Colman's)

1 teaspoon ground sage

2 tablespoons salt

1 tablespoon freshly ground black pepper

Spice Rub for Pork or Beef

Try this spicy rub on pork ribs of all types, pork tenderloins, and roasts. It's also delicious sprinkled on steak or pork chops.

. . . .

■ Mix all the ingredients, taking care to crush any lumps of brown sugar or spices. Make up a double or triple batch and store in a covered jar for up to 2 months.

Source: Bruce Aidells and Denis Kelly, *The Complete Meat Cookbook*. Houghton Mifflin, 1998.

Mike Lopez's Steak

I can remember the first steak I ever tasted that was seasoned with anything other than salt and pepper. Now there's nothing wrong with salt and pepper on tender beef hot off the grill, but when you add some garlic or chile or herbs you get a different experience altogether.

My family being Irish, seasoning food in general was not something that was done on a regular basis. My dear mother, God bless her, was a good cook in her own way. She would cook roast beef on the rare side and didn't boil the vegetables to a dull gray the way my aunts and grandma always did. Mom cared about good ingredients and always served us wholesome food, seasoned with salt and pepper, and maybe a touch of garlic salt and dried herbs if she was feeling adventurous.

I grew up in Southwest Los Angeles and went to St. Michael's Grammar School in a neighborhood that was a lively mix of ethnic groups: Irish, Italian, Mexican, Cuban, Latvian, and Croatian; black kids from Alabama and Haiti; Asian kids from China and the Phillipines. The schoolyard was an interesting place and I learned many of life's lessons there: keep your chin down and your fists up; stick with friends through all difficulties; watch out for nuns and other authorities at all times; and, with food, always try to find something to put in your mouth that tastes good.

We had an active barter system out there in St. Michael's school-yard: I could always trade the roast beef or lamb or ham sandwiches my mother lovingly prepared for food with real flavor: meatball sand-wiches or salami heroes; homemade tamales; piroshki stuffed with spicy meat, raw onions and hunks of stinky cheese; fried pork skin and hot pepper sauce; dim sum filled with barbecued pork; and *lumpias,* greasy Filipino spring rolls.

Mike Lopez was my best pal (and still is for that matter—he's up in the Sierras now creating ceramic art and going fishing every chance he gets). I'd go to his house and eat the delicious carne asada his mom would make; he'd come to mine for roast lamb and boiled corned beef. One Saturday afternoon we had some money we made from mowing lawns and we decided to have a feast. We went to the butcher's shop over on Hoover and bought the biggest and thickest steak we could afford, a top sirloin as I remember.

We took the beautiful steak over to my place and fired up the grill in the backyard. And then the argument began. I was for a little bit of salt and pepper and cooking the steak rare. Mike wanted garlic, chile powder, some oregano, and well done. We argued and argued about it until we got really hungry. And so we compromised: we put on salt and pepper and garlic and chile powder and dried oregano. In effect, a spice rub. And we grilled that magnificent steak brown and crisp on the outside and rosy pink in the middle: medium-rare.

I was a convert with my first bite and have never looked back since that day. Seasoning meat of any kind before you cook it is the only way to really get flavor into your mouth. That's why I have a shelf full of dry rubs and use them every chance I get. And whenever flavors explode in my mouth when I take that first bite of a perfectly sea-soned sirloin, I remember Mike's steak and the schoolyard rules. Most of them have stood me in good stead over the years. I still check for nuns over my shoulder anywhere I go.

Hot Spice Rub for Pork or Chicken

MAKES 2 CUPS

1½ cups paprika

¼ cup onion powder

2 tablespoons granulated garlic or garlic powder

2 tablespoons freshly ground black pepper

½ tablespoon salt

1 tablespoon celery salt

2 tablespoons dry mustard

1 tablespoon chile powder, or more to taste

1 tablespoon cayenne, or more to taste

1 teaspoon dried thyme

1 teaspoon dried oregano

1 teaspoon dried sage

Make up a batch of this lively mix of herbs and spices and rub on pork or chicken for a bit of extra heat and flavor.

. . . .

■ Mix all the ingredients thoroughly in a bowl. Keep in a covered jar for up to 2 months.

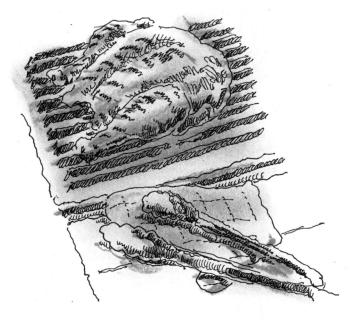

Peppery Chicken or Seafood Rub

MAKES 1 CUP

½ cup paprika

2 tablespoons granulated garlic or garlic powder

1 tablespoon dried thyme

1 teaspoon cayenne

1 tablespoon lemon pepper

1 teaspoon freshly ground black pepper

2 teaspoons celery salt

1 tablespoon salt

Use this peppery rub on grilled chicken, fish, or seafood.

. . . .

■ Combine the ingredients in a jar or small bowl. The rub will keep, covered, for a month or two.

Fish or Seafood Rub

Sprinkle this rub on fish steaks or fillets before grilling. It also works well on shrimp or scallops.

· · · · · · · · · · · · · · · · ·

■ Mix the ingredients in a jar or small bowl. The rub will keep, covered, for a couple of months.

MAKES 1 CUP

¼ cup paprika

1 tablespoon granulated garlic or garlic powder

2 teaspoons lemon pepper

1 teaspoon freshly ground black pepper

1 teaspoon Chinese five-spice powder

¼ teaspoon cayenne

2 teaspoons dried tarragon

2 teaspoons dried basil

½ tablespoon salt

Fish or Seafood Cure

This cure gives flavor while adding to the juiciness of fish or seafood. It is wonderful on Tea-Smoked Scallops with Hoisin Vinaigrette (page 113).

· · · · · · · · · · · · · · · · ·

■ In a small saucepan, combine the salt, fennel seeds, and pepper. Stirring occasionally, cook over medium-low heat for 5 minutes. Remove from the heat, cool, and add sugar. Use as directed in recipe. This mixture will last for a month in an airtight jar.

MAKES 1 CUP

½ cup salt

⅔ tablespoon fennel seeds

1 tablespoon cracked black peppercorns

½ cup sugar

Marinade for Fish

Use on fish fillets or steaks or on seafood.

· · · · · · · · · · · · · · · · ·

■ Mix the ingredients and marinate fish for up to 2 hours.

MAKES 1 CUP

½ cup olive oil

2 tablespoons lemon juice

1 small onion, finely chopped

2 tablespoons chopped fresh thyme or 1 tablespoon dried

1 teaspoon salt

½ teaspoon freshly ground black pepper

Marinade for Poultry

MAKES 1½ CUPS

1 cup olive oil

⅙ cup balsamic vinegar

4 cloves garlic, finely chopped

1 tablespoon chopped fresh oregano or 1½ teaspoons dried

1 teaspoon salt

½ teaspoon freshly ground black pepper

This marinade gives an intense Italian flavor to chicken breasts, legs, and thighs. Serve grilled chicken warm on a bed of fresh greens for a salad lunch or alongside pasta and vegetables as a dinner entrée.

. . . .

■ Whisk all the ingredients together in a small bowl. Marinate poultry 1 to 2 hours at room temperature or 8 to 12 hours refrigerated. The marinade will keep for up to a week refrigerated.

Marinade for Meat

MAKES 1 CUP

½ cup olive oil

3 cloves garlic, finely chopped

1 tablespoon chopped fresh rosemary or 1½ teaspoons dried

1 teaspoon salt

½ teaspoon freshly ground black pepper

Use on steak, pork loin, or lamb chops.

. . . .

■ Mix the ingredients and marinate for at least an hour at room temperature or 8 to 12 hours refrigerated. The marinade will keep for up to a week refrigerated.

Fish or Seafood Brine

MAKES BRINE FOR 3 TO 4 POUNDS FISH OR SEAFOOD

4 cups hot water

¾ cup salt

½ cup sugar

¼ cup freshly ground black pepper

2 tablespoons fennel seeds

1 tablespoon lemon juice

Brining fish (soaking it in a water, salt, and spice mixture) gives it a lovely flavor and firm texture. Traditionally, brines were used to preserve fish and meat. Since refrigeration, they continue to be used as a wonderful way to infuse flavor throughout the fish or seafood. The best fish for this process are halibut, rock cod, tuna, swordfish, shark, and Brined Salmon Steaks (page 131). The fish should be cut into steaks or fillets no more than 1 to 1½ inches thick. For whole salmon or large fillets (see John's Cured Smoked Salmon, page 131), double or triple the recipe as needed.

. . . .

■ Combine the water, salt, and sugar in a nonreactive container. Stir until completely dissolved. Stir in the pepper, fennel seeds, and lemon juice. Cool. Soak fish in the brine in the refrigerator as directed in recipe. The brine alone will keep for 2 weeks in the refrigerator.

Pork Brine

The high salt content of traditional brines drained the meat of moisture to preserve it. This brine, on the other hand, fills the meat with Southwestern flavors while enhancing the juiciness and texture. It's especially tasty with Brined Thick Pork Chops with Grilled Apples and Onions (page 167), or you could soak a pork tenderloin in this brine in the refrigerator for 2 to 3 hours or a loin for up to a day and enjoy delicious pork with Grilled Corn Tortillas (page 52), Salsa Roja (page 108), and Rajas: Grilled Chile and Pepper Strips (page 101). The length of time in the brine varies with the thickness and texture of the meat. The chile powder and sage in this brine will carry the appealing smells of the Southwest through your neighborhood when you barbecue.

....

■ Combine the water, salt, and brown sugar. Stir until dissolved. Add the garlic, peppercorns, chile powder, and sage. This brine will last up to 2 weeks in the refrigerator.

MAKES BRINE FOR 6 POUNDS PORK

5 cups hot water

½ cup salt

½ cup packed brown sugar

3 cloves garlic, smashed

1 tablespoon cracked black peppercorns

2 tablespoons chile powder

2 teaspoon dried sage

Appetizers

From its origins around the campfire to today's Sunday barbecue in the backyard, grilling has always been a communal and a festive activity. When we smell wood smoke and the sweet scent of browning meat, our mouths start to water and appetites build. What better place, then, for preparing appetizers, those savory morsels that excite the taste buds and stimulate hunger, than the grill itself? There's nothing more appealing than that savory bit you slice off the end of spit-roasted beef or the tip of a steak to test for doneness, toss back and forth in the fingers to cool, and then pop in your mouth for a luscious taste of what's to come.

But don't limit yourself to little bites. Use the hot grill to create delicious appetizers and first courses while the main dish cooks. While grilling or roasting larger pieces of meat or poultry to perfection, you can use other areas of the grill to quickly cook bits of fresh fish for tasty tacos (see Fish Tacos with Three Salsas, page 51), highly seasoned seafood (see Grilled Prawns or Scallops with Thai Cilantro Sauce, page 65), or stuffed mushrooms (see Luke's Pesto Crimini Bites, page 67).

The trick here, as with all grilling, is to manage your fire for maximum results. Whether you are using charcoal, hardwood coals, or a gas grill, the technique is the same. If you follow the directions in Building a Charcoal or Hardwood Fire (page 12) or The Gas Grill (page 13), you will arrange your fire into two or three areas and levels of heat. For quick grilling (page 17) and composite grilling (page 18), you should have three areas: one high, one medium, and one without a heat source. For indirect grilling (page 19), you will have two equal medium-high to medium areas, with an area in between with no heat underneath.

If you are going to roast a turkey (see Smoke-Roasted Turkey or Chickens with Three-Pepper Rub, page 146) or a piece of beef, such as a tri-tip (see Santa Maria Tri-Tips, page 176), or prime rib (see Smoky Prime Rib, Santa Maria Style, page 177), you have the opportunity to cook a wide range of appetizers and side dishes. While the turkey roasts on the cool center of the grill, use the hot sides to prepare appetizers and first courses for the feast: Bruschetta with Tomato Mozzarella Topping (page 56), or Grilled Pears with Pancetta and Pepper (page 63). Vegetables and side dishes to accompany the turkey can be cooked after the appetizers are taken off: Out-of-the-Garden Grilled Salad (page 71) or Grilled Asparagus with Roasted Garlic (page 97) or Grill-Roasted New Potatoes (page 101). And on cooler sections around the fire or in the racks of a gas grill, you can tuck whole heads of garlic (see Smoke-Roasted Garlic, page 59) to be used as appetizers squeezed onto baguettes or saved for later use in soups (see Grilled Red Pepper and Roasted Garlic Soup, page 83) and other dishes.

When quick grilling steaks or chops or chicken breasts, use the hot area of the grill to brown and mark your main dish, and then move it to a cool area. Then quickly grill your appetizers over the hottest area and serve them to guests. Check your main dish, and if it's done or close to done, remove it from the grill and cover it loosely with foil while you enjoy the appetizers or first course. If it's not done yet, leave the food on the unheated part of the covered grill and test it when you have finished the appetizers. Serve the steak or chop or chicken breast, or if it needs a bit more cooking, toss it onto high heat for a minute or two. In composite grilling, you use virtually the same technique. Brown the main dish on high heat and move it to medium heat to finish cooking. Grill your appetizer on the high-heat section of the grill until done, and serve. Test your main course and either remove it from the grill and cover loosely with foil or move it to the cooler section of the grill until you are ready to serve it.

Pizzas on the grill are great for appetizers, as a first course, or as a main course, for a light dinner or lunch. These tasty pies are easy to prepare and quick to cook on the grill. You can use your favorite pizza dough recipe or try ours (see Pizza on the Grill, page 60). Even easier, buy a precooked round of unseasoned pizza crust or focaccia from a market or delicatessen. Pizza crust can be made or purchased in small or large sizes and topped with virtually any tasty food for appetizers or first courses. Grill the pizzas as directed while other food is cooking. Anything you put on a pizza, by the way, can also be placed on a round of precooked polenta (see Grilled Polenta with Smoke-Roasted Tomato Sauce, page 98) for a delicious and easy appetizer or side dish.

Baja California: Asaderos on the Beach

All along Baja California's Pacific coast you will find little towns with shady plazas and a beachfront walk or *malecón* with deep blue water beyond and *palapas* or palm-frond huts lining a white sand beach. Along these beaches you find *asaderos,* Mexican grill masters, standing behind their *barbacoas,* grilling seafood of all kinds: spiny lobster or *langosto, langostinos* or baby lobster tails, huge prawns, albacore, shark, halibut, sea bass. You find a spot on the beach near a *palapa,* order a *cerveza con lima,* and tell the asadero what kind of seafood or fish you want. After a beer or two, the seafood arrives, smoking hot, anointed with garlic, butter, red and green chiles, or salsas frescas, whatever you've chosen. After lunch, it's a swim in the surf, a walk on the beach, or a snooze under the palm fronds, according to your age and inclination.

My first tastes of the products of these great grill masters, the Baja asaderos, were on quick trips over the border in college days. Ensenada and Rosarito Beach, just south of Tijuana, were prime destinations. We'd all pile into a car, tell our folks some lie or other, and head south for a weekend of unlimited beer, spicy food, surfing, and general carousing. In Ensenada, we'd head for Hussong's, a raucous tavern that caters to a lively mix of college kids, tourists, sailors, surfers, beachcombers, and sinister characters who look like they stepped out of a Conrad novel. After an afternoon in Hussong's, we'd walk out into the bright light and search out some good food. Trying to avoid the tourist restaurants with their picturesque fake adobe fronts and tired enchiladas, we'd look for a sign saying "Mariscos," with a little arrow pointing down some side street, and start on our trek. Often we'd follow the signs quite a way, past the end of the paved roads, where the cantinas got funkier and the mariachi music louder. And then we'd see the smoke and smell the grill. A big 55-gallon drum barbecue was the usual setup, although sometimes we'd find a regular U.S. commercial grill and once just a pit in the ground with an iron grill set up on concrete blocks. A big pile of free-form charcoal would be heaped up next to an old-fashioned soft drink cooler filled with ice, beer, and fish, and an old man always stood behind the grill, waving us on, smiling through the smoke.

We didn't need much Spanish to be understood: *camarones* or *gambas* for pink grilled shrimp, *langostinos* or *langostos* for huge prawns and spiny lobsters, *pesca* for fish: big chunks of marlin or whole red snappers, sea bass and grouper, big fish, small fish. The technique was always the same: you pointed to what you wanted and the asadero would shell it or cut off a steak or fillet, sprinkle it with lemon, chile, and salt, and toss it on the grill. As the food sputtered and smoked on the grill, you'd pull a beer from the ice and sip and watch the action. After a minute or two, you'd be handed a paper plate with a couple of grilled tortillas on it along with a pile of seafood or fish. You would wrap it all in tacos, add strips of grilled chiles and onions and salsa displayed on a rickety table near the cooler, and eat your fill. Then you would point to another fish, open another beer, and do it all over again.

Chiles: Handling Chiles

Much of the heat is found in the seeds and white inner membranes, so removing these will tone down chiles. Be careful when handling chiles, as they can burn eyes or sensitive skin: wear rubber gloves or wash hands thoroughly afterwards.

Peeling Chiles or Peppers
To peel chiles (as well as bell peppers), fire-roast on the grill or over open flame until the skin is charred and blistered. Put in a plastic or paper bag for 15 minutes to steam. Scrape the skin off under running water.

Using Dried Chiles
Soak dried chiles in hot water until soft and puree in a food processor (see Dried Chile Purée, page 108). To make your own chile powder, process dry chiles in a blender or food processor. Be careful not to inhale the dust—it can be irritating.

Other Alternatives
Buy ground New Mexico, California, or ancho chile powder from Latino groceries or by mail order (see Sources, page 225). Most commercial chile powder blends include oregano and cumin; Gebhardt is the best widely available blend.

Canned green chiles are good alternatives to fresh, or use fire-roasted and peeled bell peppers and add heat with cayenne, red pepper flakes, or hot sauce.

Chiles: Types of Chiles

There are many varieties of fresh and dried chiles used in the Southwest, ranging from mild to very hot. I give suggestions for specific chiles in the recipes, but you should feel free to substitute, depending on what is available in your market and your tolerance for heat. Chiles are found in Latino markets and are also available by mail order (see Sources, page 225). Here are some of the main types (in ascending order of heat).

Anaheim Large, mild green chile often grilled as Rajas: Grilled Chile and Pepper Strips (page 101).

New Mexico When green, New Mexico chiles are similar to Anaheim. Dried red chiles are found in *ristras* (long strings), and used in sauces and for chile powder.

Poblano Large green chile similar to above. Also called pasilla. When dried, called ancho. Used widely in sauces and for chile powder.

Mulato Medium-hot green chile similar to poblano. Chocolate brown when dry, with rich flavor. When dried, it is sweeter than ancho.

Jalapeño Hot green chile used fresh or pickled *(en escabeche)* in sauces or for garnish.

Chipotle Smoked red jalapeños can be found dried or packed in adobo sauce. Has a strong, smoky flavor.

Güero These pale yellow chiles are quite hot. They are sold fresh or packed in jars.

Serrano Small green chile, even hotter than jalapeño. Use in salsas, Thai food, and dishes with emphatic heat levels.

Habanero Very hot, light green to red chile. Also called Scotch bonnet.

Salsas Frescas

Salsas Frescas such as Salsa Cruda, Salsa Verde, and Pico de Gallo are found on tables all along the Mexican and California coast. They add spice to all kinds of grilled foods, from Carne Asasda (page 173) to Fish Tacos with Three Salsas (page 51). Salsas are best made fresh, but you can keep them for a few days, covered, in the refrigerator.

I've used Anaheim and jalapeño chiles in these recipes for lightly spicy salsas. You could heat up the salsas by increasing the jalapeños in the recipes to your taste or by using hotter chiles, such as serrano or even habanero if you want to go over the top (see Chiles, page 49). You can use a food processor if you enjoy a smoother texture; I prefer to chop the ingredients by hand for chunkier salsas.

MAKES 2 CUPS

½ cup minced onions

1 jalapeño chile, seeded and finely chopped

1 Anaheim or other mild green chile, fire-roasted and peeled

⅔ cup chopped fresh cilantro

1½ cups chopped ripe tomatoes

1 tablespoon lime juice

¼ teaspoon ground cumin

Salt to taste

Salsa Cruda

Salsa Cruda is a delicious, all-purpose salsa that is found on the table all the way from Baja to Alaska. Make it as hot or as mild as you want by varying the amount and type of chile in the mix (see Chiles, page 49).

◼ Chop all ingredients by hand or in a food processor. Mix together. Salsa will keep 3 to 5 days, covered, in a refrigerator.

MAKES 2 CUPS

8 tomatillos, husked and chopped

1 jalapeño chile, seeded and finely chopped

1 onion, chopped

½ cup chopped fresh cilantro

1 clove garlic, chopped

½ teaspoon salt

Salsa Verde

This salsa is usually blender smooth, but you can chop it by hand for a chunkier texture.

◼ Finely chop or process all ingredients. Mix together. Taste for salt and heat levels. Salsa keeps for 3 to 5 days, covered, in the refrigerator.

Pico de Gallo

You'll find this spicy salsa anywhere Mexican food is sold. It should be hot; the name means "rooster's beak," and you should expect to get pecked a bit.

·················

■ Mix all the ingredients. Serve immediately.

MAKES 3 CUPS

2 cups chopped fresh tomatoes

1 cup chopped onion

1 cup chopped fresh cilantro (about 1 bunch)

1 or more jalapeño or other hot chiles, seeded and finely chopped

Juice of ½ lime

1 teaspoon salt

Fish Tacos with Three Salsas

Fish tacos are simple and delicious: grill some fish seasoned with Mexican herbs and spices, squeeze on some lime juice, tuck chunks of fish into tortillas with some shredded cabbage or lettuce along with plenty of salsa fresca, and fall to.

This Mexican Spice Rub is great on fish, or you can use it on seafood, pork, beef, or chicken—wherever you want a touch of Southwest spice.

·················

To make Mexican Spice Rub, combine all ingredients for the rub in a bowl or jar. The rub will keep for up to a month in a sealed jar.

■ Sprinkle the fish generously with 2 tablespoons of the rub and let sit at room temperature for up to an hour.

■ Prepare the fire for direct grilling. Spray or rub the grill with oil.

■ Grill the fish over medium-high heat for 3 minutes on each side or until it flakes and is still juicy. Remove from the grill and cut into bite-size pieces. Squeeze lime juice over the fish.

■ Heat the tortillas by placing them directly on grill and turning with tongs until the edges begin to curl and the tortillas are marked by the grill.

■ Spoon fish pieces into the tortillas, top with a bit of cabbage and a slice of avocado, and serve with salsas and Corona *con lima.*

SERVES 4

MEXICAN SPICE RUB

½ cup ancho or other chile powder

2 tablespoons packed brown sugar

2 tablespoons dried oregano

2 tablespoon granulated garlic or garlic powder

1 tablespoon ground cumin

¼ teaspoon ground allspice

1 teaspoon cayenne

2 tablespoons salt

2 teaspoons freshly ground black pepper

•

4 pounds sea bass or halibut fillets or other firm white fish

2 limes

8 corn tortillas

1½ cups shredded cabbage or iceberg lettuce

1 ripe avocado, sliced

Grilled Corn Tortillas

You can buy corn tortillas or make your own. Look for the whitest tortillas when you buy because they contain less lime and have a more delicate flavor. Get them as fresh as you can; stale tortillas break easily on the grill and don't taste very good. Fresh grilled tortillas served with salsas (see Salsas Frescas, page 50) make wonderful appetizers or party snacks. If making your own tortillas, use fresh masa. Masa is a dough made from lime-soaked and ground dried corn. Make it by following the directions on the package or buy it premade from tortilla factories or Latino groceries.

1 cup fresh masa dough

■ Divide masa dough into eight balls. Roll masa between two sheets of wax paper using a rolling pin, or use a tortilla press. The tortillas should be thin, about ¼ inch, and about 5 inches in diameter.

■ Cook the tortillas on an oiled medium-hot grill. Let the edges curl and darken a bit and then flip the tortillas, using tongs or your fingertips. Grill for another minute or so until the tortillas are cooked through and marked by the grill. Keep them warm in aluminum foil. Serve while still warm.

■ You can reheat store-bought tortillas following the same method.

A 200-Mile Beach Party

It's all one long beach from Rosarito, just outside Ensenada in Baja California, up the Southern California coast to Oceanside and La Jolla above San Diego to San Clemente, Huntington Beach, and Seal Beach farther north and then the L.A. beaches—Redondo, Manhattan, Playa del Rey, and finally Malibu, Zuma Beach, Ventura, Santa Barbara, and Pismo Beach. The Pacific breaks onto a wide, sandy shore, the sun shines most of the year, and a whole culture has grown up with its own heroes and villains, myths and songs, fashions in clothes and cars and hair colors, special foods, and characteristic (and plentiful) drinks.

It's a world of surfers and boogie boarders, old station wagons called woodies with high-performance surfboards on top, and bright red jeeps with built-in beer chests. Standard attire: sun-bleached hair and bikinis for the women; Levi's cutoffs with no shirt and floppy sandals for the men. The Beach Boys and Gidget movies defined the beach scene years ago, and it hasn't changed all that much since. The boards are a little shorter, the hair a little longer, and some of the legendary surfers a bit long in the tooth, but it's still a world of blond-haired dudes and muscular surfer girls whose main activity is having fun in the sun, hanging ten on the boards, and watching for that next big wave. Plenty of Corona *con lima* and just plain Bud gets drunk, the music is loud and never seems to end, and surfers bob up and down outside the breakers all year round from dawn until sundown. Everybody is tanned, sandy, and randy, living *la vida loca,* at least on the weekends.

Food in the beach towns is good and plentiful, and the grill gets a lot of work. There's a long tradition of barbecuing in fire pits dug into the sand and on beaches that still have the old spirit and haven't put up signs saying NO to everything; you can still see plenty of folk grilling burgers and fish and seafood over charcoal or driftwood coals. Beach parties with lots of beer and music and grilled food have long been a feature of Southern California life, and the party still goes on along the 200 miles of beach. Burgers and steaks are favorites, but you're just as likely to see (and smell) fajitas, carne asada, and Asian spiced fish or seafood cooking on the grills.

The Mexican influence is powerful in all the Southern California beach towns. Everybody scarfs fish tacos at the stands and taco trucks that line the beachfronts, and restaurants feature grilled Baja lobster tails and chile-grilled prawns, snapper Ensenada style, and spicy carnitas. Legendary taco joints like Johnny Mañana's in Oceanside often have lines out into the street with everyone from close-cropped noncoms with "Semper Fi" on their biceps to surfers and long-haired hippies to pale-skinned Canadian snowbirds from the condos waiting for Johnny's famous chicken fajitas and pico de gallo.

The beaches are popular places, too, for families who want to spend a day eating, drinking, swimming, and generally having a good time together. Grandmas and grandpas guard the umbrellas while kids chase the waves and babies play in the sand. All the varied ethnic groups that make up the Pacific Coast's polyglot culture seem to end up at the beach on Sunday afternoons in summer: you'll hear Spanish and Tagalog, Thai and Japanese, Chinese and Korean, and just about every other language, including English, in all the accents you can imagine. Many Asian families catch fish or crabs from the piers or breakwaters or in the surf and grill the catch right on the beach. Fish and seafood are seasoned with soy-based marinades and grilled, and chicken, beef, and seafood are dipped into savory and sometimes fiery sauces.

Even if you don't catch your own fish, there are fish markets and food stands and restaurants on piers and along the beachfronts in many Southern California towns. Here you can buy fresh fish, crab, prawns, oysters, and other seafood, raw, smoked, or cooked in many different styles. Whole families, from grannies to toddlers and bunches of beer-drinking uncles and cousins, set up around the fire pits and big concrete tables and have seafood feasts all through the summer day and long into the night.

Some of the best food I've ever eaten has come from these beachside grills. Fish Tacos with Three Salsas (page 51), L.A. Seafood Mixed Grill with Mango Vinaigrette (page 110), Barbecued Oysters with Habanero Salsa (page 109), Shark Steaks Adobo with Chipotle Grilled Tomatoes (page 122), and Pork Tenderloins in Miso Marinade (page 164) are just a few dishes inspired by this 200-mile beach party along the Southern California coast.

Grilled Seafood Quesadillas

SERVES 4

Thick 10-inch flour tortillas work best for quesadillas. A mix of seafood is used here, but follow your own tastes. You could also put in cut-up mushrooms, cooked chicken, or just shredded cheese and salsa if you prefer.

. . . .

■ Prepare the fire for direct grilling.

■ Toss the shrimps, scallops, and fish in Mexican Spice Rub and lime juice. Let marinate for up to an hour.

■ Cut four 1½-foot-long pieces of heavy-duty aluminum foil. Spray the foil with oil. Place a tortilla on each. Divide the seafood among them, onto one side of each tortilla. Sprinkle the seafood with cheese. Fold the tortilla in half. Wrap the foil around, maintaining the shape of the tortilla. Seal the foil.

■ Cook directly over a hot grill (about 400°F) for 10 to 15 minutes, covered. Turn the quesadillas halfway through. Open the foil and check for doneness before removing. The tortilla should be crisp and the seafood tender and warm. The fish should be flaky but still juicy. If the quesadillas need more time, wrap them back up and return to the grill.

■ Serve warm with Salsa Cruda or other salsas and fresh lime.

¾ pound peeled and cleaned raw shrimp, coarsely chopped

¾ pound bay scallops or quartered sea scallops

½ pound red snapper or other white fish, cut into ½-by-½-inch chunks

2 tablespoons Mexican Spice Rub (page 51) or chile powder

1 tablespoon lime juice

4 flour tortillas

2 cups grated Monterey Jack cheese or queso fresco

1 cup Salsa Cruda (page 50) or other salsa

2 limes, cut into quarters

Grilled Mussels with Red Pepper Relish

SERVES 4 TO 6

Alice McNeil, a good friend and talented San Francisco Bay Area cook, serves these stunningly delicious mussels to hordes of friends who surround her backyard grill, risking burned fingers to snatch the tasty bivalves up as soon as they are done. The Red Pepper Relish is also tasty on pasta or as a spread for Bruschetta (page 56) instead of tomatoes.

. . . .

■ Prepare the fire for direct grilling.

To make Red Pepper Relish, roast the bell peppers on the grill over high heat for 4 to 7 minutes, rotating so all sides get toasted. Put peppers in a paper or plastic bag for 5 to 10 minutes. Peel away the skin, discard the seeds and stems, and chop the peppers finely. Cook the bacon in a frying pan on the stove until crisp, crumble,

RED PEPPER RELISH

3 red bell peppers

3 slices bacon

2 tablespoons red wine vinegar

•

24 mussels, scrubbed and debearded

½ head red leaf lettuce

and combine with the peppers. Toss the mixture with the vinegar. This relish can be prepared ahead of time and refrigerated for up to a week.

■ Grill the mussels over heat until they pop open, 3 to 5 minutes. Put a spoonful of relish in each mussel and serve over lettuce leaves. Discard any unopened mussels.

Bruschetta with Tomato Mozzarella Topping

SERVES 6

BRUSCHETTA

3 tablespoons olive oil

1 clove garlic, finely chopped

½ teaspoon salt

¼ teaspoon freshly ground black pepper

1 sourdough baguette, cut in quarters and then sliced in half lengthwise

•

TOMATO MOZZARELLA TOPPING

2 cups finely chopped ripe tomatoes

Salt and freshly ground black pepper

8 slices soft mozzarella

2 tablespoons chopped fresh basil

San Francisco is the home of chewy, tangy sourdough French bread that makes wonderful bruschetta, bread brushed with olive oil and garlic, grilled, and served with a savory topping. It's the perfect appetizer for sunny afternoons on the deck after the fog has burned off, with a glass or two of Zinfandel. Here the bruschetta is topped with tomatoes, mozzarella, and basil. You could omit these and use Smoky Eggplant Caviar (page 72), Joel's Eggplant Pesto (page 65), or even thinly sliced steak or pork tenderloin with Roasted Garlic Aioli (page 95) or Chipotle Mayonnaise (page 94). For a garlicky treat, squeeze some Smoke-Roasted Garlic (page 59) on the bruschetta and serve alongside Smoke-Roasted Turkey or Chickens with Three-Pepper Rub (page 146) or Smoke-Roasted Pork Loin or Veal Roast (page 169).

· · · · · · · · · · · · · · · · · · ·

■ Prepare the fire for direct grilling.

To make Bruschetta, combine the olive oil, garlic, salt, and pepper in a small bowl. You can also use a garlic-infused olive oil instead. Brush the cut side of the baguette slices with the oil. Place over high heat, cut side down, and grill for 2 minutes until browned and nicely marked. Turn and grill for another 2 minutes.

■ Pile tomatoes on the bread while it is still warm, sprinkle with salt and pepper, and top with a slice of mozzarella and the basil. Remove from the grill when the mozzarella has warmed through, and serve immediately.

Tapenade Toasts

These make great garnishes for Ratatouille from the Grill (page 96), salads, and grilled chicken, vegetables, or fish. They are also delicious by themselves as an appetizer or party snack.

• • • • • • • • • • • • • • • • •

To make Tapenade, mix the tapenade ingredients together in a small bowl to make a paste. For a smoother texture, pulse once or twice in a food processor or blender.

▪ Prepare the fire for direct grilling.

▪ Cut the baguettes into ½-inch rounds. Brush both sides of the rounds with olive oil or vinaigrette. Grill over medium–high heat for a minute or two per side until lightly marked and toasted.

▪ Spread the toasts with tapenade and serve.

TAPENADE

1 cup pitted kalamata or other ripe olives, finely chopped

1 anchovy fillet, rinsed and finely chopped

2 cloves garlic, finely chopped

½ cup olive oil

1 teaspoon finely chopped fresh oregano

¼ teaspoon freshly ground black pepper

•

2 baguettes or other French bread

2 tablespoons olive oil, Balsamic Basil Vinaigrette (page 96), or other vinaigrette

Garlic Madness: A Revolution of Sorts

It seems like only a few years ago that garlic was looked upon with trepidation by large numbers of Americans. In many families, including my own Irish American clan, garlic manifested itself as garlic salt, sprinkled occasionally on steak or lamb chops, with the real thing chopped sparingly into Italian meatballs or spaghetti sauce on special occasions.

Times have certainly changed. Nowadays, we get garlic in and on just about everything—soups, salads, sauces, stews, grills. We even take it in pills for our health. One of the reasons for garlic's popularity today is a revolution that took place in, naturally enough, Berkeley and the San Francisco Bay Area in the 1960s and '70s. During those exciting times, Berkeley's Chez Panisse celebrated Garlic Feasts, featuring garlic in every dish, including dessert; Gilroy started the wildly successful Garlic Festival; the official association of the garlic crazies, the Lovers of the Stinking Rose, was founded; and all of us Northern California foodies cooked with and ate and talked about and wrote of the pungent bulb as a symbol of a new attitude toward food in America. Garlic in the dish and on the breath became—like bobbed hair and hooch in the '20s, a workingman's cap and swing music in the '30s, and the zoot suit in the '40s—a talisman of our generation. We gorged on garlic and went to great lengths to include it in anything and everything we cooked and ate.

I can remember eating chocolate-covered garlic and garlic ice cream at Chez Panisse more than once. And I'll admit that I helped to create the first garlic wine ever made for one of their festivals. The taste was, as we wine professionals say when we don't want to offend, interesting. A bottle still sits on wine merchant Darrel Corti's shelf, resplendent with its beautiful designer label, wisely unopened.

Going to the Garlic Festival in Gilroy, south of San Francisco, became a pilgrimage; we endured all the dust and crowds and heat to get a chance to eat that flash-fried squid in garlic sauce and pickled garlic cloves and whole roasted heads of garlic squeezed onto French bread. Anzonini, the gypsy flamenco musician and dancer and garlic lover, threw all-night garlic parties in rented parish halls where we ate his homemade garlic sausage, garlic soup, shrimp roasted in garlic, and pasta with garlic and olive oil, accompanied by huge quantities of Zinfandel and flamenco, into the dawn. Les Blank, the Berkeley documentary filmmaker, even made a film, *Garlic Is as Good as Ten Mothers,* about Anzonini and the garlic madness.

Garlic is now a mainstay of American cooking, thanks to those revolting times, and one of the best ways to get the essence of the stinking lily is by roasting it. This can be done in the oven, of course, but roasted garlic cooked in a covered grill is even better. The smoke adds even more flavor, and the garlic cloves come out creamy and lightly smoky. I like to roast garlic heads on the grill in quantity so I can have some for later use. You can eat Smoke-Roasted Garlic (see next page) right off the grill, or squeezed onto bread or bruschetta, or you can refrigerate and save it to mix into a variety of grilled dishes. Here are a few:

- Bruschetta with Tomato Mozzarella Topping (page 56)

- Pizza with Scallops, Roasted Garlic, and Bitter Greens (page 62)

- Luke's Pesto Crimini Bites (page 65)

- Grilled Red Pepper and Roasted Garlic Soup (page 83)

- Grilled Portobello Mushroom Caps (page 94)

- Grilled Asparagus with Roasted Garlic Oil (page 97)

- Smoke-Roasted Tomato Sauce (page 98)

Smoke-Roasted Garlic

Roasting whole heads of garlic in a smoky grill gives the pungent bulb an unforgettable flavor and smooth texture. My gas grill has a rack that swings out when the cover closes, and when I'm cooking anything that requires a bit of time—Smoke-Roasted Pork Loin or Veal Roast (page 169) or Smoke-Roasted Turkey or Chickens with Three-Pepper Rub (page 146), for example—I put five or six heads of garlic in the rack to roast along with the main dish. If you don't have a rack on your grill, just put as many separately wrapped garlic heads on the unheated portion of the grill when cooking with indirect heat.

1 or more heads of garlic

Extra-virgin olive oil

••••••••••••••••••

■ Pull off some of the papery cover from the garlic head, but leave enough so that the head is still intact. With a serrated knife, slice off about ¼ to ½ inch of the top or stem end of the head, exposing the tops of individual garlic cloves. Place each head on a piece of heavy-duty aluminum foil, pour a little olive oil over the top of the garlic, and wrap in the foil.

■ Place foil-wrapped heads on an unheated part of the grill when using indirect heat. Check the garlic after 30 or 40 minutes. The garlic cloves should be soft and cooked through. I like to open up the foil for 10 to 15 minutes or so to let the garlic pick up a bit of the smoke flavor. Remove garlic from the grill and unwrap the foil. Pry the garlic cloves out of the head with a fork or small knife and squeeze onto bruschetta or into whatever dish or gravy you want. Foil-wrapped garlic heads will keep for a week in the refrigerator.

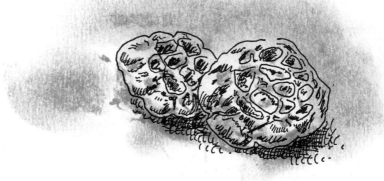

Chester Aaron's Grilled Elephant Garlic

Chester Aaron writes novels and books about food and grows some very special garlic up in the hills above Occidental in California's northern Sonoma County. And by special, I mean special. He not only grows and sells tasty varieties such as ajo rojo or rosé de Provence, but also rare types of garlic such as a Transylvanian strain that is guaranteed to repel vampires. And it's done a good job up to this point, Chester reports.

Chester has authored two best-selling books on the stinking lily and loves to cook with and talk about his favorite subject. When I asked him for a recipe, though, he started talking about elephant garlic, a huge-bulbed vegetable that is not garlic at all, but a member of the leek family. When I asked Chester if he grew elephant garlic, he snorted derisively, "Hell, I wouldn't put any in the ground up here. I'd insult the whole community and nobody would grow anymore. But I sure love to grill elephant garlic and eat it as a vegetable."

Chester peels the enormous bulbs and, if they are very thick, slices them in half lengthwise. He brushes the slices with olive oil and grills them for a few minutes on both sides until tender. They make a great garnish for grilled steak, chicken breasts, or portobello mushroom caps. Another way to use elephant garlic is to skewer the whole cloves, brush them with olive oil, and grill them. They can also be interspersed between small pieces of chicken or fresh prawns for a wonderful appetizer.

One drawback, though: elephant garlic does not keep vampires away. Keep plenty of real garlic in the house at all times, suggests Chester the garlic guru. You never know when you might need it!

Pizza on the Grill

Use this dough recipe with any of your favorite pizza toppings.

MAKES ENOUGH FOR TWO 10-INCH PIZZA CRUSTS

1 package (¼ ounce) active dry yeast

1 teaspoon sugar

¾ cup warm water

2 cups all-purpose flour, plus more as needed

½ teaspoon salt

¼ cup olive oil, plus more for brushing

1 tablespoon cornmeal

■ Combine the yeast, sugar, and water and let stand in a warm place for 5 minutes or until bubbles form. In a separate bowl, combine 2 cups of the flour and the salt. Make a well in the dry ingredients and add the yeast mixture and ¼ cup of the olive oil. Mix the dough with your fingers until it forms a ball; if it's too sticky, add more flour.

■ On a lightly floured surface, knead the dough for about 10 minutes. If you have a food processor with a dough hook, you can use this for about 8 minutes on high speed. Dust the dough with flour and put it in a large bowl; cover with a lid or plastic wrap. Put the bowl in a warm place for 1 to 2 hours or until the dough has doubled in size.

■ Prepare the fire for indirect grilling. Spray or rub the grill with oil.

■ Punch the dough down with your fists. Divide into two pieces. On a floured surface, knead each section. (At this point, you can wrap the balls in plastic wrap and store in the refrigerator for up to a week.) Stretch each ball with your hands and then roll from the center to the edges to form a 10-inch circle about ¼ inch thick. Fold the dough onto itself to seal any holes. Crimp the edges of the circle to form a rim. Brush each side with olive oil and dust both sides with cornmeal.

■ Place the dough on the unheated part of the grill and cook each side for 3 to 5 minutes, covered, or until the dough is firm to the touch and beginning to brown. Use a metal spatula to flip the dough, taking care not to tear it.

■ Spread toppings on the crust and grill for another 5 minutes or more on indirect heat.

Cherry Tomato, Chard, and Goat Cheese Pizza

Roasting pizzas on the grill is easy, and the smoky taste you get is absolutely delicious. I like to add hickory or oak chips to give grilled pizza an even smokier flavor, but you can leave the smoke out if you wish. The possibilities for pizza on the grill are endless: here I use some chard plucked from the garden, but just about any greens will do. Try kale or mustard greens, bok choy, or Napa cabbage. Use our recipe for Pizza on the Grill, your favorite pizza dough recipe, or one of the precooked pizza crusts available in most supermarkets today.

• • • • • • • • • • • • • • • • • •

■ Prepare the fire for indirect grilling. Add hickory or oak to the smoke box (see Smoke on the Grill, page 21). Spray or rub the grill with plenty of olive oil.

■ Grill whole stalks of chard for 1 to 2 minutes over medium-high heat, turning often. Remove the chard from the grill and chop into bite-size pieces.

■ If you have made your own pizza dough, divide the dough into two balls. On a lightly floured surface, knead each section. Stretch each ball with your hands and then roll from the center to the edges to form a 10-inch circle about ¼ inch thick. Brush each side with olive oil and dust with cornmeal.

SERVES 4

2 large stalks chard

1 recipe Pizza on the Grill (page 60) or two 10-inch precooked pizza rounds

Flour for dusting

Olive oil for brushing

Cornmeal for dusting

½ cup cherry tomatoes, halved

1 cup fresh goat cheese, crumbled

2 tablespoons chopped fresh basil

Salt and freshly ground black pepper

■ Put pizza rounds on the unheated part of the grill and grill each side for 3 to 5 minutes. When the dough is firm to the touch and beginning to brown, layer on the chard, tomatoes, goat cheese, and basil. Sprinkle with salt and pepper.

■ Roast the pizzas on the unheated part of the grill, covered, for another 5 minutes or until the cheese melts. Cut each pizza into quarters and serve.

Pizza with Scallops, Roasted Garlic, and Bitter Greens

When roasted on the grill, garlic takes on a luscious, smoky flavor. The mixture of chopped greens and roasted garlic with olive oil also makes a quick and tasty sauce for pasta.

SERVES 4

12 large scallops

•

SEASONINGS

1 tablespoon Fish or Seafood Rub (page 41)

OR

1 tablespoon dried tarragon

½ teaspoon salt

½ teaspoon pepper

•

2 cups bitter greens, such as kale, mustard, turnip, or curly endive, chopped, steamed briefly, and drained

2 tablespoons extra-virgin olive oil, plus more for brushing

4–8 cloves Smoke-Roasted Garlic (page 59) or 1 table-spoon finely chopped raw garlic

1 recipe Pizza on the Grill (page 60) or two 10-inch precooked pizza rounds

Flour for dusting

Cornmeal for dusting

1 cup fontina cheese, grated

■ Prepare the fire for indirect grilling. Spray or rub the grill with oil. If you wish, add hardwood chips to the smoke box (see Smoke on the Grill, page 21).

■ Cut the scallops into bite-size pieces. Combine the scallops and spice rub or tarragon-salt-pepper mixture in a medium-size bowl. Toss so the scallops are well coated; let sit for up to an hour.

■ Put the greens in a bowl, toss with olive oil, and squeeze four cloves of roasted garlic on them or add chopped garlic and mix well.

■ If you have made your own pizza dough, divide the dough into two balls. On a lightly floured surface, knead each section. Stretch each ball with your hands and then roll from the center to the edges to form a 10-inch circle about ¼ inch thick. Crimp the edges. Brush each side with olive oil, and dust with cornmeal.

■ Place the dough on the unheated part of the grill and cook each side for 3 to 5 minutes. When the dough is firm and beginning to brown, layer on chopped greens, then scallops. If you are a garlic lover, you can peel a few more roasted cloves and scatter them on the pizzas. Finally, sprinkle on the cheese.

■ Roast the pizzas on the unheated part of the grill for 5 minutes or more until the cheese melts and the scallops are firm. Remove from the grill, cut into quarters, and serve.

Pizza with Sour Cream and Smoked Salmon

SERVES 4

The variations of grilled pizza are endless: here Northwest ingredients meet cutting-edge L.A. chefs to create a delicious appetizer or first course. The wine: Washington state White Riesling.

. . . .

■ Prepare the fire for indirect grilling. Spray or rub the grill with oil.

■ If you have made your own pizza dough, divide the dough into two balls. On a lightly floured surface, knead each section. Stretch each ball with your hands and then roll from the center to the edges to form a 10-inch circle about ¼ inch thick. Crimp the edges. Brush each side with olive oil and dust with cornmeal.

■ Place the dough on the unheated part of the grill and cook each side for 3 to 5 minutes or until firm and beginning to brown. If using precooked pizza rounds, grill for 1 to 2 minutes per side until marked and warmed through.

■ Put pizzas on a platter and spread each with a layer of sour cream, salmon, and onions and a dollop of caviar. Sprinkle dill over the whole pizza and serve while still warm.

1 recipe Pizza on the Grill (page 60) or two 10-inch precooked pizza rounds

Flour for dusting

Olive oil for brushing

Cornmeal for dusting

¾ cup sour cream

4 ounces smoked salmon, thinly sliced

½ sweet onion (preferably Walla Walla), sliced very thinly

2 tablespoons Columbia River golden caviar or other caviar

2 teaspoons chopped fresh dill

Grilled Pears with Pancetta and Pepper

SERVES 4

Serve these tangy pears and pancetta with an Oregon Pinot Gris. Crisp winter pears such as Anjou or Bosc work better here than softer and sweeter Bartletts.

. . . .

■ Prepare the fire for direct grilling. Spray or rub the grill with oil.

■ Wrap each pear quarter with a slice of pancetta. Use a toothpick or skewer to secure it. Grill on medium heat for a total of 8 minutes. Be sure to rotate the pears thoroughly to cook the pancetta through. Remove from the grill and sprinkle generously with black pepper. Serve warm.

4 pears, cored and quartered

16 thin slices pancetta

Freshly ground black pepper

Penthouse Party: Grilling with a View

My daughter, Meghan, did a great job testing recipes and helping with this book. As she describes below, she and her friends enjoyed doing research and contributing their favorite recipes.

"Luke Putnam, a good friend, has the best apartment in Oakland, a city without many tall buildings. Manhattan it's not, thank God; it has mostly family houses and just a few skyscrapers downtown. In another city, Luke's fourth-floor penthouse wouldn't give you much of a view. But here in the East Bay, standing on his huge deck, you can see the Golden Gate Bridge, Alcatraz, towering Mount Tamalpais and the Marin headlands, the toylike buildings of the far-off San Francisco skyline, and, just about every evening, wisps of fog moving in from the Bay.

"Not only is Luke's apartment wonderful, but Luke, who works at Pixar, the computer animating company, and his roommates are generous hosts who love to throw frequent impromptu barbecues. They call all their friends and talk about the beautiful sunset they can see from the deck. Everybody shows up with food for the grill— chicken breasts with garlic and herbs, fresh fish and seafood skewers, marinated vegetables. Luke supplies lovely wines from his home town, Napa, and makes some of the most delicious appetizers I've ever eaten.

"Luke prepares hummus to dip raw veggies in, fresh salsas for blue corn chips, and tasty grilled mushrooms stuffed with pesto (see Luke's Pesto Crimini Bites, next page). We all watch the sunset until the fog comes in and mixes with the smoke from the grill. When it gets too cold, we move inside to sit around the big table and eat the good food we've grilled. The deck door stays open, though, so Buddy, Luke's big tomcat, can meander in and out and we can watch the fog swirl above the glowing coals."

Luke's Pesto Crimini Bites

In one bite, maybe two, you'll taste three great flavors: basil, Parmesan cheese, and mushrooms. This easy appetizer will keep the hungry hordes busy while the rest of the food is grilling. And if the main course needs extra time, you can whip a few more up to be snatched right off the grill.

This pesto recipe is also good on vegetable brochettes, grilled corn, or burgers. For a variation, you can fill the mushrooms with Cilantro Pesto (page 91), Joel's Eggplant Pesto (page 65), or Smoky Eggplant Caviar (page 72).

Crimini mushrooms are small portobellos. Use them or medium-size white button mushrooms.

This recipe is from the talented young griller, Luke Putnam.

....

■ Prepare the fire for direct grilling. Spray or rub the grill with oil.

To make Luke's Pesto, blend all pesto ingredients in a food processor or blender, making sure to scrape the sides.

■ Brush both sides of the mushroom caps with olive oil. Grill over medium heat, gills up, for about 4 minutes or until liquid collects in the cap. Flip over, dumping the liquid, and grill the gill side for about 4 minutes. Turn the caps over and fill with pesto or other stuffing. Sprinkle with Parmesan cheese and serve.

LUKE'S PESTO

2 cups basil leaves

½ cup grated Parmesan cheese

3 cloves garlic, peeled

3 tablespoons extra-virgin olive oil

Salt and freshly ground black pepper

•

12 crimini mushroom caps, stems removed

Extra-virgin olive oil

Parmesan cheese

Joel's Eggplant Pesto

My friend Joel Herman is a good man on the grill. Joel worked as a film editor in Hollywood for many years, and together we pursued the Holy Grail of grilling—The Perfect Steak—in his garden amid the Bohemian bustle, roaring police helicopters, and never-ending salsa music of the polyglot beach community of Venice (see The Perfect Steak: So Cal Style, page 181). Joel's version of grilled eggplant can be eaten in a number of ways: right off the grill as a side dish, processed with basil and garlic into a delicious pesto to be scooped up with a baguette, or used as a stuffing for mushrooms (see Luke's Pesto Crimini Bites, above). The pesto is also delicious on pasta or as a topping for Grilled Polenta (page 98) or Bruschetta (page 56). Leftover slices of eggplant can be served cold on an Eggplant Hero Sandwich (page 66). Joel's trick is to

4 Japanese eggplants or 1 globe eggplant, sliced lengthwise ¼ inch thick

Olive oil

4 cloves garlic, minced

½ cup chopped fresh basil

2 tablespoons balsamic vinegar

Salt and freshly ground black pepper

¼ cup extra-virgin olive oil

¼ cup freshly grated Parmesan cheese

grill enough eggplants for three recipes: one for quick eating that night, one for pesto, and another for sandwiches.

. . . .

■ Prepare the fire for direct grilling. Spray or rub the grill with oil.

■ Brush the eggplant slices with olive oil and sprinkle with garlic, ¼ cup of the basil, balsamic vinegar, salt, and pepper. Grill the slices over medium high heat for 3 to 4 minutes per side or until they are browned and tender. Move to a cooler area of the grill if flare-ups occur. (Note: you can serve these directly from the grill as a side dish or use them to continue preparing Eggplant Pesto.)

■ To continue making pesto, cool the grilled eggplant slices or refrigerate them 8 to 12 hours. Process into a paste with olive oil, the remaining ¼ cup basil, and Parmesan. Serve as a dip with a baguette or stuffed into mushrooms.

Eggplant Hero Sandwich

SERVES 1

1 French or Italian sourdough roll, split

Extra-virgin olive oil

2 tablespoons Luke's Pesto (page 65) or Roasted Garlic Aioli (page 95)

2–3 slices grilled eggplant

3–4 large basil leaves

½ plum (roma) or other fresh tomato, sliced

¼ red onion, thinly sliced

Shredded lettuce

1–2 slices provolone cheese

Salt and freshly ground black pepper

Use leftover grilled eggplant slices from Joel's Eggplant Pesto (page 65), or grill slices especially for this hearty sandwich. Use the best quality sourdough French- or Italian-style rolls you can find.

. . . .

■ Brush the cut sides of the roll with oil and spread with Luke's Pesto or Roasted Garlic Aioli. Lay slices of eggplant on one side and top with basil leaves, tomato, onion, lettuce, and provolone. Salt and pepper to taste. Add top half of roll and serve immediately.

Grilled Prawns or Scallops with Thai Cilantro Sauce

SERVES 4

Thai seasonings, such as lime, cilantro, and chiles, are perfect for seafood and are especially good on grilled prawns or scallops. Serve this tangy appetizer with Thai Mango Tomato Salsa (page 68) and a cold, hoppy ale from the Northwest such as Redhook India Pale Ale.

• • • • • • • • • • • • • • • • •

To make Thai Cilantro Sauce, combine all ingredients.

■ Peel and devein prawns. Marinate the prawns or scallops for up to 2 hours. Reserve ¼ cup of the sauce.

■ Prepare the fire for direct grilling. Spray or rub the grill with oil.

■ Remove the prawns or scallops from the marinade and pat dry. Slide two parallel skewers through the seafood. (Skewered prawns and scallops are easier to turn, but you can put them on the grill individually if they're large enough.) Use a fish basket, if needed (see Equipment, page 27). Rub or spray the grill with oil. Grill the prawns or scallops over high heat for 2 minutes on each side until firm and no longer translucent. Cool.

■ Serve prawns or scallops garnished with bean sprouts and cilantro, with reserved sauce as a dipping sauce.

THAI CILANTRO SAUCE

½ cup soy sauce

1 tablespoon Thai fish sauce (*nuoc cham* or *nam pla*)

4 cloves garlic, finely chopped

½ cup chopped fresh cilantro (about 1 bunch)

2 tablespoons lime juice

1 serrano chile, seeded and minced

•

16 jumbo prawns or large scallops

•

GARNISH

Bean sprouts

Cilantro sprigs

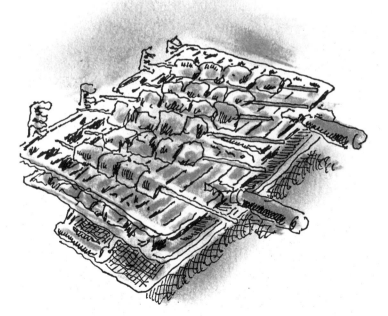

MAKES 4 CUPS

2 cups peeled diced mango

2 tomatoes, seeded and
chopped

1 cup chopped red onion

2 tablespoons chopped
fresh mint

2 tablespoons chopped fresh
basil, preferably Thai

1 serrano or jalapeño chile,
or more or less to taste,
seeded and finely chopped

2 tablespoons rice wine
vinegar

1 tablespoon Thai fish sauce
(nuoc cham or nam pla)

2 tablespoons peanut oil

2 tablespoons soy sauce

Dash or more Sriracha or
other Asian hot sauce

Salt and freshly ground
black pepper, if needed

Thai Mango Tomato Salsa

Serve this lively Thai salsa with grilled fish or chicken, or try it in Fish Tacos (page 51). Adjust the heat level as you want: serranos are decidedly hotter than jalapeños (see Chiles, page 49). Sriracha is a popular Thai chile sauce, widely available in Asian grocery stores or by mail order (see Sources, page 225). Use it or other Thai or Chinese hot sauces or chile oils to spice up the salsa if you want. Asian fish sauce (nuoc cham or nam pla) is made from fermented fish and adds a characteristic pungency to many Southeast Asian dishes. It's available in many groceries or by mail order.

• • • • • • • • • • • • • • • • • •

■ Mix all ingredients in a bowl. Taste for salt and pepper. Salsa will last for 2 or 3 days refrigerated.

Salads and Soups

It might seem strange to be talking about grilled salads. After all, isn't a salad a bunch of greens heaped on a plate or in a bowl with "salad dressing" on top? Well, in recent years, especially in California restaurants, the simple salad has been redefined. Under the influence of health-conscious diners and with the rich profusion of fresh natural ingredients available along the Pacific Coast, chefs keep on adding ingredients so that the salad has become a meal in itself.

Actually, this expanded role for the salad hearkens back to European *salades composées* such as salade niçoise (see Salade Niçoise with Grilled Tuna, page 77) and classic American salads such as the Waldorf and Cobb salads. But West Coast chefs took these salads a step further and used the base of cool greens in a tangy dressing as a platform for serving grilled foods such as chicken (see Grilled Chicken Salad, page 76), duck breast, fish and seafood (see Grilled Lobster or Monkfish Salad with Blood Orange Vinaigrette, page 78), vegetables (see Asian Noodle and Grilled Baby Bok Choy Salad with Orange Ginger Vinaigrette, page 75), and even fruit (see Grilled Apple and Goat Cheese Salad with Walnut Oil Vinaigrette, page 79). Salads like these are substantial enough to serve as a main course for lunch or a light dinner and make wonderful first courses or buffet dishes.

The grill comes in especially handy here. On a hot summer day, what can be more delightful than a mound of cool greens and ripe tomatoes spread out on a plate, tossed with a flavorful vinaigrette, and topped with a mix of fresh summer squash and peppers plucked from the garden and cooked briefly on the grill (see Out-of-the-Garden Grilled Salad, page 71; Grilled Tomato and Yellow Pepper Salad with Lemon Mustard Aioli, page 73)?

But grilled soup? Now he's really stretching it, I can hear readers say. Well, I'm not suggesting that we pour Mom's chicken soup on the grill, stand back, and hope for the best. I haven't gone that far 'round the bend, yet. But think of grilled vegetables heated in a savory stock (see Garden Grill Minestrone, page 81), grilled chicken breasts and smoky grilled chiles in chicken broth (see Grilled Chicken and Chile Soup, page 82), or smoke-roasted garlic and charred red peppers with cream (see Grilled Red Pepper and Roasted Garlic Soup, page 83).

Soups are a great use for any leftovers from a grilling session. Whenever I fire up the grill, I always make sure to cook a lot more food than my family and guests can handle. Why not take advantage of the fire and wood smoke and nicely seasoned meat or poultry or fish or vegetables? It's just as easy to grill eight chicken breasts as four or five, twelve ears of corn cook as quickly as six; and if you're making up vegetable or shrimp or chicken skewers, why not make a double recipe and have leftovers?

I love using extra grilled foods in tacos and quesadillas, salads, and sandwiches, of course, but they can also really dress up a soup. I've given a few suggestions in this section, but use your imagination and create your own "grilled" soups. What about an eggplant bisque made from Smoky Eggplant Caviar (page 72) or Ratatouille from the Grill (page 96) puréed with Smoke-Roasted Garlic (page 59) and Cilantro Pesto (page 91)? Use the following soup recipes as examples or templates, and add your own ingredients as you will.

To make soups into main courses, serve them with Bruschetta (page 56), with the topping of your choice, to sop up the delicious broth.

Out-of-the-Garden Grilled Salad

SERVES 4

This recipe is flexible: use whatever is ready in your garden or looks great at the produce store or farmers' market in the bountiful summer months. Grilled vegetables carry their own delicious flavors, so you only need to dress this salad lightly. All the vegetables should be a little underdone to add crunch to the salad.

. . . .

■ Prepare the fire for direct grilling. Spray or rub the grill with oil.

To make Garden Vinaigrette, mix the ingredients in a small bowl.

■ Brush the bell peppers, zucchini, onion, tomatoes, and string beans with vinaigrette.

■ Place the peppers on high heat, cover, and grill for 3 to 4 minutes, turning often. Remove from the grill, peel off the skin and any charred spots, and cut into strips.

■ Put the zucchini and onion on the grill, cut side down. Turn them after 3 minutes, and add the tomatoes, cut side down. After 2 more minutes, turn the tomatoes and add the string beans (you may want to use a fish basket if they are small). Grill the vegetables for 1 to 2 minutes more.

■ Remove the vegetables as they are done. Take the skin off the onion. Chop all the vegetables into bite-size pieces.

■ Put the spinach in a bowl or on a platter, top with warm vegetables, and drizzle on vinaigrette.

GARDEN VINAIGRETTE

½ cup extra-virgin olive oil

2 tablespoons red wine vinegar

1 clove garlic, finely chopped

Juice of ½ lemon

Salt and freshly ground black pepper

•

2 red or yellow bell peppers, cut in half, seeded, and flattened

2 zucchini or other summer squash, cut in half lengthwise

1 red onion, cut in half crosswise

4 tomatoes, cut in half crosswise

1 dozen medium to large string beans

1 bunch spinach leaves (10 ounces), washed and dried

Smoky Eggplant Caviar

SERVES 4

1 large globe eggplant

¼ cup olive oil, or more if needed

1 tablespoon balsamic vinegar

3–4 cloves garlic, finely chopped

1 tablespoon fresh oregano or 1½ teaspoons dried

¼ teaspoon dried red pepper flakes

¼ cup chopped fresh parsley

Salt and freshly ground black pepper

This grilled eggplant spread is excellent on Bruschetta (page 56), as a dip, or as a filling for pita bread. You can serve it as an appetizer or as a light lunch. Eggplant caviar makes a great combination with Out-of-the-Garden Grilled Salad (page 71) or Grilled Tomato and Yellow Pepper Salad with Lemon Mustard Aioli (page 73) for a vegetarian dinner. Serve a grassy Sauvignon Blanc from California's Dry Creek Valley or a light-bodied California Zinfandel with the smoky, garlicky eggplant.

. . . .

■ Prepare the fire for direct grilling. Add mesquite or other hardwoods to the smoke box (see Smoke on the Grill, page 21). Spray or rub the grill with oil.

■ Leave the eggplant whole, and place it directly over high heat. Grill the eggplant, covered, turning often, until the skin begins to char and the eggplant softens, for 7 to 10 minutes. Check with a skewer or thin knife to see if the center is tender. If not, move the eggplant to a cooler part of the grill, cover, and cook until tender.

■ Remove the eggplant from the grill and let cool. Remove charred bits of skin, and chop the eggplant flesh coarsely. In a bowl, mix the chopped eggplant with the rest of the ingredients. Start off with ¼ cup of oil and add more if needed.

■ Serve at room temperature.

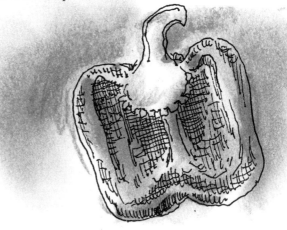

Grilled Tomato and Yellow Pepper Salad with Lemon Mustard Aioli

SERVES 4

Lemon Mustard Aioli is also delicious on grilled chicken, fish, or Summer Vegetable Skewers (page 95). For a quicker version, or if you're worried about salmonella when using raw egg yolks, omit the egg yolks and olive oil and mix the remaining ingredients with a cup of good-quality commercial mayonnaise.

····················

To make Lemon Mustard Aioli, put the egg yolks in a bowl. Whisk constantly, slowly adding the oil. Check the consistency often; when it becomes a runny mayonnaise, stop adding the oil. Stir in the mustard, lemon, and garlic. Whisk well. Add salt and pepper to taste.

(Alternative: You can also make this in a food processor. Pulse the egg yolks, and then add oil slowly with the motor running. Add the mustard, lemon juice, and garlic and pulse again. Add salt and pepper to taste.)

■ Prepare the fire for direct grilling. Spray or rub the grill with oil.

■ Spray or drizzle oil on the cut side of the tomatoes and sprinkle with salt and pepper. Place the tomatoes on high heat, cut side down, for 2 to 3 minutes, covered. Turn and grill for another 2 minutes. Remove to a platter. Grill the peppers cut side down for 3 to 4 minutes; turn and grill for another 2 to 3 minutes. Remove the peppers from the grill, slice them lengthwise, and arrange them on a platter with the tomatoes.

■ Serve the tomatoes and peppers warm with Lemon Mustard Aioli drizzled on top.

LEMON MUSTARD AIOLI

2 egg yolks

2 tablespoons extra-virgin olive oil

2 teaspoons Dijon mustard

Juice of ½ lemon

3–4 cloves garlic, pressed

Salt and freshly ground black pepper

•

4–6 tomatoes, cut in half crosswise

Olive oil

Salt and freshly ground black pepper

2 yellow peppers, cut in half lengthwise, seeded, and flattened

SERVES 4

SOY GINGER DRESSING

½ cup soy sauce

¼ cup sake or dry sherry

¼ cup vegetable oil

2 tablespoons sesame oil

2 tablespoons chopped fresh ginger

4 cloves garlic, finely chopped

¼ cup chopped green onions

¼ cup lightly toasted sesame seeds (see Toasting Sesame Seeds, page 80)

½ teaspoon Asian chile oil (optional)

•

4 chicken breasts, bone in or boneless, skin on or skinless

Salt and freshly ground black pepper

1 pound thin Asian noodles or capellini or vermicelli

•

GARNISH

½ cup chopped green onions

½ cup bean sprouts

2 tablespoons chopped peanuts

2 tablespoons chopped cilantro

Asian Noodle Salad with Soy Ginger Chicken

This dressing adds savory Chinese flavors to chicken breasts here, but it can also be used on chicken thighs, pork tenderloin, and pork chops. The salad can also be served without the chicken as a light, tasty side dish.

· · · · · · · · · · · · · · · · · · ·

To make Soy Ginger Dressing, mix the dressing ingredients in a small bowl.

■ Pour half of the dressing over the chicken. Marinate for up to 2 hours at room temperature or 8 to 12 hours, covered, in the refrigerator. Turn occasionally. Pat dry and sprinkle with salt and pepper before grilling.

■ Prepare the fire for direct grilling. Spray or rub the grill with oil.

■ Place the breasts skin side down over high heat. Sear and mark the breasts for 2 to 3 minutes per side, moving to a cooler spot if flare-ups occur. Move the chicken to the cooler part of the grill, cover, and cook until the internal temperature reaches 155°F or the meat shows no pink but is still juicy, about 10 minutes. Slice the chicken into bite-size pieces.

■ Cook the noodles, following the directions on the package. Drain and put into cold water. Drain again and toss in the remaining dressing. Add the chicken and sprinkle garnishes on top.

■ Serve warm or cold.

Asian Noodle and Grilled Baby Bok Choy Salad with Orange Ginger Vinaigrette

This Chinese-influenced vinaigrette can also be used as a marinade for grilled fish, seafood, pork, or chicken. If marinating fish, poultry, or meat, use half the amount of vinaigrette. Use the other half as a dressing for pasta and/or greens. Any of these can be added to the salad to make it a main course.

• • • • • • • • • • • • • • • • • •

To make Orange Ginger Vinaigrette, whisk together the vinaigrette ingredients in a small bowl.

■ Prepare the fire for direct grilling. Spray or rub the grill with oil.

■ Brush the bok choy with vinaigrette. Grill the bok choy for 4 minutes, covered, turning often. They should still be a bit crunchy. Chop into bite-size pieces.

■ Cook the noodles following the directions on the package. Drain and put into cold water. Drain again and toss with the vinaigrette. Add the bok choy and garnish with cilantro, green onions, and bean sprouts.

ORANGE GINGER VINAIGRETTE

¼ cup fresh orange juice

2 tablespoons soy sauce

2 tablespoons Asian peanut oil

1 clove garlic, minced

1 tablespoon minced fresh ginger

1 tablespoon sugar

2 tablespoons rice vinegar or sherry vinegar

1 teaspoon Asian chile oil

1 teaspoon Asian sesame oil

½ teaspoon Chinese five-spice powder

•

4–6 baby bok choy or 2 large bok choy, cut in half lengthwise

1 pound very thin noodles or Asian rice noodles

•

GARNISH

2 tablespoons chopped cilantro

¼ cup chopped green onions

½ cup bean sprouts

Grilled Chicken Salad

SERVES 4

4 boneless, skinless chicken breasts or 4 cups chopped cooked chicken

Olive oil

SEASONINGS

2 tablespoons dried oregano

Salt and freshly ground black pepper

OR

1 tablespoon Herb Rub for Pork and Chicken (page 37) or herb or spice rub of your choice

½ cup finely chopped onion

¼ cup finely chopped celery

¼ cup chopped broadleaf parsley

½ cup Chipotle Mayonnaise (page 94), Roasted Garlic Aioli (page 95), or commercial mayonnaise

Salt and pepper

1 head butter lettuce, cleaned, leaves separated

GARNISH

Rajas: Grilled Chile and Pepper Strips (page 101)

This is a great way to use up leftover grilled chicken, but this salad is so tasty you might want to grill some chicken just to make it. Grilled boneless, skinless chicken breasts are best for the salad, but any kind of cooked chicken will do. Boneless breasts cook quickly, so be sure not to overcook them. A flavored mayonnaise such as Chipotle Mayonnaise or Roasted Garlic Aioli provides an added dimension to the salad. Spoon this salad between two slices of sourdough French bread for a special sandwich.

■ To grill the chicken breasts, brush breasts with olive oil and sprinkle both sides with dried oregano and salt and pepper or your favorite herb or spice rub.

■ Prepare the fire for direct grilling. Spray or rub the grill with oil.

■ Place the chicken breasts directly over medium–high heat and grill for 3 to 5 minutes per side until internal temperature reaches 155°F or the meat is no longer pink but still juicy when cut. Remove from the grill and cool before chopping.

■ To make the salad, mix chopped cooked chicken with onion, celery, parsley, and mayonnaise. Taste for salt and pepper. Spoon over butter lettuce leaves and garnish with Rajas: Grilled Chile and Pepper Strips, if you wish.

Salade Niçoise with Grilled Tuna

SERVES 8 AS A FIRST
COURSE OR 4 AS A
MAIN COURSE

Salade Niçoise originated along the Mediterranean coast, but Southern California restaurants have made a specialty of the tangy salad, with their own variations. Seared tuna steaks should be almost raw, but you can cook them longer if you desire. This is the perfect dish for a summer dinner on the deck with a bottle of crisp Sauvignon Blanc from California or from Washington state's Yakima Valley.

1 pound small new potatoes

Olive oil

Salt and freshly ground black pepper

1 pound fresh tuna, cut into 4 steaks

1 teaspoon chopped garlic

1 teaspoon dried *herbes de Provence* or dried thyme

1 pound green beans

1 head butter lettuce or other lettuce

1 cup pitted niçoise or kalamata olives

1 cup thinly sliced red onions

16 cherry tomatoes

• • • • • • • • • • • • • • • • • •

■ Prepare the fire for direct grilling. Spray or rub the grill with oil.

■ Toss the potatoes in olive oil, salt, and pepper. Grill the potatoes, covered, over medium-high heat for 20 to 25 minutes, turning often. Use a grill basket, if needed (see Equipment, page 27). When the potatoes are tender, remove from the heat, cool, and dice coarsely.

■ Rub the tuna steaks with olive oil and sprinkle both sides of each steak with garlic, dried herbs, salt, and pepper. Grill over high heat for 2 to 3 minutes per side until seared outside but virtually raw inside. Let cool.

■ Toss the green beans in olive oil and grill on high heat until they are lightly marked and still crunchy, about 3 to 4 minutes, turning often. Use a grill basket, if needed. Or poach the beans for 3 to 4 minutes in boiling salted water. Cool and chop into 1-inch pieces.

■ Arrange the lettuce on individual plates with green beans, potatoes, and olives, and top with onions. Place the tuna steaks in the center (half on each for a first course) and garnish with tomatoes.

To make Niçoise Dressing, blend the mustard, anchovies, and vinegar in a food processor or blender. With the motor running, pour in the extra-virgin olive oil to emulsify.

■ Pour the dressing over the fish and salad. Garnish with parsley.

NIÇOISE DRESSING

1 tablespoon Dijon mustard

1 or 2 anchovies, oil drained, rinsed with water

2 tablespoons red wine vinegar

½ cup extra-virgin olive oil

•

GARNISH

Chopped fresh parsley

Grilled Lobster or Monkfish Salad with Blood Orange Vinaigrette

SERVES 4

1 pound lobster meat or monkfish fillets, cut into 1-inch chunks

Vegetable or olive oil

•

SEASONINGS

1 tablespoon chopped fresh tarragon or 1½ teaspoons dried

½ tablespoon ground fennel seeds (see Toasting and Grinding Spices, page 149)

½ teaspoon salt

¼ teaspoon freshly ground black pepper

OR

2 tablespoons Fish or Seafood Rub (page 41)

OR

2 tablespoons Asian Spice Rub (page 110)

•

BLOOD ORANGE VINAIGRETTE

2–3 blood or other oranges, peeled and thinly sliced

1 red onion, thinly sliced

Juice of 1 lime or lemon

Juice of ½ orange

½ teaspoon finely chopped lemon or lime zest

1 tablespoon balsamic vinegar

⅓ cup extra-virgin olive oil

Salt and freshly ground black pepper

•

1 head frisée or curly endive or 4 Belgian endives

Use West Coast spiny lobster tails or chunks of monkfish or anglerfish for this tangy salad. Monkfish is a deepwater fish that has the flavor and texture of lobster. You could also use large prawns. Blood oranges are delicious and colorful. Use them when they are in season, or substitute any ripe orange. Serve for a first course or light lunch with a dry Gewürztraminer from California or Washington state.

• • • • • • • • • • • • • • • • • •

■ Brush the lobster or monkfish chunks with oil and toss with the tarragon, fennel seeds, salt, and pepper or the spice rub of your choice. Thread the pieces on four large or eight small skewers.

■ Prepare the fire for direct grilling. Spray or rub the grill with oil.

■ Grill the skewers directly over high heat for 3 to 4 minutes per side. Do not overcook.

To make Blood Orange Vinaigrette, mix the orange slices and onion. Whisk the citrus juices and zest with the vinegar and olive oil in a small bowl. Mix with the oranges and onions. Add salt and pepper to taste.

■ Divide the frisée onto four plates and spoon on some of the Blood Orange Vinaigrette. Place one or two skewers on top of each plate and serve with more vinaigrette on the side.

Grilled Apple and Goat Cheese Salad with Walnut Oil Vinaigrette

Washington state abounds in apples of every kind, from old standbys such as Jonathans and pippins and heirloom varieties such as Northern Spy to newcomers such as Granny Smiths. For this recipe, choose a tangy, high-acid apple for grilling: Granny Smiths are ideal. The Walnut Oil Vinaigrette is good over greens or used as a sauce for Brined Salmon Steaks (page 131).

••••••••••••••••••

■ Prepare the fire for indirect grilling.

To make Walnut Oil Vinaigrette, mix the ingredients thoroughly in a small bowl or jar.

■ Core the apples and stuff 2 tablespoons of goat cheese into the center of each. Wrap in foil and put on the unheated part of the grill for 5 to 7 minutes. Remove from the foil and slice each apple in half horizontally.

■ Toss the greens with the Walnut Oil Vinaigrette and sprinkle with salt and pepper. Divide the greens among four salad plates and top with the apple halves. Garnish with chopped walnuts.

SERVES 4

WALNUT OIL VINAIGRETTE

½ cup walnut oil

2 tablespoons sherry or other white wine vinegar

1 tablespoon lemon juice

1 teaspoon honey

½ teaspoon salt

¼ teaspoon freshly ground black pepper

•

2 apples, cored but not peeled

4 tablespoons fresh goat cheese

1 head red leaf lettuce, loosely shredded

1 head arugula, loosely shredded

Salt and freshly ground black pepper

2 tablespoons coarsely chopped walnuts

Grilled Japanese Eggplant Salad with Tahini Dressing

SERVES 4

4 Japanese eggplants, cut in half lengthwise, or 1 globe eggplant, cut into ½-inch rounds

4 cloves garlic, finely minced

¼ cup sesame oil

1 teaspoon ground cumin

Salt and freshly ground black pepper

Olive oil

•

TAHINI DRESSING

½ cup tahini

½ cup olive oil

2 tablespoons sherry or other wine vinegar

1 tablespoon sesame oil

2 cloves garlic, finely minced

¼ cup pitted and chopped kalamata or other ripe olives

Salt and freshly ground black pepper

•

4 cups mixed garden greens, shredded

½ medium red onion, thinly sliced

1 cup chopped broadleaf parsley

¼ cup toasted sesame seeds

Armenian farmers have made California's great Central Valley their home for many years, and this dish is typical of what you'd find served with Fresno Shish Kebab (page 206) or Grilled Lamb Chops with Rosemary Garlic Paste (page 207). Tahini, a Middle Eastern sesame seed paste popular with California cooks, is delicious on grilled vegetables and in salad dressings. It is available in many markets and by mail order (see Sources, page 225).

I like to use Japanese eggplants on the grill, but you could also slice globe eggplants into ½-inch-thick rounds for this savory dish.

• • • • • • • • • • • • • • • • • •

■ Slash the cut side of the eggplants with a sharp knife. Mix the garlic with the sesame oil and brush on the cut sides of the eggplants. Sprinkle with cumin, salt, pepper, and olive oil.

■ Prepare the fire for direct grilling. Spray or rub the grill with oil.

■ Grill the eggplants, cut side up, for 3 to 4 minutes over medium-high heat. Turn and grill for another 3 to 4 minutes. If flare-ups occur, move to a cooler part of the grill. Test with a skewer: the eggplants are done when they have softened and are nicely marked by the grill. Remove and let cool while you prepare the dressing and the rest of the salad.

To make Tahini Dressing, whisk the ingredients together in a small bowl. Taste for salt and pepper.

■ Mix together the greens, onion, and parsley. Reserve 2 tablespoons of the dressing and toss the rest lightly with the greens, onion, and parsley. Divide the salad into four bowls or plates. Place the eggplants on top of the greens. Spoon reserved dressing over the eggplants and sprinkle with sesame seeds and salt and pepper to taste.

■ Serve with grilled lamb or as a first course or light lunch.

Toasting Sesame Seeds

Heat a nonstick frying pan over medium-high heat. Place a single layer of sesame seeds in the pan and toast lightly for 2 to 3 minutes, stirring and tossing the seeds until golden and aromatic. Cool before using.

Garden Grill Minestrone

SERVES 4 TO 6

This hearty soup is based on whatever is plentiful in the garden or farmers' market; it's very adaptable and can be put together in a few minutes using precooked beans. The soup makes a substantial first course but is satisfying enough for dinner along with some crusty sourdough French bread and a bottle of California Zinfandel.

If you'd prefer a vegetarian version, use vegetable stock or tomato juice and omit the grilled sausages.

....

■ Prepare the fire for direct grilling. Spray or rub the grill with oil.

■ Cut the zucchini or crookneck squash in half lengthwise, the pattypan squash in half horizontally. Slice the Japanese eggplants in half lengthwise, or cut the globe eggplant into ½-inch-thick rounds. Leave the tomatoes whole and unpeeled. Cut the unpeeled onion into ½-inch-thick rounds. Cut the red and yellow bell peppers in half lengthwise, seed, and flatten. Wash and dry the chard stalks. Brush all these vegetables with olive oil and sprinkle with salt, pepper, and oregano.

■ Put the squash and eggplants on the grill first, and grill, covered, over medium-high heat for 3 to 5 minutes. If flare-ups occur, move to a cooler part of the grill. Put the tomatoes over medium-high heat and grill for 3 to 4 minutes total, turning often, until they are nicely marked and beginning to soften. Do not overcook. Turn the squash and eggplants when they are marked and brown, and put the onion and bell peppers on the grill. Grill the vegetables for 3 to 5 minutes more. Test the squash and eggplants with a skewer; if they are tender and nicely marked, remove from the grill. If not, cook longer. Turn the onions and peppers, and put the chard stalks on the grill. Check the onions and peppers: they should be softening and marked by the grill. Remove the vegetables when done. Turn the chard stalks after 1 minute and grill for another minute or two. The greens should be wilted and the stalks marked by the grill. Remove from the grill. When the vegetables have cooled, chop them all coarsely, discarding charred bits of skin if you wish.

■ Grill the sausages over medium high heat for 7 to 10 minutes, turning often or until firm to the touch and cooked through (the internal temperature should be 165°F with no pink showing). Move to a cooler part of the grill if flare-ups occur.

---

4 medium zucchini or crookneck squash or 8 pattypan squash

4 Japanese eggplants or 1 globe eggplant

6 medium tomatoes

1 large onion

1 red bell pepper

1 yellow bell pepper

6 stalks chard, leaves on

Olive oil

Salt and freshly ground black pepper

Dried oregano

4 Italian or other spicy sausages

6 cups chicken stock

1 head Smoke-Roasted Garlic (page 59) or 8 cloves raw garlic, chopped

2 cups cooked cannellini or other beans

½ cup chopped fresh basil

•

GARNISH:

Bruschetta (page 56)

Parmesan cheese, grated

■ Bring the stock to a boil and stir in the vegetables. Squeeze the roasted garlic into the stock or stir in the chopped garlic. Add the cooked beans and fresh basil. Reduce the heat to a simmer and cook for 10 minutes. Slice the cooked sausages into rounds and add to the soup. Simmer for 5 more minutes.

■ Put a piece of Bruschetta in each bowl and ladle the soup over. Garnish with grated Parmesan.

Grilled Chicken and Chile Soup

SERVES 4 TO 6

4 boneless chicken thighs, skin on or off, or 2 boneless chicken breasts, skin on or off, or 2 cups coarsely chopped cooked chicken

2 tablespoons chile powder (preferably Gebhardt)

1 tablespoon dried oregano

Salt and freshly ground black pepper

2 Anaheim or poblano chiles

1 jalapeño or other hot green chile

6 tomatoes

1 onion, unpeeled, cut into ½-inch rounds

4–6 corn tortillas

6 cups chicken stock

2 cups cooked hominy (if canned, rinsed under cold water)

1 tablespoon chopped garlic

1 teaspoon ground cumin

1 tablespoon dried oregano

•

GARNISH

Thin lime slices

Pico de Gallo (page 51) or other Salsas Frescas (page 50)

You can make this spicy soup with leftover Mexican-style chicken (see Chicken Fajitas with Lime Tequila Marinade, page 141; Chicken Breasts Adobo, page 142; Smoke-Roasted Whole Chicken with Chipotles under the Skin, page 145; or Chicken, Chile, and Onion Skewers, page 143), or you can grill your own, as in this recipe. Either way, the soup makes a delightful opening to a Southwest meal or a main course for a light dinner.

Instead of using chile powder, oregano, salt, and pepper, as in this recipe, you could substitute 2 tablespoons Mexican Spice Rub (page 51) or Chipotle Spice Rub (page 145). Canned hominy is widely available in supermarkets and Latino groceries. Rinse it under cold water before using.

Garnishing with grilled tortillas is a good way to use up tortillas that have been around for a while.

• • • • • • • • • • • • • • • • • • •

■ Prepare the fire for direct grilling. Spray or rub the grill with oil.

■ If you are grilling chicken, sprinkle with chile powder, oregano, salt, and pepper. Grill the chicken pieces on medium-high heat, turning often, until done, about 10 to 12 minutes total. The internal temperature of the chicken thighs should be 160°F, breasts 155°F, and the meat should be juicy but not pink when cut. Remove, cool, and chop coarsely.

■ Place the chiles, tomatoes, and onion slices on the grill over medium-high heat. Grill the chiles, turning often, until charred and blistered, about 3 to 7 minutes depending on size. Remove from the grill. Grill the tomatoes 4 to 5 minutes total, turning often, until well marked and beginning to soften. Do not overcook. Grill the onion slices 2 to 3 minutes per side until nicely marked by the grill. Peel, deseed, and chop the chiles. Chop tomatoes and onions coarsely, discarding any charred pieces of skin if you wish.

■ Grill the tortillas until marked and beginning to curl.

■ Bring the stock to a boil in a large pot. Add the chicken, chopped vegetables, hominy, garlic, cumin, and oregano. Simmer for 10 minutes. Taste for salt and pepper. Shred at least one tortilla in each serving bowl and ladle soup over. Garnish with limes and Pico de Gallo or other salsa if diners want some extra heat.

Grilled Red Pepper and Roasted Garlic Soup

SERVES 4 TO 6

I love to make this soup in midsummer when bell peppers are at their ripest and reddest, but you can make it year-round if you wish. If you can find fresh pimientos, use them. The red (ripe) jalapeños are optional but add a bite of heat to the soup. You could also add a chipotle or two (see Chiles, page 49), if you wish. For a vegetarian dish, substitute vegetable stock, tomato juice, or water for chicken stock.

When I grill chicken, pork loin, turkey, anything that needs time on the grill, I like to take the opportunity to roast five or six whole heads of garlic). That way, I can serve some with the dish and have plenty left over. Roasted garlic will keep for up to a week tightly wrapped in the refrigerator. Just mash or chop cloves of roasted garlic into whatever sauce, soup, or other dish you want, or mix it with olive oil to make Roasted Garlic Oil (page 98).

6 red bell peppers or pimientos

1 red jalapeño chile or chipotle en adobo (optional)

6 cups chicken stock

¼ cup tomato paste

1 head Smoke-Roasted Garlic (page 59)

Salt and freshly ground black pepper

•

GARNISH

Sour cream

Fresh basil, cut into fine strips or chiffonade

. . . .

■ Prepare the fire for direct grilling. Spray or rub the grill with oil.

■ Place the peppers on medium–high heat and grill, turning often, until the skin is blistered and charred. Remove. When cool, peel, seed, and chop coarsely.

■ Bring the stock to a boil and whisk in the tomato paste. Squeeze or mash the garlic and whisk into the soup. Add chopped peppers and simmer for 5 minutes, until the peppers are soft. Cool a bit and process until smooth in a food processor or blender. Taste for salt and pepper.

■ Serve the soup hot or cool. Garnish each bowl with a dollop of sour cream and some fresh basil.

Grilled Corn and Salmon Chowder

SERVES 4

4 ears of corn, husks removed

2 red onions, thickly sliced, skins on

2 salmon fillets, ½ pound each

Olive oil

2 tablespoons Peppery Chicken or Seafood Rub (page 40) or other spice rub

6 cups chicken or fish stock

1 tablespoon chopped fresh thyme or 1½ teaspoons dried

2 cloves garlic, finely chopped

1 tablespoon cornstarch

¼ cup sherry

½ cup half-and-half or heavy cream

Salt and freshly ground black pepper

•

GARNISH

1 tablespoon chopped green onions

1 tablespoon chopped parsley

You can either grill the corn and salmon especially for this hearty chowder as described below or use leftover Grilled Corn (page 91), Sweet Onions on the Grill (page 100), and Tom's Spice-Rubbed Salmon (page 130). Serve with crusty sourdough bread or Bruschetta (page 56).

· · · · · · · · · · · · · · · · · ·

■ If you are grilling especially for the chowder, prepare the fire for direct grilling and spray or rub the grill with oil. If using wood chips, add them.

■ Brush the corn, onions, and salmon with olive oil and sprinkle with spice rub. Grill corn and onions, covered, for 8 to 12 minutes total, turning often with tongs. Grill salmon, covered, for 4 to 5 minutes each side or until firm. Remove from grill.

■ In a large, heavy pot, combine the stock, thyme, and garlic. Bring to a boil, then reduce to a simmer. Stir the cornstarch into the sherry and whisk it into the stock. Remove onion skins and chop the onions coarsely; cut the corn kernels from the cobs; and coarsely chop the salmon. Stir the onions, corn, and salmon along with the half and half or cream into the stock and simmer for 5 minutes. Taste for salt and pepper.

■ Garnish with chopped green onion and parsley.

Thai Roasted Tomato, Prawn, and Basil Bisque

SERVES 4

This recipe is inspired by a spicy prawn and roasted tomato soup made by a talented Thai chef, Ponnarong Nimearm-on, who performs wonders in his tiny kitchen at Ninna Restaurant in Oakland, California.

....

■ Prepare the fire for direct grilling. Spray or rub the grill with oil.

■ Rub the tomatoes with olive oil. Butterfly prawns by cutting through the back almost to the other side when you devein them. Squeeze lime juice on the prawns. Sprinkle tomatoes and prawns with spice rub. Grill the tomatoes, covered, on high heat for 5 minutes, turning often, until they are lightly charred and beginning to soften. Remove and chop coarsely.

■ Chop the shallots and combine with the stock, garlic, jalapeño, and chopped basil in a large, heavy pot along with the tomatoes. Bring to a boil. Reduce heat and let simmer for ½ hour, stirring often.

■ While the stock is simmering, grill the prawns over high heat for 2 minutes per side or until they are no longer translucent. Remove from grill.

■ Strain the stock mixture and discard the solids. Whisk in the fish sauce and tomato paste. Mix the sherry and cornstarch together and stir it into the bisque. Simmer for 5 minutes, stirring occasionally. Add Sriracha, salt, and pepper to taste.

■ Place two prawns in each of four shallow bowls. Ladle hot bisque over prawns and garnish with basil and lime slices.

8 whole roma (plum) or other fresh tomatoes

Olive oil

8 large prawns, cleaned, deveined, and butterflied, tails on

Juice of 1 lime

2 tablespoons Asian Spice Rub (page 110)

4 shallots

6 cups chicken stock

2 cloves garlic, chopped

1 jalapeño chile or more to taste, finely chopped

¼ cup chopped fresh basil, preferably Thai

1 teaspoon Asian fish sauce (nuoc cham or nam pla)

½ six-ounce can tomato paste

¼ cup sherry

1 tablespoon cornstarch

Sriracha or other Asian hot sauce

Salt and freshly ground black pepper

•

GARNISH

12 basil leaves

1 lime, thinly sliced

Vegetables

My friend Ron di Giorgio owns a house and 40 acres near my house and land in the hills of western Sonoma County. We're both on Creighton Ridge, 5 miles in and 1,500 feet straight up from Fort Ross, the old Russian colony on the coast about 60 miles north of the Golden Gate. Ron spends most of his time these days tending his large organic garden and growing vegetables and medicinal herbs (the legal kind, not the other Sonoma County crop), while I only seem to get up to my place on weekends. It's Ron's dream to live off his land, eating the food he grows and selling fresh produce and herbs at farmers' markets and to restaurants and health-food stores.

I got to know Ron when he was owner-chef of Ti Bacio Ristorante, an Italian restaurant that emphasized healthful cooking and organic ingredients. The menu had a few chicken and seafood dishes, but the main focus of Ron's cooking was vegetarian and Italian

macrobiotic. Ron's philosophy was to use the freshest organic vegetables and cook them briefly and simply to conserve their natural flavors
and health-giving nutrients. His favorite way to cook vegetables is on
the grill.

"Grilling vegetables is the best way I know to keep flavors fresh and
preserve their essential vitamins and minerals," says Ron. "Cooking
vegetables in water can leach out nutrients, and there's always the tendency to leave them in the pot too long. On the grill, you can watch
vegetables cooking, poke them with a skewer or sharp knife, and take
them off when they are still al dente and crunchy. You'd be surprised at
the number and types of vegetables that you can cook on a charcoal or
gas grill. The trick is to get the grill good and hot, spray or rub it
and/or the vegetables with a little olive oil, and then cook the vegetables until they are barely done. Just as with chicken or meat, the heat
of the grill seals the outside of the vegetable and keeps the juices in.
The caramelization of the surface also brings out vegetables' natural
sweetness and punches up the flavors. I season vegetables lightly with
salt and pepper, and maybe some herbs with a little olive oil before
grilling. Afterward you can add lemon or garlic or pour on vinaigrettes
or flavored oils for extra taste. Grilled vegetables can be eaten as is or
added to pasta, salads, sauces, or even soups. To me there's nothing better
than some grilled asparagus, say, anointed with a bit of garlic-flavored
olive oil, grilled on high heat for a couple of minutes, and then served
over pasta with a little grated Parmesan or shaved pecorino."

Here are some of Ron's tips for choosing and grilling vegetables:

"First of all, get the freshest vegetables you can find. Grow them
yourself, if you can, like so many of us here in California do. Planting a
garden in your backyard (or even your frontyard—who needs lawns
anyway?) can give you all the vegetables you need year-round if you
are blessed with our West Coast climate. If you can't grow your own,
buy vegetables at a farmers' market, roadside stand, or reputable produce store. And always buy what's in season; it doesn't make any sense
to grill week-old imported vegetables. You can grill all year 'round.
Just find out what's ripe and plentiful, and give it a try.

"**Corn** is a good example. When corn is ripe in late summer, I eat
it just about every day. Buy fresh corn the morning of the day you are
going to cook it; look for firm ears with plump fat kernels and bright,
abundant silk. Some like to soak corn in water before grilling, but I
don't think that's necessary if it's fresh. You can pull out some of the
silk and grill the corn in its husk, if you like. But I prefer to husk the
corn, rub it with a little oil, and toss it right on the grill (see Grilled
Corn, page 91). You get a little crunch to the kernels this way, and the
corn seems extra sweet. When it's done, sprinkle on a little salt, rub the

corn with a flavorful butter, such as Lime Ancho Chile Butter (page 107) or Roasted Garlic Oil (page 98) or Cilantro Pesto (page 91), and you've got a real treat.

"**Asparagus** is another seasonal delight. When the plump stalks poke their heads up through the mulch in the spring, I start to feast. And by the time they stop coming up in midsummer, I've had my fill. When you buy asparagus, get the biggest and fattest stalks you can find. Thin asparagus is bitter and a little tough, and it doesn't take well to grilling, my favorite way of cooking the tender spears (see Grilled Asparagus with Roasted Garlic Oil, page 97).

"**Zucchini and summer squash** produce abundantly in my garden, and I never get tired of them. When they're tiny, just toss them raw into salads, and when they get big, you can stuff them. But when summer squash are just right—big enough to have plenty of flavor, small enough to be tender and without seeds—I think they are best grilled. I like to marinate summer squash for a bit before grilling (see Summer Vegetable Skewers, page 95). Their somewhat bland flesh picks up flavor from a garlicky vinaigrette or a soy-based Asian marinade. Be sure not to overcook summer squash. A few minutes on the grill is usually enough time. Zucchini and other summer squash can be cooked whole or on skewers; they are delicious served over pasta or in salad. Leftovers make a very tasty appetizer when sliced onto Bruschetta (page 56).

"**Eggplants** are wonderful on the grill. The meaty flavor and rich texture of eggplant make it a good choice for the centerpiece of a vegetarian meal. And when you grill eggplant, you avoid excess oil. Sautéed eggplant has an unpleasant tendency to soak up all the oil in the pan and can end up soggy and unappealing. When you grill eggplant, a light brush of olive oil (just enough to keep it from sticking) is all you need. I like to grill Japanese or Chinese eggplants, but globe eggplants can be sliced into rounds and grilled. When choosing eggplants, look for deep glossy colors and a firm, plump skin.

"When **tomatoes** are in season we harvest them by the bucketful. I love to grill ripe tomatoes, whole or cut in half, and serve them as side dishes or in sauces (see Smoke-Roasted Tomato Sauce, page 98). If you have a freezer, grill tomatoes and put them, skin and all, into plastic cartons to freeze. In the middle of winter, you'll love the sweet, smoky taste of these fresh tomatoes. They will be immeasurably better than the pale pink cardboard imitations that pass for tomatoes in most supermarkets. In fact, when tomato season is over, I just stop eating fresh tomatoes. Either I use canned Italian-style tomatoes or tomato paste or I dip into my store of frozen grilled tomatoes when I want to make a sauce. Grilling tomatoes is simple: rub with a little olive oil and place over high heat, turning often. When the tomatoes are marked and just beginning to soften, take them off the grill. It's easy to slip the skin off then, or you can leave it on for a bit of char and smoke taste, as I do.

"Peppers of all kinds, from mild bell peppers to medium-hot Anaheims or pasilla chiles to hot jalapeños, seem made for grilling. Simply put whole peppers over high heat and grill and char them, turning often, until the skin is blistered and the peppers are getting soft. Just scrape off most of the skin and deseed the peppers and they are ready to use in a sauce or on pizza, to tuck into a taco, or to put on a hero sandwich. I like to grill a bunch of red bell peppers when they are at their sweetest and ripest, peel them, and pour on the best extra-virgin olive oil I can find. Keep the peppers in the refrigerator, or freeze them to use later in the winter for a taste of summer.

"Onions seem to get sweet on the grill. If you can get Maui or Walla Walla or Vidalia or another of the very sweet onions, you are in for a treat. Just cut them into thick rounds with the skins on, brush with oil, and grill. Eat the onion rounds as side dishes, on sandwiches, or chopped into a sauce. **Leeks** and their relative, **elephant garlic,** are also delicious when grilled.

"Garlic heads can be roasted when cooking on the grill using indirect heat. Cook up a few heads when you roast a chicken or turkey and use them with the dish and for delicious leftovers (see Smoke-Roasted Garlic, page 59). Roasted garlic can also be used to flavor oil (see Roasted Garlic Oil, page 98) or in sauces and soups (see Grilled Red Pepper and Roasted Garlic Soup, page 83).

"Mushrooms, especially the large brown portobello mushrooms, are delicious grilled. Their huge caps can be used as vegetarian burgers (see Grilled Portobello Mushroom Caps, page 94) or as "steaks" for a vegetarian banquet. If you can find fresh porcini mushrooms in your market, they are an extra treat.

"Artichokes, especially small or baby artichokes, are delicious when grilled. Split down the middle and remove the choke and most of the leaves. Brush with olive oil and grill over direct heat.

"Fruits of all kinds, surprisingly, become even sweeter when grilled. Any firm ripe fruit will do, from pineapple to apples to pears and even figs. Grilled fruits can be incorporated into spicy relishes (see Ono with Grilled Pineapple Relish, page 127), used in salads (see Grilled Apple and Goat Cheese Salad with Walnut Oil Vinaigrette, page 79), or served as dessert (see Grilled Peaches with Amaretto Mascarpone, page 218).

Grilled Corn

SERVES 4

One of the great pleasures of hanging around the beaches of Baja is grilled corn. Everywhere you go, grills are smoking and crunchy ears of corn are for sale. Rubbed with Cilantro Pesto or Lime Ancho Chile Butter, grilled corn is irresistible. Use leftovers in soups, salads, or tacos.

. . . .

■ Prepare the fire for direct grilling. Spray or rub the grill with oil.

■ In a bowl, mix the olive oil, chile powder, cumin, 1 teaspoon of the salt, and 1 teaspoon of the pepper. Rub the corn with the oil and chile mixture.

■ Place the corn on medium-high heat, cover the barbecue, and grill on all sides for 7 to 10 minutes, turning often to cook evenly. The corn is done when the kernels are lightly browned and tender (husks will char if left on—don't worry). Remove any husks and silk and rub the ears with Cilantro Pesto or Lime Ancho Chile Butter. Salt and pepper to taste.

2 tablespoons olive oil

1 teaspoon chile powder

1 teaspoon ground cumin

1 teaspoon salt, plus more to taste

1 teaspoon freshly ground black pepper, plus more to taste

4–6 ears fresh corn, husked or unhusked

1 recipe Cilantro Pesto (see below) or Lime Ancho Chile Butter (page 107)

Cilantro Pesto

MAKES 2 CUPS

Rub this garlicky cilantro sauce on Grilled Corn (see above) for a real treat. The tangy pesto is also delicious on grilled seafood and fish, chicken, pork, and grilled vegetables. Try it as a sauce on Southwest Black Bean Burgers (page 93) or Grilled Portobello Mushroom Caps (page 94). Cilantro Pesto will keep, covered, for up to a week in the refrigerator.

. . . .

■ Put all ingredients except the salt and pepper into a food processor and blend to make a smooth paste. Taste for salt and pepper.

2 cloves garlic

¼ cup grated Asiago or Parmesan cheese

¼ cup shelled walnuts or pine nuts (optional)

2 cups fresh cilantro, packed

2 tablespoons fresh lime juice

½ cup or more olive oil

Salt and freshly ground black pepper

Asian Tofu Burgers

MAKES 8 BURGERS

4–5 slices stale or toasted bread, torn into large pieces

12 ounces firm tofu

2 tablespoons miso paste

1 egg

1 tablespoon grated fresh ginger

1 clove garlic, chopped

½ teaspoon salt

1 teaspoon freshly ground black pepper

1 tablespoon vegetable oil

½ teaspoon black bean hot oil or other hot Asian oil

1 tablespoon soy sauce

½ teaspoon ancho chile powder or other chile powder

½ cup chopped green onions

½ cup chopped mushrooms

Flour for dusting

8 buns

•

GARNISH

Lettuce

Sprouts

Tomatoes

Mayonnaise

Spicy Ketchup (see next page)

I know the image: Berkeley, hippies, granola, tie-dyed shirts, Birkenstocks. And I know what you're thinking: the only folks who could enjoy this recipe are vegetarians who, in a moment of subconscious meat craving, make due with a bland, crunchy meat substitute to put between two buns and pour ketchup on.

But these tofu burgers taste so good they'll tempt those who enjoy the real thing. The black bean hot oil, soy sauce, and miso add moisture and wonderful flavor that will make even the carnivores come running.

• • • • • • • • • • • • • • • • • •

■ Process the bread in a food processor to make soft bread crumbs. Crumble in tofu; add miso and egg. Process briefly. Remove the mixture from the food processor and mix in the rest of the ingredients, except the flour and buns. The green onions and mushrooms should remain a bit chunky. If the mixture is too sticky, add more bread crumbs. Form eight patties about ½ inch thick. Dust with flour. You may freeze the patties at this point.

■ Prepare the fire for direct grilling. Spray or rub the grill copiously with oil.

■ Grill the burgers for 5 minutes on each side or until heated through and nicely browned. Serve on buns with lettuce, sprouts, tomatoes, mayonnaise, and Spicy Ketchup.

Spicy Ketchup

MAKES 1½ CUPS

Sriracha, a tangy, mildly hot Thai chile sauce, is widely available in Asian markets and by mail order (see Sources, page 225). You'll be surprised what it does to that all–American kitchen standby, ketchup, when combined with lime juice and soy sauce. Ketchup's ancestor is the spicy Indonesian sauce *ketjap bentang,* so perhaps the Asian flavors are not really so strange after all. If you can't find Sriracha, try another Asian hot sauce or paste or some Chinese hot chile oil.

Spicy Ketchup is also tasty on grilled fish or seafood.

1 cup ketchup

1 tablespoon Sriracha or other Asian hot sauce, or more to taste

Juice of 1 lime

¼ cup soy sauce

. . . .

■ Mix and serve with Asian Tofu Burgers (see previous page). Spicy Ketchup can be refrigerated, covered, for up to a week.

Southwest Black Bean Burgers

SERVES 4

These tangy burgers have plenty of flavor and pack a bit of spice. Serve them on a bun with Chipotle Mayonnaise and sliced tomatoes, onions, and avocado for a real surprise. You can also grill the burgers and crumble them up for vegetarian tacos or burritos with plenty of Salsa Cruda (page 50).

. . . .

■ Put the bread in a food processor and process to form soft bread crumbs. Add the egg and garlic and pulse briefly. Remove from the food processor and add the remaining ingredients except the flour and buns. Mix by hand or using a wooden spoon. The mixture should still be a bit chunky. Form into eight patties. Dust with flour. Freeze or refrigerate, if you want, for later use.

■ Prepare the fire for direct grilling. Spray or rub the grill with oil.

■ Grill each side of the patties for 5 minutes or until browned and heated through. Serve on buns with lettuce, tomato, avocado, onion, and Chipotle Mayonnaise.

4 slices bread

1 egg

2 cloves garlic, chopped

1 cup black beans, cooked

½ cup corn kernels, fresh or frozen

½ cup jack cheese

½ white onion, chopped

½ cup chopped mushrooms

1 teaspoon ancho chile powder or other chile powder

1 teaspoon dried oregano

½ teaspoon cumin

1 teaspoon salt

1 teaspoon freshly ground black pepper

Flour for dusting

4 buns

•

GARNISH

Lettuce

Tomato

Avocado

Onion

Chipotle Mayonnaise (page 94)

MAKES 1 CUP

1 chipotle en adobo, seeded, or 1 tablespoon dried chipotle purée or 1 tablespoon chipotle powder or other chile powder

1 cup mayonnaise

Chipotle Mayonnaise

This mayonnaise is fantastic with Southwest Black Bean Burgers (page 93). Latino groceries sell chipotle en adobo: dried, smoked jalapeño chiles in a spicy tomato sauce. Another choice is to use dried chipotles (see Dried Chile Purée, page 108), if you can find them. If you can't find either of these, use 1 tablespoon of chipotle powder or other chile powder.

....

■ Purée ingredients in a food processor or blender. Chipotle Mayonnaise will keep 1 week, covered, in the refrigerator.

SERVES 4

2 garlic cloves, chopped

¼ cup Roasted Garlic Oil (page 98) or other flavored oil or extra-virgin olive oil

4 large portobello mushroom caps, stems removed

Salt and freshly ground black pepper

Grilled Portobello Mushroom Caps

Portobello mushrooms are large brown domestic mushrooms (called crimini when they are small) that are widely available in markets today. Portobello caps are easy to grill. Marinate them briefly in flavored oil and grill the large caps whole, just like a small steak or burger. The meaty, earthy mushrooms can serve as a vegetarian main course, on a split roll as a mushroom burger, or as a side dish with grilled beef or chicken.

....

■ Mix the garlic and oil in a small dish. Rub both sides of the mushroom caps with the mixture.

■ Prepare the fire for direct grilling. Spray or rub the grill with oil.

■ Grill the caps, skin side down, on a medium-hot fire. Cover the barbecue and move the mushrooms to a cool spot on the grill if flare-ups occur. Turn the caps carefully once or twice for a total cooking time of 5 to 6 minutes. The caps are done when the skin side is brown and nicely marked and the mushrooms are tender. Sprinkle with salt and pepper to taste before serving.

Roasted Garlic Aioli

1 cup good-quality commercial mayonnaise

3 cloves or more Smoke-Roasted Garlic (page 59), pressed or mashed

This easy-to-make garlicky mayonnaise is great on Grilled Portobello Mushroom Caps (see previous page), Asian Tofu Burgers (page 92), or Southwest Black Bean Burgers (page 93). It is another example of how Smoke-Roasted Garlic can dress up the simplest ingredients.

••••••••••••••••••

■ Combine the ingredients by pulsing briefly in a blender or food processor. Roasted Garlic Aioli will last, covered, for up to 2 weeks in the refrigerator.

Summer Vegetable Skewers

4 medium yellow and/or green zucchini

2 red and/or yellow bell peppers

2 Japanese eggplants

2 large red onions

2 tablespoons Roasted Garlic Oil (page 98) or other flavored oil or olive oil

Salt and freshly ground black pepper

When summer comes to California gardens and the zucchini and eggplants and peppers are ripening faster than you can pick them, I like to fire up the grill for a special treat. Grilling brings out the innate sweetness of these sun-ripened vegetables, and when brushed with a flavored oil and paired with pasta or fresh greens, grilled vegetables can be the basis of a healthful and delicious summer meal. They also make a colorful accompaniment to grilled chicken, meat, or fish. The skewers could be served with Cilantro Pesto (page 91) or Lime Ancho Chile Butter (page 107) in addition to or in place of the flavored oil.

••••••••••••••••••

■ Prepare the fire for direct grilling. Spray or rub the grill with oil.

■ Cut the zucchini into quarters and the bell peppers, eggplants, and onions into eighths. Pieces should be roughly uniform, about 1½ to 2 inches on each side. Thread the vegetable and onion pieces alternately on eight metal or bamboo skewers to create a colorful pattern. Brush with oil, sprinkle with salt and pepper, and grill directly over moderate heat for 5 to 7 minutes, turning often, until the vegetables are tender and nicely marked. Brush again with oil, pesto, or flavored butter of your choice before serving.

SERVES 4

BALSAMIC BASIL VINAIGRETTE

1 cup olive oil

¼ cup balsamic vinegar

4 cloves garlic, finely chopped

¼ cup chopped fresh basil

½ teaspoon salt

¼ teaspoon freshly ground black pepper

•

2 medium zucchini

2 pattypan or yellow summer squash

1 globe eggplant

1 large red onion, peeled

4 medium tomatoes

4 portobello or other large mushroom caps

1 red bell pepper

1 yellow bell pepper

½ cup chopped fresh broadleaf parsley

Salt and freshly ground black pepper

•

GARNISH

Tapenade Toasts (page 57)

Ratatouille from the Grill

Chez Panisse in Berkeley defines the California style of cooking: everything is fresh and locally grown, cooked with a minimum of fuss and a lot of flavor. Chez Panisse's Alice Waters and other Northern California chefs look to Provence in the south of France for inspiration. Vegetables, fish, poultry, and meat there are grilled quickly and seasoned with plenty of garlic and fresh herbs.

One of Provence's classic dishes is ratatouille, a savory mix of tomatoes, peppers, squash, eggplant, and lots of garlic. We like to garnish ratatouille with grilled French bread slathered with tapenade, a pungent mix of garlic, olive oil, and chopped olives. Serve this for a light lunch, first course, or side dish with grilled chicken, lamb, or fish, and complement with California Sauvignon Blanc.

· · · · · · · · · · · · · · · · · ·

To make Balsamic Basil Vinaigrette, mix the vinaigrette ingredients in a small bowl or jar.

■ Prepare the fire for direct grilling. Spray or rub the grill with oil.

■ If the squash are large, slice them in half lengthwise. If medium or small, leave them whole. Slice the eggplant, unpeeled, into ½-inch-thick rounds. Slice the onion into ½-inch-thick rounds. Leave the tomatoes whole, unpeeled, with stems on. Reserve at least ½ cup of the vinaigrette, and use the rest to brush the squash, eggplant, onion, tomatoes, and mushroom caps.

■ Place the bell peppers directly over medium-high heat, turning often as they char and blister, until soft. Remove from the grill.

■ Cook the squash, eggplant slices, onion slices, and mushroom caps over medium-high heat, turning occasionally, until they are well marked and beginning to soften. Move to a cooler part of the grill if flare-ups occur. The onion slices will cook quickly, 2 to 3 minutes per side; the mushrooms, squash, and eggplant will take a little longer, depending on the thickness and heat levels, 3 to 5 minutes per side. Remove to a platter when done.

■ Grill the whole tomatoes over medium-high heat, turning often with tongs for 3 to 4 minutes, just long enough to mark the skin and soften them slightly. Do not overcook or they will fall apart.

■ Peel and chop the peppers and place them in a large serving bowl. Coarsely chop the squash, eggplant, onions, and mushrooms and add to the bowl. Remove the stems and skins from the tomatoes, chop coarsely, and add to the bowl. Stir in the chopped parsley and the reserved Balsamic Basil Vinaigrette. Taste for salt and pepper.

■ Serve with Tapenade Toasts on the side.

Grilled Asparagus with Roasted Garlic Oil

SERVES 4

Look for fat asparagus right at the peak of the season for best results. Unlike other vegetables, small does not mean beautiful for asparagus. Thick stalks have more flavor and a tender but crunchy texture.

Many flavored olive oils are on the market, but they are also easy to make. This garlicky asparagus could be served with The Perfect Steak: So Cal Style (page 181) for a traditional summer dinner or with Grilled Lamb Chops with Mint Cilantro Relish (page 208). The trick here, as for all vegetables, is not to overcook; allow the natural flavor and crunch of the asparagus to come through.

2 pounds thick asparagus

2 tablespoons Roasted Garlic Oil (page 98) or other flavored oil or olive oil

Salt and freshly ground black pepper

. . . .

■ Prepare the fire for direct grilling. Spray or rub the grill with oil.

■ Snap the tough ends off the asparagus. Brush the asparagus with Roasted Garlic Oil. Place the stalks directly over high heat and grill, turning often, for 3 to 5 minutes until done. The asparagus should be nicely marked and tender but still crunchy to the bite. Do not overcook. Salt and pepper to taste.

Roasted Garlic Oil

MAKES 1 PINT

4–6 cloves Smoke-Roasted Garlic (page 59)

1 teaspoon salt

1 pint good-quality extra-virgin olive oil

Using flavored oil is an easy way to give extra flavor to vegetables, stirfrys, salad dressings, and poultry. Just brush it on or pour it into a pan and avoid the hassle of chopping garlic; the taste is all in the oil.

....

■ Mash the roasted garlic cloves and salt together in a small bowl. Add this mixture to olive oil (in either a jar or a bowl). Let steep 8 to 12 hours. Strain. This flavored oil will last up to a week.

Grilled Polenta with Smoke-Roasted Tomato Sauce

SERVES 4

1 pound cooked and cooled polenta, cut into 1-inch-thick squares or rounds, or 1-inch-thick slices of premade polenta

Olive oil

1 tablespoon dried oregano

1 tablespoon dried basil

Salt and freshly ground black pepper

SMOKE-ROASTED TOMATO SAUCE

1 red or yellow bell pepper

2 tablespoons olive oil, plus more for brushing vegetables

1 large onion, sliced into ½-inch-thick rounds

2 portobello mushroom caps

6 medium tomatoes

Salt and freshly ground black pepper

4 cloves Smoke-Roasted Garlic (page 59) or raw garlic, finely chopped

¼ cup chopped fresh basil

Freshly grated Parmesan or Romano cheese (optional)

You can make your own polenta (follow the directions on the package) or buy premade rolls of the tasty cornmeal mush from Italian groceries or delicatessens. Brushed with olive oil, sprinkled with herbs, grilled, and served with Smoke-Roasted Tomato Sauce, polenta is a great side dish for North Beach Grilled Chicken (page 135) or Boned Leg of Lamb with Wild Mushroom and Fresh Herb Stuffing (page 205). Polenta also makes a delicious first course or light lunch when topped with the tomato sauce and grated cheese.

....

■ Prepare the fire for direct grilling. Spray or rub the grill with oil.

■ Brush the polenta with olive oil and sprinkle with oregano, basil, salt, and pepper. Place polenta pieces directly over high heat and grill until nicely marked and golden brown on both sides, 3 to 5 minutes per side. Remove from the grill and keep warm in a low oven.

To make Smoke-Roasted Tomato Sauce, add mesquite, oak, or other hardwood chips to the smoke box, or add hardwood as described in Smoke on the Grill, page 21. Place the bell pepper directly on medium–high heat and char and blister, turning often, until soft. Remove from the grill. Reserve 2 tablespoons of the olive oil and use the rest to brush the onion slices, mushroom caps, and tomatoes. Sprinkle with salt and pepper. Grill the onions and mushrooms over medium–high heat until nicely marked and softened, 3 to 4 minutes per side. Remove from the grill. Place the tomatoes directly over medium–high heat and grill, turning often with tongs, for 2 to 3 minutes total, until marked and starting to soften. Do not overcook. Remove from the grill.

■ Peel, seed, and coarsely chop the pepper. Coarsely chop the onion, mushrooms, and tomatoes. Sauté the garlic in the remaining 2 tablespoons of olive oil over medium-high heat for 1 to 2 minutes. Add the grilled vegetables and sauté for 2 to 3 minutes more. Stir in the chopped basil and taste for salt and pepper.

■ Arrange the grilled polenta slices on a platter and top with tomato sauce. Sprinkle with grated cheese, if you wish.

Miso-Marinated Grilled Eggplant

This Japanese-style marinade is also excellent on fish or pork. You can garnish the eggplant with bean sprouts, avocado slices, or toasted sesame seeds. Grilled eggplants make a tasty side dish for Chinatown Prawn and Baby Bok Choy Skewers (page 112) or L.A. Seafood Mixed Grill with Mango Vinaigrette (page 110). They can also become a vegetarian main course when served in place of the chicken on Asian Noodle Salad with Soy Ginger Chicken (page 74). Miso is a tangy paste made from fermented soybeans. It is available from Asian markets or by mail order (see Sources, page 225).

. . . .

■ Prepare the fire for direct grilling. Spray or rub the grill with oil.

■ Cut the eggplants lengthwise and score each on the cut side a few times with a sharp knife.

To make Miso Ginger Paste, combine all marinade ingredients.

■ Coat the eggplant with the paste and let marinate for up to 2 hours at room temperature.

■ Grill the eggplants over medium-high heat for 4 to 5 minutes per side until nicely marked by the grill and tender when pierced with a skewer.

■ Serve immediately.

SERVES 4

8 Japanese eggplants

•

MISO GINGER PASTE

½ cup miso

2 tablespoons chopped fresh ginger

3 cloves garlic, chopped

¼ cup sake or dry sherry

1 tablespoon sesame oil

2 tablespoons hoisin sauce

2 tablespoons lime or lemon juice

1–2 teaspoons black bean chile paste or other Asian hot paste

Sweet Onions on the Grill

SERVES 4 AS A SIDE DISH

Walla Walla onions are the best and sweetest onions you'll ever find. Use them or their cousins, Maui onions or Vidalia onions. If you can't find any of these, use large red onions.

2 large Walla Walla or other sweet onion, skins still on, thickly sliced (about ½ inch thick)

½ cup olive oil

. . . .

■ Prepare the fire for direct grilling. Spray or rub the grill with oil.

■ Brush the onion slices with olive oil. Lay the onions on the grill, cover, and grill over medium-high heat for 3 minutes. Turn and continue grilling until tender, about 4 more minutes.

■ Serve hot.

Penne with Grill-Roasted Vegetables

SERVES 4

Use Roasted Garlic Oil (page 98) or a very high quality extra-virgin olive oil. If you use garlic oil, you don't need the extra garlic, unless you're a diehard garlic fan, as I am. Serve with Bruschetta (page 56) or Tapenade Toasts (page 57).

4 small yellow or green zucchini

2 large red onions

2 red bell peppers

2 Japanese eggplants

16 small fresh mushrooms

2 tablespoons olive oil or flavored oil

4–6 cloves Smoke-Roasted Garlic (page 59) or 2 cloves raw garlic, chopped (optional)

4 medium tomatoes

1 pound penne or other dried pasta

Salt and freshly ground black pepper

¼ cup grated Parmesan cheese

. . . .

■ Prepare the fire for direct grilling. Spray or rub the grill with oil.

■ Cut the zucchini into quarters and the onions, peppers, and eggplants into eighths; leave the mushrooms whole.

■ In a large bowl, toss the vegetables, oil, and garlic. Save the bowl to serve pasta in. Begin to boil a large pot of water for penne pasta; add a pinch of salt.

■ Thread the vegetables, except the tomatoes, alternately on skewers. Grill for 5 to 7 minutes, covered, over medium-high heat, turning often, until the vegetables are tender. Grill the tomatoes for 3 to 4 minutes, turning often, until nicely marked and beginning to soften. Do not overcook. Take the vegetables off the grill and remove the skewers. Cool and then chop all the vegetables, including the tomatoes, and put them in the large bowl.

■ Cook the pasta until tender, following the directions on the package. Drain and toss in the bowl with the vegetables. Taste for salt and pepper, and sprinkle on Parmesan cheese.

Grill-Roasted New Potatoes

SERVES 4

20 to 24 small new potatoes

2 tablespoons olive oil

•

FRESH GARLIC AND HERB RUB

4 cloves garlic, finely chopped

1 tablespoon fresh rosemary, chopped, or 2 teaspoons dried

1 teaspoon salt

½ teaspoon freshly ground black pepper

These crisp, small potatoes make a great accompaniment to grilled fish, meat, or poultry. Many delicious varieties of smooth-skinned potatoes are available today: Yukon Gold, Russian Blue, Banana, and Fingerlings, to name a few. Use your favorite or mix them up for color and flavor contrast.

Use the Fresh Garlic and Herb Rub included here, or for a variation, toss potatoes in 2 tablespoons of the same spice mix that you've used on the main dish: Spice Rub for Pork or Beef (page 38), for example, or Herb Rub for Beef or Lamb (page 37), or Asian Spice Rub (page 110).

. . . .

■ Prepare the fire for direct grilling. Spray or rub the grill with oil.

■ Scrub potatoes and dry thoroughly. Put the olive oil in a large bowl and toss the potatoes well.

To make Fresh Garlic and Herb Rub, combine the garlic, rosemary, salt, and pepper.

■ Toss the potatoes with the herb rub, coating them thoroughly.

■ Grill the potatoes directly over medium–high heat for 4 to 5 minutes, turning often. Move them to the cooler part of the grill and roast them at about 350°F until they can be pierced easily with a skewer or a sharp knife. This could take 15 minutes or longer depending on the size of the potatoes and the heat level.

■ Serve immediately.

Rajas: Grilled Chile and Pepper Strips

SERVES 4

2 poblano, Anaheim, or pasilla chiles (see Chiles, page 49)

2 red bell peppers

2 red or green jalapeño chiles (optional)

2 tablespoons olive oil

Salt

Grilling chiles and peppers accentuates their natural sweetness, and touches of char and smoke can add flavor interest to the many foods they can accompany. Rajas are delicious tucked with grilled meat or chicken into tacos and burritos, and they make a beautiful and tasty garnish for roast chicken or grilled fish. The grilled peppers are usually cut into strips, but they can be left whole for an elegant and colorful platter to serve as a vegetable course. Mild chiles and bell peppers are usually used, but you can add a couple of jalapeños if you want more heat.

. . . .

■ Prepare the fire for direct grilling. Spray or rub the grill with oil.

■ Place the peppers directly on the grill, cover, and cook, turning often, over high heat until blistered, charred, and softened, 10 to 15 minutes total, depending on the size of the peppers and the heat of the fire. Remove the peppers from the grill as they are done: jalapeños will take the least amount of time, bell peppers the most. Peel off the skin and charred spots; remove and discard the stems and seeds. Cut into strips, toss with oil, and sprinkle with salt. Rajas keep covered in the refrigerator for up to a week.

Tony's Spanish Rice with Smoke-Roasted Tomato Sauce

SERVES 4

3 cloves garlic, minced

½ cup corn oil

1 cup long-grain white rice

1 cup Smoke-Roasted Tomato Sauce (page 98) or other tomato sauce or 4–6 medium tomatoes

¼ cup salsa of your choice

2 cups chicken stock or 2 cups water plus 1 chicken bouillon cube

Salt and freshly ground black pepper

Spanish rice is a good use for leftover Smoke-Roasted Tomato Sauce. Serve as an accompaniment to Smoke-Roasted Whole Chicken with Chipotles under the Skin (page 145) or Jalapeño-Stuffed Turkey Thighs (page 147). This is a family recipe from a good friend, Tony Salinas.

· · · · · · · · · · · · · · · · · ·

■ Prepare the fire for direct grilling; add flavorful wood to the smoke area. Spray or rub the grill with oil.

■ If using tomatoes, grill them for 6 minutes total, turning often. Remove, cool, and skin, and chop coarsely.

■ To make the rice, sauté the garlic in hot oil until it begins to brown. Add the rice and sauté until it is coated in oil and browning a bit. Continue to stir, adding the tomatoes or tomato sauce and salsa. Reduce heat to medium. Add the chicken stock or water and bouillon cube and stir. Cover and simmer 20 to 25 minutes, or until the rice is tender. Stir once or twice during this time. Taste for salt and pepper.

Gene Cattolica is a masterful grill cook, especially with fish and seafood. He comes from a family of Sicilian-American fishermen and fishmongers and grew up in the San Francisco Bay Area knowing all there is to know about choosing, seasoning, and cooking the rich harvest of the sea that's brought in each day through the Golden Gate. His seafood-grilling tips? Make sure it's fresh, keep it simple, and, above all, don't overcook it.

When you see Gene filleting salmon or shelling shrimp or splitting lobsters, he looks like a surgeon at work, which, in fact, he is. He carries his same concern for technique over to the grill. "I like to season large prawns and scallops lightly, with a little oil and a touch of garlic and herbs and a bit of hot pepper," Gene says, "and then skewer them and grill them as briefly as I can over a hot fire. You can serve them as is, as an appetizer, or put them over bitter greens for a salad or on pasta tossed with a little garlic, olive oil, lemon, and parsley." Gene serves his own award-winning homemade Chardonnay with this dish, but a store-bought Chardonnay would be almost as good.

Large prawns and big sea scallops work well on the grill. They are best skewered or cooked in a grill basket. Smaller bits of seafood can fall through and also cook too quickly and can become tough. Lobster tails or spiny lobsters (see Baja Lobster or Prawns with Lime Ancho Chile Butter and Salsa Roja, page 107) are especially delicious.

Shellfish such as mussels, clams, and oysters can be cooked directly on a covered grill. Clean and scrub them well and place the shellfish, unopened, on direct heat. When the shells open, you may add salsas or other flavorings (see Grilled Mussels with Red Pepper Relish, page 55; Barbecued Oysters with Habanero Salsa, page 109).

The prime rule here is not to overcook seafood. It's better to serve seafood a little raw in the middle (think sushi or clams on the half-shell) than overcooked. Often seafood is done in a minute or two, so be alert and taste and test. When seafood is firm to the touch and opaque white or pink, it is usually done. Pull it off the fire and serve it up.

Gene's Prawns on the Grill

SERVES 4

16 huge prawns or 32 large prawns, peeled and deveined

Olive oil

1 cup dry bread crumbs

4–6 cloves garlic, finely chopped

¼ cup chopped broadleaf parsley

1 teaspoon salt

½ teaspoon lemon pepper

My friend Gene Cattolica has a way of grilling prawns that keeps guests crowded around the barbecue on his deck overlooking San Francisco Bay, snatching the skewers off the grill as soon as the prawns are done. His Sicilian-American family fished the waters outside the Golden Gate for years and sold fish and seafood retail in Oakland when he was growing up. His father and uncles would take the biggest prawns they could find, rub them with oil and garlic, parsley and bread crumbs, and toss them on a hot grill. "They always left the tails on," Gene says, "so they could grab the prawns right off the grill.

. . . .

■ Prepare the fire for direct grilling. Spray or rub the grill with oil.

■ Rub the prawns with olive oil and thread onto skewers.

■ Mix the bread crumbs, garlic, parsley, salt, and pepper on a platter or large plate. Coat the prawns with the bread crumb mixture, pressing the crumbs on to make a crust. Drizzle or spray a little more olive oil over the prawns.

■ Grill the prawn skewers over high heat for 2 to 3 minutes per side, until the crumbs are golden and the prawns pink and cooked through. Try to put the skewers on a platter before all the guests snatch them off the grill. Good luck!

Prawn-and-Scallop Skewers in Wasabi Dipping Sauce

SERVES 4

Instead of running a single skewer down the center of the scallops and prawns, run two parallel skewers down the sides. This makes them easier to turn. Use the largest prawns and the largest scallops you can find for these tasty skewers. Wasabi, the pungent and powerful Japanese horseradish, can be found in powdered form or as a paste in Asian groceries or by mail order (see Sources, page 225). Serve with Asian Noodle and Grilled Baby Bok Choy Salad with Orange Ginger Vinaigrette (page 75).

. . . .

To make Wasabi Dipping Sauce, combine all ingredients in a small bowl and whisk. This mixture can last refrigerated for up to 4 days.

■ Prepare the fire for direct grilling. Spray or rub the grill with oil.

■ Alternate scallops and prawns on skewers. Brush liberally with Wasabi Dipping Sauce. Grill the skewers over high heat for 2 minutes. Turn and brush again with dipping sauce. Grill for 2 to 3 more minutes until the shrimp are pink and the scallops firm. Do not overcook.

■ Serve the seafood on skewers with dipping sauce on the side. Garnish with pickled ginger and wasabi paste.

WASABI DIPPING SAUCE

¼ cup peanut oil

1 tablespoon rice vinegar

2 tablespoons soy sauce

1 tablespoon sake

1 tablespoon wasabi paste

1 clove garlic, finely chopped

•

12 large scallops

12 large prawns, shells removed, deveined

•

GARNISH

Pickled ginger

Wasabi paste

Puerto Nuevo: The Lobster Village

The road below the border in Baja California travels along the ocean, and if you're lucky, the water and the sun will shine bright. About 40 minutes south of Tijuana on the highway, you'll find the village of Puerto Nuevo, a small cluster of buildings just to the west of the main road. If there's a port here, new or old, I've never seen it. This tiny roadside town has only one product: lobster. There are about twenty small restaurants here. You turn off the highway and bump down a one-lane road, which becomes the main street. Park any which way you can (it's not a bad idea to make a deal with one of the street kids to watch your car) and walk down the slope toward the water. Make your choice—the restaurants are all pretty much the same—although I've come to prefer Ortega's over the years.

The menus feature lobster (the Pacific Coast spiny kind, so don't expect any claws here), with other grilled fish and seafood. Most people order grilled lobster served with limes and chiles and butter. I would stay away from any fancy lobster preparations such as lobster Thermidor, and stick to the basics. Lobsters are served half or whole, and the decision is obvious. Not only should you get the whole lobster (a fantastic bargain by U.S. standards), you should be ready to order more than one, if you are a lobster lover as I am. Side dishes of beans and rice and tortillas are served, but I concentrate on what I come here for—lobster. You pull the tail out of the shell, dip it in melted butter and lime juice and spicy Salsa Roja if you want, and dig in. I know it sounds impossible ever to eat enough lobster at one sitting, but at Puerto Nuevo, I've come close. Margaritas and other drinks are served, along with wine at a few places. The choice again is obvious, for me at least: ice-cold Mexican beer with a lime squeezed into the top. But just about anything tastes good with these delicious lobsters.

The waiters in Puerto Nuevo, as in most Baja establishments, are friendly and speak enough English to get everybody what they want. Sometimes, after a long afternoon of lobsters and beer, with the table covered with shells and empty bottles, a waiter will toss a "mouse" on the table (actually a cute little radish cut and shaped like a mouse). This usually wakes everybody up and is good for a scream and a laugh or two. And most times the "mouse" excitement gets the group started on the way home, which is maybe what the waiter had in mind all along.

Baja Lobster or Prawns with Lime Ancho Chile Butter and Salsa Roja

SERVES 4

Use Pacific Coast spiny lobster if you want to be authentic, but frozen lobster tail, large or baby, is also delicious. Large prawns work well, too, or you could skewer chunks of lobster with pieces of escolar, swordfish, or shark and brush with Lime Ancho Chile Butter before and during grilling. Serve the lobster meat or prawns with Salsa Roja or Salsas Frescas. Lime Ancho Chile Butter is also tasty on Grilled Corn (page 91).

· · · · · · · · · · · · · · · · · ·

■ Using a strong knife or cleaver, split spiny lobsters in half lengthwise, or have your fishmonger do it for you. Defrost and split lobster tails. If using large prawns, split the shells along the back, devein the prawns, and skewer them so they lie flat.

To make Lime Ancho Chile Butter, whisk the ingredients together in a small saucepan or bowl.

■ Brush the flesh side of the lobsters or prawns with Lime Ancho Chile Butter.

■ Prepare the fire for direct grilling over high heat. Spray or rub the grill with oil.

■ When the grill is very hot, lay the lobsters or lobster tails on the grill, flesh side down. Place prawn skewers on the grill. Grill the seafood for 2 to 3 minutes. Move to a cooler spot if flare-ups occur. Turn the seafood and brush liberally with more Lime Ancho Chile Butter. Grill until the flesh is firm to the touch and no longer translucent. This might take as little as 2 to 3 more minutes for prawns or baby lobster tails, or it could be 5 or 10 minutes more for whole lobsters and lobster tails, depending on the size. Cut with a knife to check the inside of the meat for doneness.

■ Remove from the grill and brush liberally with more Lime Ancho Chile Butter. Remove the lobster meat and prawns from the shells and serve with Salsa Roja or other Salsas Frescas.

4 whole spiny lobsters or large lobster tails or 16 baby lobster tails or 24 large prawns

•

LIME ANCHO CHILE BUTTER

1 stick salted butter (¼ pound), melted

4 cloves garlic, minced

2–3 tablespoons Dried Chile Purée (page 108) or ancho chile powder, or more to taste

Juice of 1 lime

Salt to taste

•

Salsa Roja (page 108) or other Salsas Frescas (page 50)

Salsa Roja

MAKES 2 CUPS

1 large onion, peeled and cut into thick slices

6 or more plum (roma) or other fresh tomatoes (enough to make 2 cups chopped tomatoes)

1 clove garlic, minced

2–3 tablespoons Dried Chile Purée (see below) or ancho or other chile powder, or more to taste

1 tablespoon fresh chopped oregano or 1½ teaspoons dried

½ teaspoon ground cumin

Salt

Tabasco or other hot sauce to taste (optional)

This popular sauce is easy to make and adds zest to everything from seafood and fish tacos to grilled chicken or fish. Grilling the tomatoes and onions is optional but gives the sauce a delicious smoky undertone.

....

■ Prepare the fire for direct grilling. Spray or rub the grill with oil.

■ Grill onion slices on high heat for 1 to 2 minutes per side until lightly browned. Grill whole tomatoes, turning often, 4 to 6 minutes, until lightly blistered and softened, over a hot fire. Remove the stems and tomato skins if you wish and chop or process the tomatoes coarsely.

■ Chop the onion by hand or in a food processor and add to the tomatoes. Mix in the garlic, Dried Chile Purée, oregano, and cumin. Taste for salt and heat levels.

■ If you like salsa hotter, add Tabasco or other hot sauce to taste. Salsa Roja keeps, covered, in the refrigerator for up to a week.

Dried Chile Purée

MAKES ABOUT 1 CUP

4 dried chiles such as anchos, chipotles, or pasillas, or more to taste

1 tablespoon tomato paste (optional)

1 teaspoon salt

You can use anchos or any other dried chiles, such as chipotles or pasillas, to make a spicy puree. The puree can be used as a salsa by itself or added to other salsas, flavored butters, or other dishes to add a spicy undertone. I mix a tablespoonful of tomato paste into the purée for texture and consistency. This is optional. If you want the sauce hotter, leave it out.

Be careful when handling chiles (see Chiles, page 48). Wear rubber gloves or wash your hands thoroughly afterward.

....

■ Cover the chiles with hot water and soak for 20 to 25 minutes. Weigh down the chiles to keep them under water while they soak. Reserve the soaking water when done. Tear the soaked chiles apart and discard the stems and seeds. If you want a hotter sauce, leave the seeds in.

■ Put the torn-up chiles in a food processor. Start by adding ½ cup strained soaking water and then running the processor. Depending on the chiles, you may need to add more water to make a paste, often another ½ cup. Blend in the tomato paste, if desired, and taste for salt. Dried Chile Purée will keep, covered, in the refrigerator, for up to a week.

Barbecued Oysters with Habanero Salsa

SERVES 4

Barbecuing fresh oysters right out of the Pacific Ocean is a pleasant practice found up and down the coast from Baja to Puget Sound. Seasonings range from hot chile salsas like this one to a couple of shots of Worcestershire and Tabasco or melted butter with garlic and herbs.

Pacific, Kumamoto, or Hog Island oysters are tasty in this dish, or choose another large variety. You can remove the top shell if you want; leave the deep bottom shell on and be sure not to spill out the juice. Or put the oysters right on the grill (deep shell down) and let the shells open in the heat. Either way, be sure to get some savory sauce into the oysters while they're still on the grill.

A word of warning: habanero chiles are as hot as they come. Be careful in handling them (see Chiles, page 48). If you prefer a milder salsa, use serranos or jalapeños.

HABANERO SALSA

6 plum (roma) or other fresh tomatoes

1 large onion, thickly sliced

½–1 habanero or other fresh chile, seeded and finely chopped

Juice of 2 limes or 1 orange

Salt

•

24 large oysters

· · · · · · · · · · · · · · · · · ·

■ Prepare the fire for direct grilling. Lightly spray or rub the grill with oil.

To make Habanero Salsa, grill the whole tomatoes, turning often for 4 to 5 minutes, until blistered and softened. Grill slices of onion 1 to 2 minutes per side until lightly browned. Put the tomatoes and onions into a food processor along with the chile and citrus juice and pulse once or twice to chop roughly. Taste for salt and heat levels. If the salsa is too hot, grill two or three more tomatoes and add to the food processor. If you want it hotter, add more chopped habanero or some hot sauce. The salsa will keep up to a week, covered, in the refrigerator.

■ Place the oysters on the grill over high heat. If you remove the top shells, spoon some salsa on top of each oyster and cover the grill for 2 to 3 minutes. Serve when the oysters are heated through and plump. If the oysters are unopened, cover and cook them on high heat for a few minutes until they open up.

■ Spoon some salsa into each oyster and serve. Discard any unopened oysters.

L.A. Seafood Mixed Grill with Mango Vinaigrette

SERVES 4

MANGO VINAIGRETTE

1 ripe mango, peeled and cut into chunks

1 one-inch piece of fresh ginger, peeled and chopped

Grated zest of 1 lemon

2 cloves garlic

¼ cup packed fresh mint leaves

¼ cup rice vinegar

⅔ cup vegetable oil

Sriracha or other Asian hot sauce to taste

Salt and freshly ground black pepper

•

ASIAN SPICE RUB

¼ cup paprika

1 tablespoon granulated garlic or garlic powder

1 tablespoon onion powder

2 teaspoons lemon pepper

¼ teaspoon cayenne

1½ teaspoons Chinese five-spice powder

½ tablespoon salt

•

12 large prawns, removed from shells and deveined

12 large scallops

1 pound swordfish, cut into 1-inch chunks

1 pound albacore, ahi, or other tuna, cut into 1-inch chunks

Oil or oil spray

It seems as if everybody's at the L.A. beaches on Sunday afternoons, drawn by the waves and a chance to beat the heat. When the beach grills start smoking, you can get quite an appetite just walking by. Try these Asian seafood treats dipped in Mango Vinaigrette, a tangy sauce that is delicious with fish, seafood, or grilled chicken or served as a dressing for grilled vegetables or salads. Or substitute Papaya Jicama Red Onion Salsa (page 124) or Grilled Pineapple Relish (page 127) for the Mango Vinaigrette.

You can skewer the seafood or use a special basket for cooking seafood on the grill (see Equipment, page 27). Skewers have the advantage of portion control and ease of eating for a picnic. Cooking with the basket is handy if you are going to serve the seafood in a salad (see Asian Noodle and Grilled Baby Bok Choy Salad, page 75) or over rice.

· · · · · · · · · · · · · · · · ·

To make Mango Vinaigrette, process all the ingredients except the chile sauce, salt, and pepper in a food processor until smooth. Add chile sauce, salt and pepper to taste. The sauce keeps, covered, in the refrigerator for up to a week.

To make Asian Spice Rub, mix the ingredients together in a small bowl or jar. The rub will keep, covered, for a month or two.

■ Prepare the fire for direct grilling. Spray or rub the grill lightly with oil.

■ Sprinkle the seafood and chunks of fish generously with about 2 tablespoons of Asian Spice Rub. If you are using skewers, divide the seafood and fish into fourths, and thread alternately onto skewers. Brush lightly with oil or spray all sides. If you are using a basket, lightly brush or spray the basket, seafood, and fish and arrange in a single layer.

■ Grill over high direct heat, turning once or twice, until just done. Do not overcook; remove pieces or skewers as they are done. Taste a piece of fish or seafood after a few minutes of cooking. Total cooking time should be less than 8 minutes.

■ Serve the seafood immediately on the skewer or in a salad or over rice with Mango Vinaigrette or other suggested sauces.

Source for Mango Vinaigrette: Bruce Aidells and Denis Kelly, *Flying Sausages.* Chronicle Books, 1995.

Chinatown: More Fun than the Movies

The movie *Chinatown* paints a bleak and depraved picture of a place I love to go every week. Film noir is certainly not my image of the West Coast's bustling Asian markets. Whenever I get a craving for *pho* (spicy Vietnamese beef soup) or *char su* (savory Chinese barbecued pork) or dim sum or clams in black bean sauce—or when I suddenly run out of my favorite hot sauce, Sriracha Thai Hot Chile Sauce—I just jump into my jeep and head for Oakland's Chinatown.

As you can tell, the name Chinatown is not exactly right. Whether in the International District in downtown Seattle, or San Francisco's sprawling Asian neighborhoods near North Beach or out in the Avenues, or L.A.'s not-so-sinister Chinatown, you'll find Thai restaurants next to Hong Kong seafood houses, sushi masters plying their trade across from Korean barbecues, Chinese pork butchers and Japanese fish markets displaying their wares side by side. And Asian markets in these polyglot and vibrant neighborhoods carry virtually every product from just about anywhere east of Suez, from dried sea slugs to galangal, 1,000-year-old eggs to Japanese tea noodles, lemongrass to wonton wrappers.

Whenever I need an Asian ingredient, if I've heard about it, I can usually find it a few minutes from my house in Oakland's hills. But if you don't have the great luxury of living near an Asian district or Chinatown, don't despair. Many Asian markets sell whatever you need by mail order (see Sources, page 225).

So don't be shy about visiting the nearest Asian neighborhood and looking for what you read about in this or other books. Just head to Chinatown, wherever that might be for you, and let yourself wander. The best way to visit is by walking slowly along, looking at the food, and nibbling as you go. I find that a carton or two of chopped *char su* or some Peking duck helps to settle the mind and keep the taste buds alert.

Chinatown Prawn and Baby Bok Choy Skewers

SERVES 4

16 large prawns, peeled and deveined

8 baby bok choy, cut in half lengthwise

•

SZECHUAN DIPPING SAUCE

2 tablespoons peanut oil

½ cup soy sauce

1 tablespoon finely chopped fresh ginger

¼ cup finely chopped green onions

1 teaspoon finely chopped garlic

2 tablespoons finely chopped cilantro

3 teaspoons dry mustard (preferably Colman's)

1 teaspoon Szechuan peppercorns, ground (see Toasting and Grinding Spices, page 149)

1 teaspoon Asian hot chile oil

Serve these Asian-accented skewers as a party snack or a first course with a full-bodied Semillon from Washington state. They also make a great main course when paired with Asian Noodle and Grilled Baby Bok Choy Salad with Orange Ginger Vinaigrette (page 75) or Grilled Asparagus with Roasted Garlic Oil (page 97). I used baby bok choy here, but pieces of mature bok choy or wedges of Napa cabbage would also work well. The Szechuan Dipping Sauce is also tasty on Tea-Smoked Scallops (see next page) in place of Hoisin Vinaigrette.

. . . .

■ Prepare the fire for direct grilling. Spray or rub the grill with oil.

■ Alternately skewer the prawns and bok choy diagonally. Use two skewers to stabilize the prawns or bok choy if necessary.

To make Szechuan Dipping Sauce, mix the ingredients thoroughly in a small bowl.

■ Brush the skewers generously with the sauce and let marinate for up to an hour. Place directly on high heat. Grill for 2 minutes and then turn. Brush with sauce again. Grill until the prawns are pink and firm and the bok choy tender, another 2 to 3 minutes. Move to a cooler part of the grill if flare-ups occur.

■ Serve skewers with the remaining dipping sauce.

Tea-Smoked Scallops with Hoisin Vinaigrette

SERVES 4

Tea-smoking is a Chinese technique that lends a delicate hint of smoke to seafood and is easy to do using a kettle-style grill. I like to use the cheapest grade of Lapsang Souchong, a smoky China black tea, but just about any bulk tea will do. Once you try tea-smoking, you might want to experiment with flavored teas: Earl Grey is scented with orange-smelling bergamot oil; other specialty teas such as mango or jasmine would add interesting notes.

Allen Kuehn of Rockridge Fish shared this recipe with me. We use his Fish or Seafood Cure for a salty tang, but this is optional if you are concerned about sodium in your diet. This recipe is for 2 pounds of large sea scallops; they are so tasty, you'll love the leftovers if there are any. Serve scallops on Asian Noodle Salad (page 74) in place of the chicken, or as a filling for Fish Tacos (page 51) with Thai Mango Tomato Salsa (page 68). Szechuan Dipping Sauce (see previous page) can replace the Hoisin Vinaigrette.

• • • • • • • • • • • • • • • • • •

■ Combine the scallops and cure and refrigerate for 1 to 2 hours. Remove the scallops, rinse briefly in cold water, and dry.

■ Prepare the fire for indirect grilling at a medium–hot temperature (350°F). Spray or rub the grill with oil.

■ Prepare a foil packet of rice, brown sugar, cinnamon, and tea leaves; seal the foil and poke holes in it with a large fork or skewer (see Smoke on the Grill, page 21). Place the foil pack right on the coals or fire. Cover the grill.

■ Rub or spray the scallops with oil. You may skewer the scallops, use a special mesh basket for seafood (see Equipment, page 27), or, if the scallops are large enough, place them directly on the grill.

■ Once the rice-tea mixture is smoking well, place the scallops on the unheated portion of the grill. Cook until the scallops are firm, heated through, and no longer translucent inside, turning once or twice. This should take about 10 minutes, depending on the heat of the grill and the size of the scallops. Do not overcook.

To make Hoisin Vinaigrette, whisk all the ingredients together in a small bowl.

■ Serve the scallops over Asian Noodle Salad or wilted Chinese mustard greens and rice with Hoisin Vinaigrette spooned over.

2 pounds large sea scallops

1 recipe Fish or Seafood Cure (page 41), optional

1 cup rice

2 tablespoons brown sugar

1 tablespoon cinnamon

1 cup Lapsang Souchong or other bulk tea leaves

Olive oil or oil spray

•

HOISIN VINAIGRETTE

½ cup soy sauce

2 tablespoons rice vinegar

2 tablespoons minced green onions

2 tablespoons sesame oil

1 tablespoon minced fresh ginger

2 tablespoons hoisin sauce

Dash hot chile oil or other hot sauce

Fish

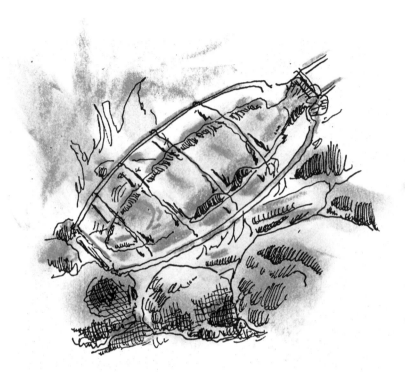

The Pacific, from Baja to Alaska, abounds in fish. Weather permitting, fishing boats set out every morning all along the coast from the lagoons of Baja California and San Diego Harbor, Monterey and San Francisco Bay, Seattle and Puget Sound, and ports on the Gulf of Alaska. Most West Coast fishmarkets carry fresh fish year-round. Fish is one of the easiest and most delicious foods to cook on the grill, and most recipes and techniques are quick and simple. Mildly flavored spice rubs and marinades can add flavor and moisture, while a squeeze of lemon or lime and a brush of oil accentuates natural tastes.

High-heat direct grilling is one of the best ways to cook fish. The intense heat of the grill seals the surface to hold juices in, and the fish cooks quickly so it doesn't have a chance to dry out. You want a really hot fire for fish: I use mesquite charcoal because it burns hottest, but you could also use briquettes or hardwoods in a double or triple layer for extra heat (see Building a Charcoal or Hardwood Fire, page 12). With a gas grill or indoor grill, try to get the heat as high as you can. Use the hand-over-the-fire method to test for heat: Hold your hand on inch or so over the hottest part of the grill and start counting slowly. If you can get to 3 without removing your hand, the fire is probably not hot enough.

Most fish are not very fatty, so use either an oil-based marinade or a bit of oil rubbed on the fish before grilling. Even with fattier types of fish, such as salmon and escolar, a light brushing with oil is a good idea. This will keep the fish from sticking to the grill and tearing when it is removed. For best results, brush or scrape your grill clean and spray it with oil. The grill should also be preheated well before any fish are put on. If the fillet has skin on one side, start with the skin side up so that you'll end up with a handsome presentation. Try to turn fish only once on the grill to prevent the pieces from flaking or tearing apart.

Fish grill baskets and screens are widely available these days (see Equipment, page 27). They can be very helpful when grilling fish, especially tender varieties and thin fillets. Baskets can keep fish from flaking and falling through the grill; they also help hold the fish together. Oil baskets or screens well before using.

Fish steaks cut across the length of the fish or thick fillets are best for grilling. These thicker cuts keep their shapes well on the grill and also help prevent overcooking. Tuna, which can dry out easily, is often grilled in thick blocks on all sides so that the outside is seared and the interior still raw (see Seared Tuna with Togarishi Pepper and Wasabi Mustard Sauce, page 126).

Firm-fleshed fish in relatively thick pieces are best for grilling. These include tuna, salmon, swordfish, shark, halibut, grouper, sea bass, anglerfish (also called monkfish), and true cod. More delicate, flakier fish—such as Pacific rockfish (often called red snapper), rock cod or ling cod, flounder, sole, sand dabs, black cod (also called sablefish or butterfish)—can be grilled, but care should be taken. These delicate fish should be placed in a well-oiled grilling basket and cooked for only a short period of time.

I usually don't use smoke from wood chips with fish because it can be too strong for the delicate flavors of fish. I make an exception, though, for salmon. This fatty fish takes well to smoke, especially alder or cherry wood (see Tom's Spice-Rubbed Salmon with Grilled Corn Relish, page 130, and John's Cured Smoked Salmon, page 131).

Hawaii has a long tradition of fish and seafood grilled over kiawe wood (mesquite). Hawaiian cooks often marinate and season fish with Asian ingredients such as soy, ginger, miso, wasabi, togarishi pepper, and sesame oil and seeds. Salsas and relishes that incorporate tropical fruits such as mango, pineapple, and papaya go beautifully with grilled fish. Some Hawaiian fish suitable for grilling are ahi (tuna), ono, mahimahi, escolar, and marlin. Many of these are increasingly available fresh in West Coast markets.

Always buy fresh fish from a reputable fishmonger (see Allen's Tips on Grilling Fish, below). Don't buy frozen fish, and never freeze fresh fish for later use; cook fish the day you buy it. If you have leftover grilled fish, use it the next day in a dish such as Fish Tacos with Three Salsas (page 51) or Grilled Seafood Quesadillas (page 55).

Allen's Tips on Grilling Fish

Allen Kuehn, owner of Rockridge Fish Market in Oakland, gives his customers good advice on cooking the fresh fish and seafood he sells. His background as a chef at Bay Area landmarks such as PJ's Oysterbed and Narsai's helps him guide people to the best way of cooking different varieties of fish and seafood. His favorite way to cook most fish? Grilling, of course.

"Grilling provides an intense flavor that you can only get by searing the surface. The seasonings merge with the distinctive taste of the fish itself, and a tasty crust forms.

"The first tip for successful grilling is to get the bars of the grill really hot. Up to a little while ago, mesquite charcoal was my main choice, but I recently purchased a gas grill, and I use it all the time now. Both types of grill give me enough heat for grilling fish or seafood. Scrub the grill bars with a wire brush, and rub them with a little oil. Preheat the grill so that when you put the fish down you hear it sizzle. This way, you'll get the searing effect you want and the fish won't stick to the grill.

"Seasoning fish correctly is also important. I tell my customers that the marinade or seasonings determine the ultimate flavor of the fish. When they ask me how to season fish, I ask them, 'What country do you want to visit tonight?' If it's Mexico, I recommend rubbing the fish with oil and sprinkling it with a bit of chile powder and oregano; if Italy, it's olive oil, garlic, and some basil. I don't like to overdo the seasonings, though: rub the fish with a little oil, some chopped garlic, salt and pepper, and add just a touch of whatever herbs you like. Using a spice rub or herb rub is another good way to add flavor.

"The key to successful grilling is not to overcook the fish or seafood. If you are cooking a fish fillet or steak about an inch thick, 4 minutes per side is a good rule of thumb. Check the fish just before you think it's done. The flesh should be firm and not translucent inside and should flake slightly when you probe with a skewer or a thin knife. I think that most fish should be just cooked through, although some fish, like ahi, can be served rare. Seafood, such as shrimp or scallops, cooks quickly. A couple of minutes per side is usually enough. When seafood is firm and no longer translucent, take it off the grill.

"The fat content of fish makes a big difference in how long is needed to cook it. Here are some of my recommendations:

"Halibut is one of the best fish for the grill, because it is firm-fleshed and buttery. I sell locally caught California halibut, which is a bit leaner than the Alaskan halibut found in Northwest markets. The key with halibut is to season it lightly and not to overcook it.

"Salmon is a great favorite on the grill. Fat content varies in salmon depending on the type you are cooking and where it is from. Alaska-caught salmon is the richest, with fish from the Copper River a seasonal delicacy. I like to leave salmon just a bit rare inside, pink with a lightly translucent center. Salmon is one fish that really goes with smoke and can also be brined for extra flavor and texture.

"Escolar is a rich-tasting fish from tropical waters that has a high oil content. It really sizzles on the grill and stays very juicy. White-fleshed escolar is delicious with tangy citrus-based salsas. Escolar's high oil content can occasionally cause some people digestive problems, but most of my customers love it and keep coming back for more.

"Ono, or **King Mackerel,** is a firm-fleshed tropical fish that has a high oil content. It is excellent grilled and is often served with Salsas Frescas (see page 50). **Swordfish** and **Marlin** are dense-fleshed and rich enough for successful grilling. **Opah,** or **Hawaiian Moonfish,** is similar in texture to swordfish and has a taste somewhat like tuna. **Ahi, Tombo,** and other tunas are delicious grilled, but care must be taken or they can end up a bit dry. Ahi is often served rare, especially by Asian-influenced chefs, with a spicy dipping sauce based on wasabi and soy.

"I love to grill whole fish, especially various types of snapper (Thai or red). Here the fish is gutted and scaled and then stuffed with aromatics such as onions, fennel, and other fresh herbs. Score the skin, rub it with oil, and sprinkle with salt and pepper. Grill 4 to 5 minutes per side or until the flesh at the backbone flakes slightly.

"Another way to grill fish is to use the indirect method for large cuts of salmon and other fish. I cut a flap in the flesh of a large, skin-on salmon fillet and stuff the fillet with some chopped spinach and lightly sautéed mushrooms and onions. Roll and tie the salmon roast, and then cook it by indirect heat until done. This is a favorite with my customers and also with guests at Sunday barbecues."

Ahi Skewers with Miso-Sesame Crust

SERVES 4

Japanese cooks often grill fish and seafood with a miso–sesame seed topping. Hawaiian chefs use this style of cooking, called *dengaku,* with ahi and other types of tuna. Tuna dries out quickly on the fire, so leave the inside of the fish rare to medium rare. Get your grill very hot, and grill the skewers briefly just to sear the surface. These skewers are very tasty with Wasabi Mustard Sauce, or try them with Grilled Pineapple Relish or Papaya Jicama Red Onion Salsa.

• • • • • • • • • • • • • • • • •

To make Miso-Sesame Crust, mix all the ingredients except the sesame seeds together in a small bowl.

▧ Coat the tuna pieces with the miso paste. The fish can then marinate for up to an hour at room temperature.

▧ Thread fish pieces onto skewers and sprinkle with sesame seeds.

▧ Prepare the fire for direct grilling. Spray or rub the grill with oil.

▧ Grill the skewers over high heat for 3 minutes; turn and baste the fish with any extra miso-sesame mixture. Grill another 2 to 3 minutes until the fish is medium-rare. Do not overcook.

▧ Serve skewers with dipping sauce, relish, or salsa of your choice.

MISO-SESAME CRUST

¼ cup white miso

2 tablespoons sake, mirin, or dry sherry

1 tablespoon rice wine vinegar

1 teaspoon sesame oil

1 tablespoon chopped fresh ginger

2 tablespoons sesame seeds

•

2 pounds ahi or other fresh tuna, cut into 2-inch pieces

Wasabi Mustard Sauce (page 126), Grilled Pineapple Relish (page 127), or Papaya Jicama Red Onion Salsa (page 124)

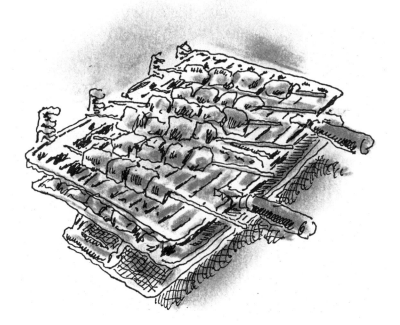

Grilled Escolar with Lime Tequila Relish

SERVES 4

4 escolar fillets (about 1 pound total)

•

SEASONINGS

1 tablespoon dried thyme or tarragon

Salt and freshly ground black pepper

OR

1 tablespoon Asian Spice Rub (page 110)

OR

1 tablespoon Fish or Seafood Rub (page 41)

•

LIME TEQUILA RELISH

1 cup chopped tomatoes

1 or more jalapeño chiles, minced

½ cup chopped onion

¼ cup chopped cilantro

1 tablespoon tequila

2 tablespoons lime juice

¼ teaspoon cayenne, or more to taste

1 teaspoon salt, or more to taste

¼ teaspoon freshly ground black pepper

A dash or two Tabasco or other hot sauce (optional)

Escolar is a white, firm-fleshed tropical fish that is perfect for grilling. Its rich, oily flesh literally sizzles on the grill and makes the phrase "melt in the mouth" believable. Its high oil content can cause problems for some folk's tummies, but I've never had any cause for complaint. You can grill whole escolar fillets and serve with Lime Tequila Relish, or you could substitute escolar chunks in any skewered fish or seafood recipe. Escolar is also delicious with any of our Salsas Frescas (page 50) or with Salsa Roja (page 108).

....

■ Prepare the fire for direct grilling. Spray or rub the grill with oil.

■ Trim the escolar of any skin or bones. Sprinkle with dried herb, salt, and pepper or spice rub of your choice.

To make Lime Tequila Relish, combine the ingredients in a small bowl.

■ Make sure the grill is very hot. Place the fillets over high heat and grill for 3 to 4 minutes per side.

■ Serve with Lime Tequila Relish or a salsa of your choice.

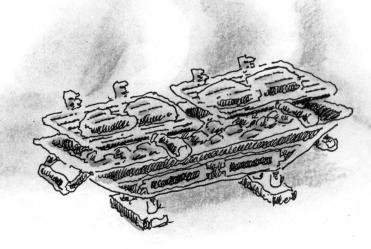

Grilled Snapper on the Beach

SERVES 4

Red snapper, or *huachinango,* is delicious grilled whole and served with a traditional chile and caper sauce. You could also use any West Coast rockfish or farm-raised striped bass. Fillets of firm white-fleshed fish such as sea bass, halibut, rock cod, or grouper could also be grilled. Fillets require less time and are more delicate than whole fish. Use a fish basket and turn carefully (see Equipment, page 27).

Even though Vera Cruz is on the east coast of Mexico, you'll find *huachinango* Vera Cruz style grilled on the beach all along the coast of Baja. If you want a bit more heat in the sauce, add more jalapeños or use hotter serrano chiles. Serve with Grilled Corn Tortillas (page 52) and Summer Vegetable Skewers (page 95). Leftovers will be tasty the next day in a salad or in Fish Tacos with Three Salsas (page 51).

....

■ Gut and scale the fish. Slash the skin on both sides in two or three places. Rub with oil and lime juice. Sprinkle with chile powder, oregano, and salt and pepper or spice mix.

■ Prepare the fire for direct grilling. Spray or rub the grill with oil.

■ Grill the fish directly over high heat for about 4 minutes per side or until the flesh flakes when probed with the point of the knife. Remove to a platter.

To make Vera Cruz Sauce, grill the onion slices over medium-high heat for 3 to 4 minutes per side. Remove the skins and chop coarsely. Grill the tomatoes for 3 to 4 minutes, turning often, until the skin is blistered and the tomatoes begin to soften. Cut off the stems, peel, and chop coarsely. Grill the pepper on high heat until charred and blistered, about 5 to 7 minutes. Peel, seed, and chop coarsely. Mix the vegetables in a bowl with the remaining ingredients.

■ Spoon the sauce over the fish and garnish with fresh lime slices and cilantro sprigs.

2 whole red snappers (about 2 pounds each)

Olive or vegetable oil

Juice of 1 lime

•

SEASONINGS

1 tablespoon chile powder

1 teaspoon dried oregano

1 teaspoon salt and freshly ground pepper

OR

2 tablespoons Mexican Spice Rub (page 51)

OR

2 tablespoons Chipotle Spice Rub (page 145)

OR

2 tablespoons Fish or Seafood Rub (page 41)

•

VERA CRUZ SAUCE

1 onion, unpeeled, cut in ½-inch rounds

6 plum (roma) tomatoes

1 red bell pepper

2 cloves garlic, chopped

1 or more jalapeño chiles, seeded and finely chopped

2 tablespoons chopped capers

2 tablespoons chopped pitted green olives

1 tablespoon lemon juice

Salt and freshly ground black pepper to taste

•

GARNISH

Limes, thinly sliced

Cilantro sprigs

Shark Steaks Adobo with Chipotle Grilled Tomatoes

SERVES 4

4 shark steaks

½ cup adobo or 2 tablespoons puréed chipotles en adobo

Salt and freshly ground black pepper

•

CHIPOTLE GRILLED TOMATOES

4 large fresh tomatoes, cut in half

Vegetable or olive oil

Salt and freshly ground black pepper

2 tablespoons puréed chipotles en adobo or 2 tablespoons dried chipotle purée

•

GARNISH

Limes, sliced

Fresh cilantro, chopped

Shark is a delicious, dense-textured fish that takes well to the grill. Baja cooks like to marinate shark steaks in a spicy adobo sauce made from tomatoes, vinegar, and chiles before grilling. You can make your own adobo (see Chicken Breasts Adobo, page 142) or use canned chipotles en adobo. For the tomatoes, use canned chipotles, or make a purée from dried chipotles (see Dried Chile Purée, page 108). A nice accompaniment for this dish is Out-of-the-Garden Grilled Salad (page 71). Any leftover shark is great in Fish Tacos with Three Salsas (page 51).

• • • • • • • • • • • • • • • • •

■ Coat both sides of the shark steaks with adobo or puréed chipotles en adobo (use a food mill or strainer to purée the chipotles en adobo). Marinate for up to 2 hours before cooking. Sprinkle with salt and pepper.

■ Prepare the fire for direct grilling. Spray or rub the grill with oil.

■ Grill the shark steaks over high direct heat for 3 to 5 minutes per side, until done (when the fish flakes but is still moist). Remove from the grill and keep warm.

To make Chipotle Grilled Tomatoes, spray or rub the cut sides of the tomatoes with oil and sprinkle with salt and pepper. Place the cut side down over high heat to sear and mark the tomatoes for 1 to 2 minutes. Turn and move to a cooler part of the grill. Brush with chipotle purée and cook, covered, for another minute or two. Do not overcook or the tomatoes will fall apart. Remove and garnish with chopped cilantro.

■ Serve the shark steaks, garnished with lime slices, on a platter with the grilled tomatoes.

Grilled Sea Bass with Avocado Sauce

SERVES 4

Sea bass is a delightful, light-textured fish that takes well to grilling. The avocado sauce here has a delicate but spicy flavor that is delicious on fish and seafood of all kinds. Serve the sea bass steaks with Out-of-the-Garden Grilled Salad (page 71) or Grilled Tomato and Yellow Pepper Salad with Lemon Mustard Aioli (page 73). Any leftover fish and sauce can be tucked into Grilled Corn Tortillas (page 52) for a tasty fish taco.

4 sea bass steaks (about ½ pound each)

2 tablespoons lime juice

1 tablespoon salt

1 teaspoon lemon pepper

• • • • • • • • • • • • • • • • • •

■ Sprinkle the fish steaks with lime juice, salt, and lemon pepper. Let the steaks sit for up to an hour at room temperature.

AVOCADO SAUCE

½–1 jalapeño chile, seeded and minced

½ cup chopped cilantro

1 ripe avocado

1 tablespoon lime juice

2 cloves garlic

1 teaspoon salt

½ cup water

2 tablespoons sour cream

■ Prepare the fire for direct grilling. Spray or rub the grill with oil.

■ Grill the steaks for 3 minutes over high heat. Turn and cook for another 2 to 3 minutes until done. The fish should be flaky but still juicy. Do not overcook.

To make Avocado Sauce, add all sauce ingredients except the sour cream to a food processor or blender. Process until smooth. Stir in the sour cream.

■ Spoon the sauce over the fish before serving. Garnish with lime slices.

GARNISH

Limes, thinly sliced

Grilled Swordfish with Papaya Jicama Red Onion Salsa

SERVES 4

4 swordfish steaks (about ½ pound each)

Juice of 1 lime

SEASONINGS

2 teaspoons salt

1 teaspoon ground star anise or fennel seeds or anise powder (see Toasting and Grinding Spices, page 149)

½ teaspoon freshly ground black pepper

OR

1 tablespoon Asian Spice Rub (page 110)

PAPAYA JICAMA RED ONION SALSA

1 cup finely chopped red onion

1 teaspoon salt

2 tablespoons lime juice

1 jalapeño chile, seeded and finely chopped, or more to taste

2 tablespoons chopped fresh mint

4 cups chopped fresh papaya or peaches

1 cup diced jicama

I think that the best way to cook swordfish is on the grill. The firm and flavorful fish picks up hints of smoke from the fire and is delicious when served with a tangy salsa such as Papaya Jicama Red Onion Salsa. Grilled swordfish makes a delightful main course with Grilled Asparagus with Roasted Garlic Oil (page 97) and Grill-Roasted New Potatoes (page 101). A crisp and lively Sauvignon Blanc from California's Livermore Valley is a perfect match.

• • • • • • • • • • • • • • • • • •

■ Sprinkle the fish with lime juice, salt, star anise, and pepper or the Asian Spice Rub, and let the steaks sit for up to an hour at room temperature.

■ Prepare the fire for direct grilling. Spray or rub the grill with oil.

To make Papaya Jicama Red Onion Salsa, toss the onions well with the salt and lime juice in a serving bowl. Let sit for 10 to 15 minutes to pickle the onions slightly while you prepare the rest of the ingredients. Mix the onions with the remaining ingredients.

■ Grill the fish on high heat for 3 minutes; turn and cook for another 2 to 3 minutes until the fish is flaky, but still juicy.

■ Serve immediately with Papaya Jicama Red Onion Salsa.

Sesame-Crusted Yellowtail Tuna with Tahini Yogurt Sauce

SERVES 4

Tahini, a paste made from sesame seeds, is much loved by Northern California's vegetarian cooks. It packs a lot of flavor and provides a creamy, toasty character to salads, to grilled vegetables, and, as here, in a tangy yogurt sauce for grilled tuna. Hawaiian cooks love to create crunchy sesame seed crusts on grilled fish. I use yellowtail tuna in this recipe, but any firm-fleshed fish will do. Serve with Summer Vegetable Skewers (page 95) or Miso-Marinated Grilled Eggplant (page 99).

．．．．．．．．．．．．．．．．．．

To make Tahini Yogurt Sauce, mix tahini and water to form a paste. Whisk in the remaining ingredients.

■ Prepare the fire for direct grilling. Spray or rub the grill with oil.

■ Rub the fish pieces with sesame oil and sprinkle all sides with sesame seeds, salt, and pepper. Grill over high heat for 2 minutes; turn carefully using a spatula and grill for another 2 to 3 minutes. The crust should be golden brown, and the fish should flake but still be juicy.

■ Remove the yellowtail from the grill and top with sauce. Garnish with cilantro.

TAHINI YOGURT SAUCE

½ cup tahini

2 tablespoons hot water

2 tablespoons olive oil

Juice of ½ lemon

1 clove garlic

¼ cup plain yogurt

1 tablespoon toasted sesame seeds (see Toasting Sesame Seeds, page 80)

1 teaspoon ground cumin

1 teaspoon ground coriander

1 teaspoon salt

½ teaspoon freshly ground black pepper

•

4 yellowtail tuna steaks or fillets (about ½ pound each)

1 tablespoon sesame oil

¼ cup sesame seeds

Salt and freshly ground black pepper

•

GARNISH

½ cup chopped cilantro

Seared Tuna with Togarishi Pepper and Wasabi Mustard Sauce

SERVES 4

2 pounds sashimi-grade tuna, in steaks or in 1 piece

•

SEASONINGS

Kosher salt

Togarishi pepper

OR

2 tablespoons Asian Spice Rub (page 110)

•

2 cups daikon, thinly grated

2 cups carrots, shredded

1 cup pickled ginger

•

WASABI MUSTARD SAUCE

1 tablespoon rice wine vinegar

1 tablespoon wasabi paste, or more to taste

¼ cup soy sauce

Juice of 1 lime

1 tablespoon dry mustard (preferably Colman's)

For this recipe, get the best-quality fresh tuna you can find: sashimi grade, if you have access to a Japanese fishmonger. And get it either in one thick piece or cut into thick (at least 1-inch and preferably 2-inch) blocks. The trick is to sear the tuna over a very hot fire, marking it and cooking only about ¼ inch of the fish. The center should still be raw. You then slice the tuna into bite-size pieces and serve with pickled ginger and Wasabi Mustard Sauce. Togarishi pepper is a seasoned Japanese pepper available in Asian groceries or by mail order (see Sources, page 225).

Serve as a first course or as a light dinner with Miso-Marinated Grilled Eggplant (page 99) and Asian Noodle and Grilled Baby Bok Choy Salad with Orange Ginger Vinaigrette (page 75).

■ Prepare the fire for direct grilling. Spray or rub the grill with oil.

■ Sprinkle the tuna all over with salt and togarishi pepper or Asian Spice Rub.

■ Place the tuna over very high direct heat and sear on all sides, about 2 minutes per side, marking and coloring the outside but leaving the inside quite rare. Remove from the grill and slice the tuna into thick, bite-size pieces. Arrange the slices over thinly grated daikon and carrots and garnish with pickled ginger.

To make Wasabi Mustard Sauce, combine the vinegar and wasabi. Whisk in the soy sauce, lime, and mustard. Taste and adjust the wasabi level as desired.

■ Spoon a little sauce over the fish and serve the rest on the side.

Ono with Grilled Pineapple Relish

SERVES 4

Ono is a flavorful Hawaiian fish, a member of the mackerel family. Its rich, succulent flesh cooks perfectly on the grill and is complemented by this fruity and spicy relish. If ono is not available, other white, firm-fleshed fish such as sea bass, grouper, or swordfish can be substituted.

The Grilled Pineapple Relish has a spicy citrus flavor that is perfect with Pork Tenderloins in Miso Marinade (page 164), Asian Tofu Burgers (page 92) or Ahi Skewers with Miso-Sesame Crust (page 119). At a supermarket near my home, I found pineapple that was peeled, cored, sliced, and ready to use. It was fresh and stored in its juices. This made using fresh pineapple easier and a lot less messy.

Serve with Asian Noodle and Grilled Baby Bok Choy Salad with Orange Ginger Vinaigrette (page 75).

• • • • • • • • • • • • • • • • • •

■ Prepare the fire for direct grilling. Spray or rub the grill with oil.

To make Grilled Pineapple Relish, grill the pineapple slices on a hot grill for 3 to 5 minutes. Turn and grill for another 3 to 4 minutes or until tender and marked by the grill. Remove and chop into ¼-inch pieces. Mix with the other relish ingredients in a bowl.

■ Rub the fish pieces with oil and sprinkle lightly with five-spice powder, lemon pepper, and salt or spice rub. Grill the fish for 3 minutes over high heat. Turn and grill for another 2 to 3 minutes until done. The fish should be flaky but still juicy.

■ Serve immediately with Grilled Pineapple Relish.

GRILLED PINEAPPLE RELISH

4 slices of pineapple. ½ inch thick

1 orange, peeled and cut into ¼-inch pieces

1 tablespoon lime juice

1 serrano chile, seeded and finely chopped

¼ cup chopped fresh cilantro

2 tablespoons chopped fresh mint

1 tablespoon chopped fresh ginger

½ cup chopped onion

2 tablespoons soy sauce

¼ teaspoon Chinese five-spice powder

¼ teaspoon Sriracha or other Asian hot sauce, or more to taste

•

4 ono fillets (about ½ pound each)

1 tablespoon vegetable oil

•

SEASONINGS

1 teaspoon Chinese five-spice powder

1 teaspoon lemon pepper

Salt

OR

1 tablespoon Asian Spice Rub (page 110)

OR

1 tablespoon Fish or Seafood Rub (page 41)

Pacific Northwest: Riches from the Sea and Land

The Pacific Northwest's resources from the sea and land create a rich and varied cuisine. The Pacific Ocean, Washington's Puget Sound, and the Gulf of Alaska provide the harvest of the sea. Valleys of rivers such as the Columbia, Willamette, Snake, and Yakima yield fresh vegetables for the table, grapes for wine, and the apples, pears, and berries the Northwest is famous for. Cool fields and meadows along the western slopes of the Cascades supply lettuces and greens, flowers and herbs, and a vast array of fruits and berries and mushrooms.

A good place to see it all is Seattle's Pike Place Market, located on a steep hill overlooking the city's thriving waterfront. Here is every kind of vegetable or fruit you could imagine for the time of year, piled high on tables alongside fresh herbs and flowers tied into bunches or growing in pots. You see prime porterhouse steaks and thick-cut pork chops in the butchers' cases with whole lambs hanging behind glass refrigerator doors. There are heaps of wild mushrooms everywhere— bright yellow and black chanterelles, ivory brown porcini, dark morels, even local truffles. And you'll find seafood and fish like you've never seen before—glistening salmon, from small cohos taken on the Columbia to huge chinooks from Alaska's Copper River, stacks and stacks of Dungeness crabs, oysters and clams from Puget Sound, and whole halibut from the Gulf of Alaska.

Grilling is a year-round activity in the Pacific Northwest. It does rain a lot here, but the barbecues in the backyards and on the decks get used anyway. I've been to many a Northwest party where the host has stood under an umbrella in the pouring rain next to a water-splashed grill with a whole salmon roasting in savory alder smoke. We guests watched through glass deck doors, contentedly sipping a rich Yakima Valley Semillon, snacking on roast oysters or grilled spot prawns, and waiting for the smoky fish (and the slightly damp cook) to come in out of the rain.

Native American cooks in the region have made a tasty tourist attraction out of their ancient practice of roasting salmon on an alder or cedar plank next to a bed of coals. Boats leave the Seattle docks for salmon feasts held on nearby islands by local tribes. Here you can dine on delicious smoked salmon while watching dancers in beautifully carved masks and listening to traditional songs.

Northwest restaurants offer tasty grilled salmon, spot prawns, and scallops, and an unparalleled array of fish and seafood of all kinds. Among the great attractions of this thriving region are the exciting dishes created by local cooks using native ingredients in striking and original ways (see Tom's Spice-Rubbed Salmon with Grilled Corn Relish, page 130).

Tom Douglas: Seattle Chef

Tom Douglas is at the center of the exciting food scene in Seattle, and one of his favorite ways to cook is on the grill. Tom owns Etta's Seafood near Pike Place Market; the sophisticated and ultra-chic Dahlia Lounge downtown; and the Palace Kitchen, which serves hearty food grilled over wood coals to crowds of hungry meat-lovers. Tom is one of the creators of an exciting and eclectic style of cooking in the Pacific Northwest that blends Asian spices, ingredients, and flavors with fresh local products.

Tom prefers cooking over a natural fire of charcoal or wood coals. He loves to grill everything from his justly famous smoke-roasted salmon at Etta's to delicious grilled bread salad at the Dahlia Lounge to whole spit-roasted prime rib at the Palace Kitchen.

Tom's Spice-Rubbed Salmon with Grilled Corn Relish

SERVES 6

SOUTH OF THE BORDER SPICE RUB

3 tablespoons packed light brown sugar

2 teaspoons kosher salt

1½ teaspoons coriander

1½ teaspoons cumin

1½ teaspoons paprika

1 teaspoon freshly ground black pepper

1 teaspoon ancho chile powder or other chile powder

¼ teaspoon cayenne

•

GRILLED CORN RELISH

4 ears corn, shucked

1 small sweet onion (preferably Walla Walla), sliced into ¼-inch-thick rings

¼ cup olive oil, plus more for brushing

3 tablespoons lime juice

Salt and freshly ground black pepper

1 small bunch fresh basil leaves, julienned (about ⅓ cup)

•

6 salmon fillets (7 ounces each)

Olive oil

•

GARNISH

Lemon or lime wedges

Tom Douglas created a slightly sweet and savory spice rub for the signature salmon dish he serves at his Seattle restaurant, Etta's Seafood. The salmon was such a hit, he developed a whole line of spice rubs—Tom Douglas's Rubs with Love—for grilling, barbecuing, and roasting meats, fish, and poultry.

The spice rub recipe Tom gives us here is a little different than his Rub with Love Salmon Rub but is equally delicious. The South of the Border notes of cumin and ancho chile in the spice rub pair well with a simple grilled corn relish. As soon as your grill is hot, you can grill the corn and make the relish, then let the corn relish rest at room temperature while you grill the salmon.

■ Prepare the fire for direct grilling. Spray or rub the grill with oil.

To make South of the Border Spice Rub, combine all the ingredients and mix well. This will keep in an airtight jar for up to 2 months.

To make Grilled Corn Relish, grill the corn over direct heat for about 8 minutes, turning often for even grilling. Remove the corn. Brush the onion rings with olive oil and grill both sides for about 2 minutes, or until soft and brown. Remove from the grill. When cool enough to handle, shave the corn from the cobs, using a serrated knife, to produce about 3 cups of corn kernels. Dice the grilled onions and combine them with the corn in a large bowl. Add the lime juice and ¼ cup olive oil and mix well. Salt and pepper to taste. Reserve basil to mix in right before serving.

■ To prepare the salmon, rub thoroughly with the spice rub, using about 3 to 4 teaspoons per fillet. Brush or spray the grill and the fish with olive oil. Grill the salmon on direct heat, covered, with vents open. When the fillets are well marked, turn and grill the other side until done. Total time will be 8 to 10 minutes on the grill. The sugar in the spice rub can burn; if flare-ups occur, move to a cooler part of the grill.

■ Mix the basil into the corn relish. Serve the salmon immediately with the corn relish. Garnish with lemon or lime wedges.

Brined Salmon Steaks

SERVES 8 TO 10

Brining adds a wonderful, lightly salty flavor to salmon that is nicely complemented by smoke. Think what happens when fresh pork is brined, smoked, and made into ham. Make plenty of this succulent and smoky salmon. Serve it hot as a main course, or cold with sliced cucumbers and sliced sweet Walla Walla onions on toasted bagels for an appetizer or light lunch.

3–4 pounds salmon steaks, about 1 inch thick

1 recipe Fish or Seafood Brine (page 42)

¼ cup vegetable oil

• • • • • • • • • • • • • • • • • •

▪ In a large nonreactive container, cover the fish with the brine. Weigh the fish down with a plate. Put the container in the refrigerator for 1 to 2 hours.

▪ Remove the fish from the brine, wash, and pat dry. Brush the steaks with oil.

▪ Prepare the fire for direct grilling. Add alder or other aromatic hardwood to the smoker box (see Smoke on the Grill, page 21). Grill the steaks over high heat for 4 to 5 minutes per side or until the fish is firm, yet still juicy. Or, if you wish to hot-smoke the salmon, follow the directions in John's Cured Smoked Salmon (see below), but begin checking the fish after 1 hour.

John's Cured Smoked Salmon

SERVES 8 TO 10 AS AN APPETIZER

John Clark is a master at the grill. He grew up in the backwoods of New Hampshire, where his family owned a country store and he started cooking over wood fires early on. John learned from his Irish father and French-Canadian mother that food should be tasty, hearty, and plentiful. When you go to a barbecue or a clambake put on by John, you know you'll be looking at huge pieces of succulent meat—whole prime ribs or hefty hams or huge turkeys are nothing for him. I've seen John set up a combination lobster roast, clambake, and beef feast for forty or fifty hungry folk at a friend's ranch in the hills near San Jose without working up much of a sweat.

One of John's specialties is this cured smoked salmon, using a recipe from a friend who hauls back immense king salmon from Alaskan fishing expeditions. John uses a commercial brine mix (see Sources, page 225), but you could use a double or triple recipe of our Fish or Seafood Brine (page 42).

1 salmon fillet (half of one fish, 4 to 5 pounds), skin on

Enough brine (8 to 12 cups) to cover fish

10–15 whole black peppercorns

1–3 large rosemary sprigs

1 cup or more dry white wine

5–6 cloves garlic, crushed

Olive oil

•

Bread or crackers

Onions, thinly sliced

Capers

Sour cream

• • • • • • • • • • • • • • • • • •

■ In a large nonreactive container, cover the salmon with brine, peppercorns, rosemary, wine, and garlic and refrigerate overnight or for at least 8 hours. Turn the salmon from time to time.

■ Remove the salmon from the brine and pat dry. If you are using a water smoker, strain the solids from the brine and reserve them. Lay the salmon, flesh side up, on aluminum foil and dry it for at least 2 hours at room temperature. Use a fan for faster drying. Wipe away any white liquids that appear on the surface of the fish.

■ Rub the skin side of the salmon and the smoker rack with olive oil. If you are using a water smoker, fill the water buffer with white wine along with the solids strained from the brine.

■ Put the salmon, skin side down, on the rack in your water smoker or covered barbecue and hot-smoke the salmon for 2½ to 3 hours (see Smoking, page 26). John prefers to use hickory chips for their intense smoky flavor, but alder, oak, apple, or other woods will also do well. Check the salmon after 2 hours. It is done when it flakes with a fork and is no longer raw at the center.

■ Remove the salmon from the smoker and let it cool. Cut on the bias across the grain into thin slices and serve on bread or crackers with thinly sliced raw onions, capers, and sour cream.

Poultry

When my kids were little, I used to cook what we called "Birdies on the Grill." These were tiny rock Cornish game hens that I'd season with garlic and chopped fresh oregano and smoke-roast in the kettle grill until they were lusciously browned and juicy. Everybody got a "birdie," and Michael and Meghan tore into the game hens like miniature Henry VIII's, waving the little drumsticks in the air and pulling the birds apart with greasy fingers (see Barbecued Small Birds, page 151).

Birds, as small as game hens or as large as turkeys, cook wonderfully on the grill. They usually have enough fat to stay moist, and the birds' delicate flesh seems to soak up flavors from spices and smoke. Poultry benefits greatly from marinating in herbs, aromatics, and pungent sauces based on soy or chiles. Spice and herb rubs add even more flavor.

While you can grill poultry directly in an uncovered hibachi or barbecue, I think the kettle barbecue or gas grill gives best results. The trick to grilling poultry, especially chicken, is to get the inside cooked through before the outside chars. The mistake of many a backyard barbecuer is to slather chicken pieces with a sweet barbecue sauce and then toss them onto a hot grill. The ensuing inferno guarantees chicken that is burned on the outside and raw on the inside—that is, inedible. When cooking cut-up chicken, season it well or marinate it in a nonsweet sauce, brown the pieces quickly over a medium-hot fire, and then move them to a cooler spot on a covered grill to finish cooking (see Composite Grilling, page 18). The interior meat should be juicy but not pink and should read 165°F to 170°F. If you wish to use commercial or another sweet barbecue sauce, brush a little on the chicken just before serving. Whole chickens should be seasoned with a spice rub or herbs and then cooked by the indirect method (see Indirect Heat, page 19).

Turkey is excellent when cooked on kettle-style barbecues or gas grills. You can leave turkey whole and cook it by indirect heat (see Smoke-Roasted Turkey or Chickens with Three-Pepper Rub, page 146) or cook turkey pieces by the composite method (see Jalapeño-Stuffed Turkey Thighs, page 147).

Duck, with its high fat content, can be a bit tricky to grill. Flare-ups and disasters are possible unless you pay strict attention. I don't recommend grilling whole ducks, but I've had good success with duck breasts (what the French call *magrets*) from both domestic ducks and, even better, muscovy or wild ducks (see Michael's Grilled Duck Breasts with Berry Pinot Noir Glaze, page 150).

All kinds of poultry take well to smoke. I like to use plenty of savory smoke with everything from game hens to turkey. The more intensely flavored hardwoods, such as oak and hickory, provide wonderfully smoky flavors, although I would use lighter mesquite or alder for delicate chicken or turkey breasts.

Chicken thighs have to be the best and easiest poultry pieces for grilling. Whether you leave the skin on and the bone in or buy the thighs already boned and/or skinned, thighs have enough fat to stand up to the heat of the grill. They also pick up flavors easily from marinades and spice rubs (see Kalbi: Hawaiian-Korean Grilled Chicken, page 140; Chicken Fajitas with Lime Tequila Marinade, page 141; North Beach Grilled Chicken, page 135; Chicken Yakitori, page 139). Grilled whole or skewered, chicken thighs are mainstay meals in my family and make great appetizers or first courses for parties and backyard barbecues.

North Beach Secrets

San Francisco's Italian neighborhood, North Beach, is a great place to party. You'll find a real mix of folk along Broadway on a Saturday night: sailors on leave and looking for action, tourists searching for Italian restaurants they've heard about, politicians and socialites glad-handing and schmoozing in fashionable cafés. My favorite times to visit, though, are on the many saint's days and other festivals when the Italian community turns out, young and old, to feast and drink and talk and generally have a good time. Big 55-gallon-drum grills are set up around Washington Square in front of St. Peter and Paul's Cathedral, and chicken and sausages and steaks send clouds of savory smoke through the crowds.

Here's a marinade recipe that I weaseled out of one of the old-timers at a festival a few years ago. He was grabbing pieces of marinated chicken out of this huge stainless steel pan and tossing them on the grill, and I asked him what the marinade was. He gave me a quick rundown on the ingredients after I bribed him with a couple of glasses of Zinfandel I carried over from the next booth, all while he was running the grill and conducting multiple conversations and financial transactions in Italian and English.

North Beach Grilled Chicken

SERVES 4

Use whatever pieces of cut-up chicken you like—breasts, thighs, or thighs and legs: skin on or skinless, bone in or boneless. North Beach Marinade is also good on vegetables or pork and can serve as a dressing for Out-of-the-Garden Grilled Salad (page 71). Serve this chicken with Grilled Polenta with Smoke-Roasted Tomato Sauce (page 98) and Summer Vegetable Skewers (page 95).

● ● ● ● ● ● ● ● ● ● ● ● ● ● ● ●

To make North Beach Marinade, mix the ingredients in a small bowl or jar. The marinade will keep, covered, in the refrigerator for up to a week.

◼ Place the chicken pieces and marinade in a nonreactive dish or zip-lock bag. Marinate for up to 2 hours at room temperature or 8 to 12 hours in the refrigerator. Turn occasionally. Remove from the refrigerator about an hour before cooking. Pat the chicken pieces dry before grilling.

◼ Prepare the fire for direct grilling. If using skinless chicken, spray or rub the grill with oil. If you'd like a touch of smoke, fill the smoke box with hardwood chips following the directions in Smoke on the Grill (page 21).

NORTH BEACH MARINADE

4 cloves garlic, finely chopped

1 cup olive oil

¼ cup balsamic vinegar

1 tablespoon dried oregano

1½ teaspoons dried basil

½ teaspoon freshly ground black pepper

½ teaspoon paprika

¼ teaspoon cayenne

1 teaspoon salt

●

12 chicken thighs or 8 thighs and legs or 4 chicken breasts

■ Sear and mark the chicken pieces, skin side down, over medium-high direct heat. Move to the cooler part of the grill, cover, and cook until done. The internal temperature of chicken breasts should be 155°F, thighs and legs 165°F—or cut to see that the meat is no longer pink but is still juicy. Cooking times will vary from 10 to 15 minutes, depending on the thickness of the chicken pieces and the heat of the fire.

D Alexander and the World's Most Expensive Chicken

D Alexander was one of the great grill cooks. He lived for years in California's coastal range near the tiny mountain town of La Honda, uphill and west of Palo Alto, and earned a reputation, if not a living, as a poet, magazine editor, Rabelaisian drinker, and master chef. D built and cooked on a 55-gallon-drum barbecue next to his ramshackle house, which happened to be right next door to Ken Kesey and his Merrie Pranksters. Get-togethers at D's often got very merry indeed.

D cooked just about anything that flew, walked, or crawled on his massive grill: whole suckling pig, for example, that he traded his home-made wine for. D would rub the pig all over with garlic and fresh herbs, rig up a spit, and then spend the afternoon drinking wine and telling stories while the savory porker dripped fat on the coals. He always said he could tell by the smell of the smoke when pig meat was done. Could be. But we made sure by slicing off little bits of juicy meat and crisp crackling skin from time to time, just to keep him honest.

D had a way with steaks, too. He'd marinate them in a bath of chopped jalapeños en escabeche with plenty of garlic, lemons, and fresh oregano. He especially loved skirt steaks and flank steaks, but his all-time favorite was the hanging tenderloin, also called the butcher's steak because meat cutters always take it home for themselves. He had a network of Latino butchers up in San Francisco's Mission District on the lookout for "hangers," as he called them, and offered a standing bribe in all the bars along Mission Street of a free drink and five bucks for anyone who could deliver the goods. D's technique was simple: marinate the steak in chiles, garlic, and lemons for at least a day or two in the fridge, burn oak or mesquite down to coals for a really hot fire, toss the steak on the grill, and cook it quickly with the lid of the big barbecue down and smoke billowing all around.

D knew when the steak was done by touch and taught his friends and disciples this grill cook's trick: Touch the ball of muscle between your thumb and index finger when it is totally relaxed. That's the texture of raw meat. Tuck your thumb under your index finger and squeeze hard to tighten the muscle. That's the texture of well-done meat. Relax the muscle a little: that's the texture of medium-rare meat. Relax it even more for the feel of rare meat. What you do, then, is touch meat on the grill and then compare it to the tension in the muscle on your hand. With a little practice touching the meat on the grill and touching your hand, you'll make the correlation and be able to take the meat off when it is exactly the way you want it. You can use an instant-read meat thermometer, of course, but it's not as much fun and doesn't amaze your friends.

D also had a way with "The Birds," as he called them. He loved to cook two or three whole turkeys on his huge covered grill and would often line up six or eight chickens down the middle. He had a heavy hand with the spices, usually ancho chile powder and lots of herbs, and he loved plenty of smoke from chunks of coastal oak soaked in a nearby stream and tossed right on the fire. Cut-up chicken he cooked long and slow, basting from time to time with a mix of oil, wine, lemon, and garlic.

When I was working for a winery in the Livermore Valley, just east of San Francisco Bay, I hired D to cook chicken at the annual Grape Stomp we put on each harvest. Five or six hundred people would show up for the good times, and not all of these were the genteel wine snobs you see in fancy magazines. Lots of good-old-boys and -gals from down the San Joaquin Valley loved "The Stomp," as they called it, and the parking lot filled up with more pickups than Mercedes on that hot September day. The deal at the Grape Stomp that attracted all these folk was simple: you paid for your ticket and, for that, you got parking, really loud country music, all the food you could eat and all the wine you could drink, and the chance to jump up and down in a huge vat of grapes after you'd consumed as much of the end product as you could hold. Things tended to get a bit raucous toward the end of the day.

Cooking for six hundred people was all in a day's work for D, and he hired a crew and we rented grills and bought plenty of charcoal. D told us not to buy any starter fluid, as he liked to start the charcoal with kindling and didn't like the smell of that starter stuff. So there we were on the big day, with marinated chicken halves for six hundred in coolers, with salad and bread and trimmings ready to go. When the time came to start up the fires, D took a look at the grills we'd rented. They were long, tablelike shallow grills with no covers and no vents for draft underneath, far different from D's usual 55-gallon drum with cover and plenty of vents to feed the fire. D fortified himself with a glass or two of wine and started the fires. Or tried to. He built small wood fires in each grill, piled charcoal on, and watched them go out. He, and we at the winery, had a problem.

The Stomp was going strong by this time, with guys in cowboy hats with rooster feathers line dancing with girls in really tight jeans, halter tops, and high heels. We realized that if we didn't get some food into these folk, God only knows what would happen. A riot would be the happiest outcome.

It seemed the only thing that would get these damn grills going was gallons of starter fluid, and the nearest store was miles away. We needed fire, and quick, to get those chicken pieces cooking to feed the hungry, and increasingly restive, crowd.

That's when inspiration hit me and turned these particular pieces of chicken into the most expensive chicken ever cooked. "What do you need for fire?" I thought to myself. "Dry wood and a flammable liquid." Well, the winery's finest reserve Cabernet Sauvignon had just been packed in fancy wooden cases for high-end consumption. This was the good stuff that sold for upward of $20 per bottle, not the less-exalted liquid that we were pouring for the gang at The Stomp. And the winery had just received a shipment of very high end grappa that was selling at a very high price indeed. Grappa, high-proof alcohol distilled from grape skins after the wine is made, had suddenly become fashionable, and the winery had packaged a goodly amount in very fancy bottles for the luxury restaurant trade.

But this was an emergency, or soon to become one. So we told the increasingly surly people lining up for their food that we were offering a special taste of our best Cabernet in the tasting room. As they rushed the bar, we started dispensing the Cabernet from the wooden cases and breaking up the cases for kindling. We piled the dry wood up high, loaded charcoal on top, and then, to really get the fire going, poured bottles of expensive grappa over everything. D stood back, lit a match, and tossed it onto the first grill. With a very aromatic *Whoosh!* grappa ignited the wood, which lit the coals, which cooked the chicken—and The Stomp was saved.

As everybody streamed out of the vineyards at the end of the day, covered with grape skins, happy and satisfied, they praised the delicious and unusual chicken and congratulated the chef. D, who had taken a great liking to the reserve Cabernet, was smiling and beaming under all the attention. He was free with advice on his chicken-cooking techniques: "Just a touch of grappa," he kept saying, "perhaps even more than a touch, is my secret for great grilled chicken."

Chicken Yakitori

SERVES 4

Japantown in San Francisco is a bustling place. There you can find all kinds of Japanese food in elegant and expensive ryori (innkeeper-style) restaurants and robata grills, crowded sushi bars and noodle shops, and yakitori barbecue stands that serve simple but very tasty skewers of chicken and vegetables. Try Yakitori Marinade on chicken, seafood, or vegetables. It's especially good on asparagus and eggplants. Use it to replace the Roasted Garlic Oil on Grilled Asparagus (page 97) or the marinade for Miso-Marinated Grilled Eggplant (page 99). Serve Chicken Yakitori with Asian Noodle and Grilled Baby Bok Choy Salad with Orange Ginger Vinaigrette (page 75).

YAKITORI MARINADE

1 cup soy sauce

¼ cup sake or dry sherry

2 tablespoons chopped fresh ginger

1 tablespoon honey

1 tablespoon finely chopped garlic

•

8 chicken thighs or chicken breasts, boneless and skinless

. . . .

To make Yakitori Marinade, combine all ingredients.

◼ Cut the chicken into 2-inch chunks and soak in half the marinade for up to 2 hours at room temperature. Reserve half the marinade for dipping sauce.

◼ Prepare the fire for direct grilling. Spray or rub the grill with oil.

◼ Skewer the chicken pieces and pat dry. Grill over medium-high heat for 3 to 4 minutes, turn, and grill for another 3 minutes. If flare-ups occur, move to a cooler part of the grill. Test the chicken for doneness: thighs should read 165°F interior temperature, breasts 155°F, and the meat should be juicy but no longer pink when cut. Cook longer if necessary, but be careful not to char the chicken, as the marinade contains sugar.

◼ Serve hot off the grill with the reserved marinade as a sauce.

SERVES 4

KALBI

½ cup soy sauce

½ cup peanut or vegetable oil

½ cup packed brown sugar

½ cup finely chopped green onions

4 cloves garlic, finely chopped

3 tablespoons chopped fresh ginger

Juice of 1 lemon

1 teaspoon Asian chile oil or other hot sauce, or more to taste

¼ cup toasted sesame seeds (see Toasting Sesame Seeds, page 80), optional

•

8 chicken thighs or 4 chicken breasts or 6 thighs and legs or any combination—bone in or boneless, skin on or skinless

Kalbi: Hawaiian-Korean Grilled Chicken

Walk down a beach just about anywhere in Hawaii on a Saturday night and you are sure to smell Kalbi, a garlicky, gingery, hot and sweet Korean-style marinade that local folks love to use on chicken, beef, and pork. Hawaiians grill spicy meat, fish, or poultry on the beach over kiawe wood fires and serve it accompanied by plenty of cold beer, slack key guitar, and old-time songs. Kiawe wood is mainland mesquite, brought over by early *panaiolos*, the cowboys who run cattle in the highlands of the Big Island. You can use mesquite wood and burn it down to coals (see Hardwood Coals, page 12) or add mesquite chips to a charcoal or gas barbecue (see Smoke on the Grill, page 21).

Kalbi is not only a great marinade, (see Korean Barbecue, page 179) it is also a terrific basting sauce for grilled vegetables and makes a delicious dressing for cooked Asian noodles. Pay attention when grilling Kalbi-marinated foods; the high sugar content makes charring a possibility. Keep a close eye and regulate heat or move food around on the grill to prevent burning.

Serve this chicken with Asian Noodle and Grilled Baby Bok Choy Salad (page 75), dressed with reserved Kalbi or another Asian marinade such as Soy Ginger Dressing (page 74).

. . . .

To make Kalbi, mix the ingredients together in a bowl.

◼ Put the chicken in a nonreactive dish and cover with marinade. If you want to use Kalbi as a basting sauce for grilled vegetables or as a dressing for cold noodles with the chicken, reserve ½ cup. Marinate the chicken for up to 2 hours at room temperature or 8 to 12 hours in the refrigerator. Remove from the refrigerator an hour or so before grilling.

◼ Prepare the fire for direct grilling. Put mesquite or other hardwood in the smoke box (see Smoke on the Grill, page 21). Spray or rub the grill with oil.

◼ Remove the chicken from the marinade and pat dry. Grill over medium-high heat, adjusting the heat or moving as necessary to avoid flare-ups or charring. Cover. Turn often and move the chicken pieces to a cooler part of the grill as they cook.

◼ Cook the thighs or legs to 165°F internal temperature, breasts to 155°F or until juices run clear and the flesh is no longer pink but is still juicy. Boneless thighs and breasts will cook quickest (check after 3 to 5 minutes per side), bone-in thighs and legs and thighs will take the longest (up to 10 minutes or more per side).

Chicken Fajitas with Lime Tequila Marinade

SERVES 4

Fajitas—lime- and chile-marinated beef or chicken strips—are popular along the Pacific Coast from Baja to Seattle. This version uses boneless, skinless chicken thighs—flavorful pieces of chicken that work well on the grill. They absorb flavors beautifully from marinades or rubs and have just enough fat to stay juicy after grilling. Boneless, skinless thighs are quick and easy to grill and become family favorites any way you season them. Thighs are easily handled if skewered after marinating, but this is not necessary. Use this tangy marinade on pork tenderloin or pork chops, or for Skirt Steak Fajitas (page 179).

· · · · · · · · · · · · · · · · ·

To make Lime Tequila Marinade, mix the ingredients together in a small bowl.

■ Marinate the chicken thighs in a nonreactive dish or zip-lock bag for up to 2 hours at room temperature or 8 to 12 hours in the refrigerator. If refrigerated, bring the chicken to room temperature. Remove from the marinade, and pat dry before cooking. Thread chicken thighs onto skewers, if you wish, for ease of handling.

■ Prepare the fire for direct grilling. Spray or rub the grill with oil.

■ Grill the thighs, covered, over medium-high heat for 3 to 7 minutes per side until done. Move to a cooler spot of the grill if flare-ups occur. The chicken is done at an internal temperature of 165°F or when the meat is no longer pink but is still juicy when cut.

■ Cut the chicken into strips or chop coarsely. Squeeze lime juice over the pieces and sprinkle with salt and pepper to taste. Garnish with sliced limes and Rajas: Grilled Chile and Pepper Strips. Tuck the meat into Grilled Corn Tortillas with Rajas and Pico de Gallo.

LIME TEQUILA MARINADE

½ cup olive oil

Juice of 2 limes

3 tablespoons tequila

3 cloves garlic, minced

1 jalapeño or other hot chile, seeded and finely chopped, or more to taste

2 tablespoons chopped fresh cilantro

1 tablespoon chopped fresh oregano or 1½ teaspoons dried

1 teaspoon ground cumin

1 teaspoon salt

•

12 chicken thighs, boneless and skinless

Lime juice

Salt and freshly ground black pepper

Lime slices

1 recipe Rajas: Grilled Chile and Pepper Strips (page 101)

Grilled Corn Tortillas (page 52)

1 recipe Pico de Gallo (page 51)

Chicken Breasts Adobo

SERVES 4

ADOBO

4 cloves garlic, peeled

1 teaspoon dried oregano

1 teaspoon salt

1 teaspoon freshly ground black pepper

2 tablespoons paprika

¼ cup olive or vegetable oil

½ cup red wine vinegar

2 tablespoons ancho, chipotle, or other dried chile purée (see Dried Chile Purée, page 108)

•

4 chicken breasts, bone in or boneless, skin on or skinless

Salt and freshly ground black pepper

•

Pico de Gallo (page 51) or Salsa Roja (page 108) or Salsa Verde (page 50)

Adobo is a spicy, vinegary sauce much loved by Latino cooks. You'll find versions from virtually every Spanish-speaking country from the Philippines to Mexico to Spain. Our version has some dried chile purée for a Mexican touch. You can use this sauce as a marinade for chicken, pork, or fish (see Shark Steaks Adobo with Chipotle Grilled Tomatoes, page 122), or use the sauce from canned chipotles en adobo (see Smoke-Roasted Whole Chicken with Chipotles under the Skin, page 145). Adobo will keep, covered, in the refrigerator for up to a week.

Serve chicken breasts with Pico de Gallo, Salsa Roja, or Salsa Verde, and Summer Vegetable Skewers (page 95). Any leftover chicken is delicious in Grilled Chicken Salad (page 76), tacos, or burritos.

. . . .

To make Adobo, process the ingredients together in a food processor or blender into a smooth paste.

▪ Trim excess skin or fat from the chicken breasts as needed and spread both sides with adobo sauce. Marinate at room temperature for up to 2 hours before cooking or in the refrigerator 8 to 12 hours. Remove chicken from the marinade and pat dry before cooking. Sprinkle with salt and pepper.

▪ Prepare the fire for direct grilling. Spray or rub the grill with oil. Add mesquite or other hardwood to the smoke box (see Smoke on the Grill, page 21).

▪ Grill the chicken breasts over medium-high direct heat, covered, for 3 to 5 minutes per side. Move to a cooler spot on the grill if flare-ups occur. Chicken breasts are done at 155°F internal temperature or when no longer pink but still juicy when cut. Bone-in, skin-on chicken breasts take the longest to cook; boneless, skinless breasts the least. Do not overcook or the meat will dry out.

▪ Serve with Pico de Gallo, Salsa Roja, or Salsa Verde.

Chicken, Chile, and Onion Skewers

These spicy skewers make a wonderful first course or picnic dish and can serve as a main course when paired with Out-of-the-Garden Grilled Salad (page 71) or Summer Vegetable Skewers (page 95). My favorite way to eat this dish is to grill a couple of corn tortillas for each skewer and then just fold the tortillas around the chicken, chiles, and onion and pull the skewer out. With a little Pico de Gallo (page 51) or Salsa Verde (page 50), you'll have the best chicken taco you've ever tasted.

Boneless, skinless chicken thighs work best here, but chicken breasts also do well. Be sure not to overcook the breasts as they can dry out quickly on the grill.

The Chile Rub is great on steaks, lamb chops, pork chops, or chicken. Use ancho chile powder if you have it or a good commercial powder such as Gebhardt.

· · · · · · · · · · · · · · · · · ·

To make Chile Rub, combine all ingredients and mix well. This will last for a month in an airtight container.

■ Cut the thighs into four pieces, the breasts into eight pieces. Sprinkle on all sides with about 2 tablespoons Chile Rub. Let sit for up to 2 hours at room temperature or 8 to 12 hours in the refrigerator.

■ Cut the chiles open, seed, and remove the veins and stems. Cut each chile into eight pieces. Peel and cut the onions into quarters. Thread the chicken, chile, and onion pieces alternately onto skewers and brush lightly with oil.

■ Prepare the fire for direct grilling. Spray or rub the grill and the skewers with oil.

■ Grill the skewers, covered, over medium–high heat, covered, turning often. They should take about 8 to 10 minutes total. The internal temperature of thighs should be 165°F, and breasts should reach 155°F. Cut into a piece of chicken to check: it should be no longer pink inside but still juicy. Don't worry about a little char on the chiles; it's traditional and adds a pleasantly smoky flavor.

SERVES 4

CHILE RUB

¼ cup paprika

2 tablespoons packed brown sugar

2 tablespoons granulated garlic or garlic powder

2 tablespoons ancho or other chile powder

1 tablespoon dried rosemary

¼ teaspoon cayenne

1 tablespoon salt

1 teaspoon freshly ground black pepper

·

8 chicken thighs or 4 chicken breasts, boneless and skinless

4 mild green chiles such as Anaheim or poblano

2 medium red onions

Vegetable oil

Spicy Indian Grilled Chicken with Tomato Chutney

SERVES 4

TOMATO CHUTNEY

¾ cup vinegar

1 cup packed brown sugar

2 cups chopped tomatoes

½ cup raisins

½ cup chopped red bell pepper

1 cup chopped onion

4 cloves garlic, finely chopped

2 tablespoons chopped fresh ginger

½ teaspoon salt

¼ teaspoon cayenne

½ tablespoon lemon juice

•

SPICY INDIAN CHICKEN RUB

½ teaspoon cayenne

1 teaspoon dry mustard

½ teaspoon coriander

½ teaspoon cardamom

½ teaspoon cumin

1 teaspoon turmeric

1 teaspoon Chinese five-spice powder

½ teaspoon salt

•

4 chicken breasts or 8 thighs, boneless or bone in, skinless or skin on

Indian spices give this chicken a fragrant, spicy character. I like to make this chutney near the end of the summer when the tomatoes come in all colors and shapes from the garden, the farmers' market, and even the grocery stores. Use any tomatoes: red, yellow, or green. Serve with Summer Vegetable Skewers (page 95).

. . . .

To make Tomato Chutney, combine the vinegar and brown sugar in a large saucepan and bring to a boil, stirring constantly. Add the remaining chutney ingredients except the lemon juice. Bring back to a boil, reduce the heat, and simmer for 15 minutes, stirring often. Turn off the heat and let cool a bit so the flavors mingle. Add the lemon juice, bring back to a boil, reduce the heat, and simmer for another 15 minutes. Serve warm or cool. Chutney will keep refrigerated for up to 2 weeks.

To make Spicy Indian Chicken Rub, combine all ingredients in a small bowl or jar.

■ Rub the chicken thoroughly with the rub and let sit for up to 2 hours at room temperature or 8 to 12 hours in the refrigerator.

■ Prepare the fire for direct grilling. Spray or rub the grill with oil. If you'd like a touch of smoke, fill the smoke box with oak, mesquite, or other hardwood chips (see Smoke on the Grill, page 21).

■ Sear and mark the chicken pieces, skin side down, over medium-high direct heat; turn and sear the other side. Move chicken to the cooler part of the grill, cover, and cook until done. The internal temperature of chicken breasts should be 155°F, thighs and legs 165°F, or cut to see that the meat is no longer pink but is still juicy; 10 to 15 minutes total time should do the trick. Serve with Tomato Chutney.

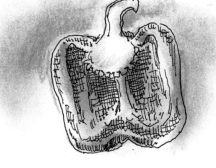

Smoke-Roasted Whole Chicken with Chipotles under the Skin

Chipotles, smoked ripe jalapeños, are hot in a lot of senses these days. They are, of course, hot to the taste, but these smoky and spicy chiles are also very popular with West Coast chefs. They provide a light touch of smoke to any dish, and their subtle spiciness lifts the flavors of chicken, pork, and fish. Chipotles are especially suited for grilled foods, where smoke is already a part of the character of the dish.

Chipotles are available in two forms: dried or canned in adobo sauce, a lively blend of tomatoes, vinegar, and spices. You can soak dried chipotles in hot water until soft and use them here. But I think the easiest (and most delicious) way to use chipotles is from the can, because the adobo sauce provides even more flavor. An added plus is that the adobo sauce can be used as a marinade for chicken, pork, or fish (see Chicken Breasts Adobo, page 142, and Shark Steaks Adobo with Chipotle Grilled Tomatoes, page 122). Canned chipotles are widely available in Latino markets and by mail order (see Sources, page 225). Herdez and La Gloria are both excellent brands.

Chipotle Spice Rub is great for Fish Tacos with Three Salsas (page 51), pork chops, or flank steak—just about anything you want to give a smoky Mexican flavor. Serve this chicken with Grilled Corn (page 91) slathered with Lime Ancho Chile Butter (page 107) and Rajas: Grilled Chile and Pepper Strips (page 101). Leftover chicken is delicious in Grilled Chicken Salad (page 76), tacos, or burritos.

· · · · · · · · · · · · · · · · · ·

To make Chipotle Spice Rub, combine the ingredients and mix well. The rub will keep in a covered jar for a month.

■ Prepare the fire for indirect grilling and put drip pan in place. Fill the smoke box with oak, mesquite, or other hardwood chips (see Smoke on the Grill, page 21).

■ Trim the chicken of any fat or excess skin. Cut open and seed the chipotles. Loosen the skin around the chicken breast and push the chipotles up under the skin. If using canned chipotles, rub some adobo over the chicken and save the leftover sauce for later use (see Chicken Breasts Adobo, page 142). Sprinkle the chicken all over with about ¼ cup of Chipotle Spice Rub.

■ You may either spit-roast the chicken (see Spit-Roasting, page 20) or roast it by indirect heat. Place the chicken on the unheated

---

SERVES 4

CHIPOTLE SPICE RUB

¼ cup ancho or other chile powder

¼ cup chipotle chile powder or other chile powder

1 tablespoon packed brown sugar

2 tablespoons dried oregano

2 tablespoons granulated garlic or garlic powder

1 tablespoon ground cumin

¼ teaspoon ground allspice

1 teaspoon cayenne

1 tablespoon salt

1 teaspoon freshly ground black pepper

·

1 whole roasting chicken (3 to 5 pounds)

4 chipotles en adobo or dried chipotles soaked in hot water (see Chiles, page 48)

part of the grill. Roast at moderate heat (350°F) until the internal temperature of the thighs reaches 165°F or until the juices run clear from the inner thighs. This will take anywhere from 45 minutes to more than an hour, depending on the size of the chicken and the heat levels. Start checking after 30 minutes.

■ Remove the chicken from the grill when done and cover loosely with foil on a platter. Let it rest for 10 minutes or so before carving.

Smoke-Roasted Turkey or Chickens with Three-Pepper Rub

SERVES 6 TO 8

THREE-PEPPER RUB

¼ cup ancho chile powder or other chile powder

¼ cup chipotle powder or other chile powder

¼ cup Hungarian sweet or hot paprika

¼ cup garlic powder

1 tablespoon dried thyme or marjoram

2 tablespoons salt

OR

½ cup Hot Spice Rub for Pork or Chicken (page 40) or spice rub of your choice

•

1 turkey (about 12 pounds) or 2 roasting chickens (4–5 pounds each)

Olive or vegetable oil

1– 2 onions, quartered

1–2 lemons, quartered

4–6 cloves garlic, smashed

Cooking a whole turkey or a couple of chickens in a covered grill over indirect heat is a lot easier than you might think. Rub the skin with oil and coat with a savory rub. Put an onion, some lemon, and a couple of garlic cloves in the cavity. You can then place the bird or birds on the center of the grill with a drip pan beneath or skewer a turkey or one or two chickens on a spit if you have a rotisserie attachment for your grill. When the bird is done, let it rest for 15 to 20 minutes, loosely covered in foil, before carving. That's it. Any leftovers are great in tacos, burritos, or salads.

I like to smoke-roast the birds using hickory or oak, but just about any hardwood will do. Use plenty of chips and replenish during cooking to give a rich smoky character to the chicken or turkey.

• • • • • • • • • • • • • • • • • •

■ Prepare the fire for indirect grilling and put drip pan in place. Load up the smoke box with hickory, oak, or other hardwood chips (see Smoke on the Grill, page 21).

To make Three-Pepper Rub, mix ingredients together in a small bowl. The rub will keep for up to a week in a covered jar.

■ Rub the turkey or chickens with oil and sprinkle Three-Pepper Rub or other spice rub all over the skin. Place the onions, lemons, and garlic cloves in the cavity of the turkey or chickens. Place in the center of the grill with a drip pan underneath and cook at 350°F or moderate heat (see Indirect Heat, page 19), or skewer turkey or chickens on a spit (see Spit-Roasting, page 20). Roast until the internal temperature of the thigh reads 165°F or the flesh at the thigh joint is no longer pink. Start testing the turkey after about 45 minutes, the chickens after 30 minutes. Remove the birds from the grill when they are done and cover loosely in foil and let rest 10 to 15 minutes before carving.

Jalapeño-Stuffed Turkey Thighs

SERVES 4

Turkey thighs make great little individual roasts on the grill. Turkey takes well to marinades and rubs and is especially delicious with a touch of smoke. Boned turkey thighs can be marinated and stuffed with a wide variety of seasonings and stuffings. You can bone the thighs yourself (a simple task with a sharp knife) or have your butcher do it. I've given the thighs a Mexican touch here with jalapeños en escabeche and chile-based rubs, but use your imagination and try your own seasonings and stuffings. For example, stuff thighs with green onions and thinly sliced shiitakes and glaze with Yakitori Marinade (page 139), or stuff them with chopped greens and garlic and brush lightly with Oakland Barbecue Sauce (page 165).

Jalapeños en escabeche (canned pickled chiles, onions, and carrots) are available in many supermarkets or by mail order (see Sources, page 225). Serve with Rajas: Grilled Chile and Pepper Strips and Grill-Roasted New Potatoes (page 101).

4 turkey thighs, skin on

1 can (7 ounces) jalapeños en escabeche

4 tablespoons Chipotle Spice Rub (page 145), Chile Rub (page 143), or chile powder (preferably Gebhardt)

Salt and freshly ground black pepper

· · · · · · · · · · · · · · · · · ·

■ To bone thighs, lay them cut side up on a cutting board and cut down against the thigh bone on both sides, loosening the meat as you go. Cut underneath and at both ends of the bone to free it from the meat.

■ Sprinkle the inside of the thighs with spice rub. Drain the jalapeños en escabeche; cut open and seed the chiles. Lay one-fourth of the chiles, onions, and carrots down the middle of the inside of each thigh. Roll the thighs around the filling and tie in two or three places with butchers' twine. Sprinkle the outside skin with more spice rub. Let the thighs sit at room temperature for up to 2 hours before cooking.

■ Prepare the fire for indirect grilling and put drip pan in place. Fill the smoke box with mesquite, oak, or other hardwood chips (see Smoke on the Grill, page 21).

■ Sear and mark the thighs on all sides over medium-high heat, for 3 to 5 minutes. Move the thighs to the unheated part of the grill, cover, and roast for 15 to 20 minutes more, until the internal temperature is 165°F or until the meat is no longer pink but is still juicy.

A California Afternoon with Michael Wild

Whenever our friend Tom Moran shows up in the Bay Area it's an excuse for a party. Tom has lived in Paris for many years, where he's gained a reputation as a great grill cook whose specialty, Côte de Boeuf au Cowboy (see page 196), based on his cowboy uncles' steaks, is famous in the Quartier Latin where we were all hungry students together.

Over the years we've thrown some lively shindigs for Tom. My all-time favorite was a huge bash that we christened "Une Cochonnerie de Moran" (*cochonnerie* might be translated as either a pig feast or a really disgusting action). D Alexander, pig-meat cook extraordinaire (see D Alexander and the World's Most Expensive Chicken, page 136), grilled a whole hog on a spit in my side yard, and the assembled multitude polished off cases of my homemade Zinfandel and a small barrel of double distilled Chenin Blanc brandy made by a scientifically oriented winemaker of our acquaintance.

We've toned down the celebrations a bit, thank God, but we still look for good food and wine and conversation whenever Tom comes to town. Michael Wild, chef-owner of the Bay Wolf restaurant in Oakland and a member of Les Anciens, a loose-knit group of survivors of many feasts, threw the last bash. Michael and his wife Jill and new son David live in a shingled Oakland home with a huge airy kitchen opening out onto a shaded deck. Michael fired up the grill on a bright, cool afternoon in late summer and put together a wonderful meal that epitomizes California grill cooking.

We started with a mix of vegetables that guests brought fresh-picked from their backyard gardens: tiny green onions, split baby leeks, skewers of cherry tomatoes and ripe red peppers, fresh corn. These were grilled quickly and set out on hand-painted Italian platters; Michael sprinkled some homemade basil oil and a little salt over them all. We drank crisp, cold Sauvignon Blanc from Sonoma's Dry Creek Valley while we nibbled and told stories and watched Michael get the lamb ready.

He boned a lamb leg and rubbed it all over with crushed garlic, fresh rosemary, lemon, salt, and pepper. Oak chunks were added to glowing coals in the grill. The lamb sizzled in fragrant smoke while Michael put together a huge salad of baby greens, tomatoes, peppers, green garlic shoots, olives, ripe cucumbers, and fresh corn cut from the cob. A dressing from local extra-virgin olive oil and lemons from a neighbor's tree went on the salad just as the lamb came off the fire.

And then we sat around Michael and Jill's immense kitchen table and ate the lamb and salad with loaves of sourdough bread and bottles of Pinot Noir made by friends down near Santa Barbara. We told the old stories again about unloading lettuce at Les Halles and spending our pay on pigs' feet and onion soup, that time Moran swung from the gargoyle and almost took a dunk in the Seine, and the night when Michael's sons, Babu and Avram, and my son, Michael, got us out of trouble with some bad dudes out beyond the Bastille.

As the fog moved in, we sat on the deck finishing off the Pinot Noir, ate goat cheese and fresh figs, and let the stories go on and on, as they will, until the dark dropped down and all we were were voices.

Toasting and Grinding Spices

Many professional chefs, including Tom Douglas (page 129) and Michael Wild (see above), prefer to toast and grind their own spices rather than to rely on dry ground spices off the shelf. Ground spices lose their flavors quickly, and grinding your own ensures a fresh and lively taste in your seasonings and rubs.

The technique is simple: toast the whole spices (cumin seeds, coriander, juniper berries, peppercorns, and so on) in a heavy skillet over medium heat for a minute or two, stirring the spices constantly, until they are lightly browned and give off a lovely aroma. Let them cool for a minute or two and then grind them.

You can use a mortar and pestle for small amounts of spices, or you can crush spices with the flat of a knife. If you want to grind larger amounts or decide you want to grind spices on a regular basis, invest in a small, handheld coffee grinder to be used only for this purpose. These grinders are quite inexpensive and can make a real difference in your cooking.

Michael's Grilled Duck Breasts with Berry Pinot Noir Glaze

SERVES 4 TO 6

6 boneless duck breasts

2 tablespoons juniper berries, toasted and ground in spice grinder

1 tablespoon coriander seeds, toasted and ground in spice grinder

Salt and freshly ground black pepper

1 cup duck or chicken stock

1 basket raspberries or other similar berries

¾ cup Pinot Noir or other dry red wine

1 shallot, minced

Michael Wild is the owner of Oakland's landmark Bay Wolf restaurant and has gained a reputation as one of the Bay Area's master chefs. Every year he travels up to Oregon to cook at the McMinnville Pinot Noir Festival, where his duck and lamb dishes go beautifully with the fragrant Pinot Noirs from the surrounding region. Michael often incorporates local berries and wines into his sauces.

The trick with grilling duck is to render the fat from the skin over a medium-low fire. You could adapt this recipe to grilled lamb chops, following the directions for cooking the meat in Grilled Lamb Chops with Rosemary Garlic Paste (page 207) but substituting the seasonings and sauce from this recipe. For instructions on toasting and grinding spices, see page 149.

Serve with fresh corn and green beans sautéed in a little rendered duck fat or olive oil.

....

■ Prepare the fire for direct grilling. Spray or rub the grill with oil.

■ Sprinkle the meat side of the duck breasts lightly with juniper, coriander, salt, and pepper. Reserve any leftover spices for the sauce.

■ Grill the duck breasts skin side down over medium-low heat until the skin is browned and crisp and the fat is rendered, about 20 to 30 minutes. Move to a cooler part of the grill if flare-ups occur. Turn the duck breasts over to seal the meat side and cook for 1 to 3 minutes more until medium-rare to medium, about 130°F to 135°F. Remove the duck breasts from the heat, cover loosely with aluminum foil, and let rest for 10 to 15 minutes while you make the sauce.

■ In a small saucepan, simmer the stock, berries (reserve ¼ cup for garnish), Pinot Noir, shallot, and remaining spices for 10 minutes, stirring constantly. Strain the sauce through a stainless steel sieve and reduce over high heat until it is thickened and glossy.

■ Pour the sauce over the duck breasts and garnish with the remaining berries.

Barbecued Small Birds

SERVES 4

The Pacific Coast is one of the world's great flyways, with myriads of migrating birds passing over our bays and inland valleys each year. Jim Bangert, a good friend who hunts quail, pheasant, and duck in California's northern Central Valley with his lovely yellow Labrador retriever Nellie Belle, grills these birds to perfection. Small game birds cook quickly on the grill, so care must be taken to keep them from drying out. Jim recommends wrapping small birds in pancetta or bacon and cooking larger birds such as pheasant in foil with bacon and onions after a preliminary browning. Many game birds are now farm raised and easily available; you can also use this and the recipe for Jim's Pheasant or Chicken on the Grill (page 153) with rock Cornish game hens or small chickens.

8 small game birds such as quail or squab or 4 rock Cornish game hens

2 tablespoons dried sage

1 teaspoon freshly ground black pepper

1 pound sliced pancetta or bacon

24 juniper berries, crushed

4 oranges, quartered

•

ORANGE GRAVY

1 cup orange juice

1 cup chicken stock

Juice of 1 lemon

1 tablespoon honey

1 teaspoon finely chopped orange zest

1 tablespoon cornstarch

¼ cup port wine

Salt and freshly ground black pepper

• • • • • • • • • • • • • • • • • •

■ Prepare the fire for indirect grilling with drip pan in place. Fill the smoke box with mesquite, cherry, or other hardwood chips (see Smoke on the Grill, page 21). Spray or rub the grill with oil.

■ Pull out any pin feathers from the birds. Mix the sage and pepper in a bowl and sprinkle all over the birds. Wrap the breast of each bird with pancetta or bacon and tie with butchers' twine. Put equal amounts of juniper berries and orange quarters into cavities.

■ Brown the birds over medium high heat for 3 to 4 minutes, breast side down; turn and brown for another 3 to 4 minutes. Move to a cooler spot on the grill if flare-ups occur. Place the birds on the unheated section of the grill, cover, and cook until the internal temperature in the breast reaches 150°F or the flesh is just slightly pink. For commercially raised game hen or chicken, make sure that the temperature of the inner thigh gets above 165°F for safety.

To make Orange Gravy, stir the orange juice, stock, lemon juice, honey, and orange zest together and cook over medium-high heat for 5 to 6 minutes. Dissolve the cornstarch in the port, add to the saucepan, and cook, stirring constantly, until the sauce thickens slightly. Taste for salt and pepper and serve with game birds.

Jim's Tips for Grilling Game

Jim Bangert is a craftsman at many levels. He makes his living restoring and rebuilding San Francisco Bay Area houses with meticulous care. He brings the same care to his cooking: making his own sausages and smoking and grilling the venison, wild boar, and game birds he brings back from hunting in the hills and valleys of Northern California.

"The key to cooking game on the grill," Jim says, "is to compensate for the low level of fat in most game meats. Venison or boar, quail or pheasant meat just doesn't have as much fat as beef or pork or chicken. These leaner meats can dry out on the grill, so you have to add fat in the form of a marinade or by wrapping small birds with bacon or pancetta.

"When I cook venison or wild boar steaks or chops, I marinate the meat overnight in the refrigerator in a mix of oil, garlic, red wine, bay leaf, and crushed juniper berries. This moistens and tenderizes the meat and adds flavor. Cook steaks or chops briefly over high heat until no more than medium-rare (see Grilled Lamb or Venison Chops with Rosemary Garlic Paste, page 207).

"For small birds on the grill such as quail or dove, I tie pancetta or bacon around the breast and tuck a bay leaf or two under the string. Small birds are best browned over medium-high heat and moved to a cool part of the grill to finish cooking (see Barbecued Small Birds, page 151). Wild duck breasts are seasoned highly with a spicy rub and then grilled over medium-high heat to medium-rare. For pheasants or other larger game birds, I season the birds with a spicy rub, brush with oil, brown, and wrap each bird in aluminum foil with onions, sliced tomatoes, juniper berries, chopped pancetta, and a little grated cheese (see Jim's Pheasant or Chicken on the Grill, next page).

"Wine and game go together. I usually drink my homemade Zinfandel with venison or wild boar; with game birds, a fragrant Pinot Noir I get from friends along the Russian River."

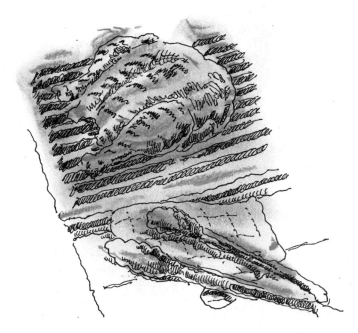

Jim's Pheasant or Chicken on the Grill

SERVES 4

Pheasants and other large game birds are best cooked with enough moisture to keep them from drying out. Jim Bangert, a master at cooking game birds, suggests browning the birds first and then cooking them in foil in a savory mix of tomatoes, onions, herbs, and cheese. Chicken, rock Cornish hens, turkey breasts, or other poultry would also be delicious.

Instead of using dried thyme or marjoram, salt, and pepper, you can substitute 2 tablespoons Herb Rub for Pork or Chicken (page 37) or Asian Spice Rub (page 110). Serve with Grill-Roasted New Potatoes (page 101) and Ratatouille from the Grill (page 96).

· · · · · · · · · · · · · · · · · ·

■ Rub the birds with oil and sprinkle with the dried herbs, salt, and ½ teaspoon pepper (or with 2 tablespoons of the spice rub of your choice).

■ Prepare the fire for indirect grilling. Fill the smoke box with alder, cherry, mesquite, or other hardwood chips (see Smoke on the Grill, page 21). Spray or rub the grill with oil.

■ Brown the birds over medium-high heat for 3 to 4 minutes breast side down. Turn and brown for another 3 to 4 minutes. Move to a cooler part of the grill if flare-ups occur.

■ Remove the birds from the grill and place each bird in the center of a piece of aluminum foil large enough to wrap it in. Spray or rub the foil with oil.

■ Lay slices of tomato and onion over the breast of each bird. In a medium bowl, mix the garlic, juniper berries, pancetta or bacon, 1 teaspoon pepper, and oregano; sprinkle over the birds. Strew equal amounts of crumbled cheese over the birds.

■ Seal the foil and return to the unheated section of the covered grill. Cook at 350°F or moderate heat for 30 to 40 minutes. Open the foil to check after 20 minutes: the pheasant should not show any pink when cut at the joints, and the cheese should be melted. Cook longer if needed. Remove the birds from the foil and serve.

4 pheasants or rock Cornish game hens or 2 small chickens

Olive or vegetable oil

2 tablespoons dried thyme or marjoram

1 teaspoon salt

1½ teaspoons freshly ground black pepper

4 plum (roma) or other fresh tomatoes, sliced

1 red onion, thinly sliced

2 cloves garlic, chopped

8 juniper berries, crushed

½ pound pancetta or bacon, chopped

1 teaspoon dried oregano

1 cup crumbled feta cheese

Pork

Far and away my favorite way to cook pork is on the grill. Pork's sweet, tender meat has just enough fat to keep the meat moist when properly grilled, and it absorbs spices and smoke flavors wonderfully. Modern pork is a leaner product than that of earlier times, though, so take care not to overcook it. If you follow the recipes from outdated cookbooks that tell you to cook pork to a well-done 170°F, you'll end up with a dry, tough, tasteless product. Grill pork correctly, and you'll sit down to some of the juiciest and most flavorful meat you'll ever eat.

The old bugaboo trichinosis is the reason most of our moms cooked pork to death. They followed the old cookbooks and believed that any trace of pink inside a pork chop would lead to a slow and agonizing death. These days we know that trichinae are killed at 138°F, or the medium stage; we also know that trichinosis has not been a health problem in the United States for many years. For most cuts, especially the leaner loin and tenderloin, pork can be taken off the grill at 150°F, when it is cooked through but still showing a little pink. If you let the pork rest for a few minutes, the temperature will end up around 155°F, perfectly juicy and tender.

It's a good idea to invest in a digital instant-read meat thermometer if you want perfection on the grill. The new models can be inserted into a chop or steak or roast or bird, and you'll know exactly what the internal temperature is. The meat thermometer is much more reliable than the cooking charts and minutes-per-pound recipes.

One of the best pork cuts for grilling is the pork tenderloin, the tender fillet that runs along the backbone of the pig. Pork tenderloins are small, cylindrical pieces of very tender, very lean meat. They can be butterflied and grilled directly (see Quick Grilling, page 17) or left whole and cooked by the composite method (see Composite Grilling, page 18). Because the meat is so lean, I recommend marinating pork tenders or rubbing them with oil before grilling (see Pork Tenderloins in Miso Marinade, page 164). Tenderloins also take well to fruits and sweet glazes (see Butterflied Pork Tenderloin with Blackberry Glaze and Grilled Fruit, page 163).

Pork loin roasts, bone in or boneless, are delicious when cooked indirectly or spit-roasted (see Indirect Heat, page 19). They are best seasoned with a spicy rub and roasted in plenty of aromatic smoke. Loin and rib pork chops are perfect for the grill. Make sure you have chops at least ¾ of an inch thick, however. Thinner chops can cook too quickly and dry out. I prefer chops cut 1 inch thick or more, and double-cut loin chops are especially suitable for grilling. Chops take well to spice rubs and marinades and are even juicer and more flavorful when brined (see Brined Thick Pork Chops with Grilled Apples and Onions, page 167).

Pork ribs are very popular, but take care to select the right type of rib for the right grill technique. Baby back ribs are tender enough to grill directly (see Thai Baby Back Ribs, page 160); country-style ribs require composite or indirect grilling (see Asian Country-Style Ribs, page 159); and tougher, fattier spareribs need long, slow indirect grilling (see Slow-Smoked Spareribs with Oakland Barbecue Sauce, page 165).

Pork becomes especially succulent when bathed in hardwood smoke while cooking. Hickory and oak are the preferred woods, but apple, alder, and mesquite also work well. I like to use plenty of smoke for pork, so load up the smoke box and replenish it when needed, or use two or three aluminum-foil packs of wood chips when cooking pork in a covered grill for any length of time (see Smoke on the Grill, page 21).

Grilled Pork Chuletas in Lime Tequila Marinade

Chuletas are tender pieces of grilled pork often served with lime and cilantro or cut up and tucked into Grilled Corn Tortillas (page 52) with Pico de Gallo (page 51) and Rajas: Grilled Chile and Pepper Strips (page 101). Use thin loin pork chops here or butterflied pork tenderloins.

Pork takes well to tangy marinades such as Lime Tequila Marinade. Be careful not to leave the tender pork pieces too long in this marinade (no more than 2 hours) as the meat picks up flavors quickly and can become mushy from the acid in the lime.

· · · · · · · · · · · · · · · · · ·

■ Place the pork and Lime Tequila Marinade in a nonreactive dish and marinate for up to 2 hours at room temperature.

■ Prepare the fire for direct grilling. Spray or rub the grill with oil.

■ Remove the pork from the marinade and pat dry. Place over medium-high heat and grill for 2 to 3 minutes, covered. Move to a cooler spot if flare-ups occur. Turn and grill for 2 to 3 more minutes until done. Cut into pork to check: it should be slightly pink and juicy inside, or 150°F to 155°F.

■ Serve garnished with slices of lime and cilantro sprigs.

SERVES 4

8 thin boneless loin pork chops or 2 butterflied pork tenderloins, cut into 4 pieces

Lime Tequila Marinade (page 141)

●

GARNISH

Limes, sliced

Cilantro sprigs

Chipotles

Chipotles are ripe jalapeño chiles that are dried and smoked (see Chiles, page 49, and Smoke-Roasted Whole Chicken with Chipotles under the Skin, page 145). They provide a distinctly smoky undertone and a nice touch of heat. You can find whole dried chipotles in Latino groceries and from mail-order sources (see Sources, page 225), but they are easier to find in powdered form or canned in adobo sauce. We use chipotle powder in our Chipotle Spice Rub (page 145) for the smoke and tang it provides.

Grilled Pork Chops with Chipotle Butter

SERVES 4

8 loin pork chops, at least 1 inch thick

2 tablespoons Chipotle Spice Rub (page 145) or Mexican Spice Rub (page 51) or commercial chile powder plus salt and pepper

•

CHIPOTLE BUTTER

¼ pound salted butter (1 stick)

Juice of ½ lime

1 chipotle en adobo, seeded and chopped, or 1 tablespoon chipotle powder or dried chipotle purée (see Dried Chile Pureé, page 108)

I love the flavor of chipotles (see Chipotles, page 157) with grilled pork chops. Use bone-in or boned chops as you like. If you can find them, large loin chops that include a bit of tenderloin (they look like little porterhouse steaks) are delicious. Any leftover chops can be cut into pieces and heated in Chipotle Butter for a tasty taco. Garnish with Rajas: Grilled Chile and Pepper Strips (page 101).

· · · · · · · · · · · · · · · · · ·

■ Slash the edges of fat around the chops in a few places to prevent curling. Sprinkle both sides generously with spice rub or chile powder plus salt and pepper.

■ Prepare the fire for direct grilling. Spray or rub the grill with oil.

To make Chipotle Butter, melt the butter in a small pan, or microwave it for 30 seconds in a small bowl. Stir in the lime juice and chipotle.

■ Place the chops over medium-high heat for 3 to 4 minutes to sear and mark the meat. Watch out for flare-ups; move to a cooler spot if necessary. Turn, brush with Chipotle Butter, cover, and grill for 3 minutes more.

■ Turn the chops and move them to the unheated part of the grill; brush again with Chipotle Butter.

■ Test for doneness with an instant-read thermometer (150°F is done), or cut into one chop. The meat should be lightly pink and still juicy. Cook longer if necessary, basting occasionally with Chipotle Butter. Remove the chops to a platter, brush with more Chipotle Butter, loosely cover with foil, and let sit for 5 to 10 minutes before serving.

Asian Country-Style Ribs

SERVES 4 TO 6

Country-style ribs are thick-cut pork shoulder chops that are meaty and full of flavor. They are ideal for slow grilling and become tender and juicy with time on the grill.

Soy Ginger Dressing can also be used to marinate pork tenderloins and chops or chicken breasts or thighs.

4–6 pounds country-style ribs

½ cup Hot Spice Rub for Pork or Chicken (page 40) or Asian Spice Rub (page 110) or Soy Ginger Dressing (page 74)

. . . .

■ Trim excess fat from the ribs and cut into manageable serving pieces. Rub with the spice rub. (If using Soy Ginger Dressing, mix the marinade ingredients in a small bowl. Pour over the pork in a nonreactive dish or zip-lock bag. Marinate the pork for up to 2 hours at room temperature or 8 to 12 hours, covered, in the refrigerator. Turn occasionally. Remove the meat from the refrigerator about an hour or so before cooking. Pat dry before grilling.)

■ Prepare the fire for indirect grilling and put drip pan in place. Add oak, hickory, or other hardwoods to the smoke box (see Smoke on the Grill, page 21). Add water to the water box if you have one, or to the drip pan if using a charcoal grill. Grill the ribs, covered, over medium–high heat for 3 to 5 minutes per side to sear and mark. Move to the unheated area of the grill and cook until done, turning occasionally. The internal temperature of the pork should be about 165°F; the meat should no longer be pink, should be tender, and should still be juicy when cut. This will take anywhere from 30 minutes up to an hour, depending on the heat and the thickness of the ribs.

■ Place the ribs on a platter, cover tightly with aluminum foil, and let rest for 10 to 15 minutes before serving.

Thai Baby Back Ribs

THAI MARINADE FOR PORK OR CHICKEN

½ cup vegetable oil

½ cup soy sauce

1 tablespoon sesame oil

1 tablespoon Asian fish sauce (*nuoc cham* or *nam pla*)

Juice of 1 lime

½ serrano chile, seeded and finely chopped

2 tablespoons finely chopped ginger

4 cloves garlic, finely chopped

2 tablespoons sugar

¼ cup chopped fresh cilantro

1 teaspoon Sriracha or other Asian hot sauce, or more to taste

•

4 slabs baby back ribs (1–1½ pounds each)

These tangy ribs cut from the pork loin are great party food and make a delicious first course for an Asian-accented meal. Look for baby back ribs with as much meat as possible. You can also use the same marinade for pork tenderloins, thin-cut boneless pork chops, or chicken breasts. Asian fish sauce (*nuoc cham* or *nam pla*) is a pungent fermented sauce widely used in Southeast Asian cooking. It is available in Asian groceries or by mail order (see Sources, page 225). Serve back ribs with Spicy Ketchup (page 93) or Wasabi Dipping Sauce (page 105).

....

To make Thai Marinade for Pork or Chicken, mix the ingredients in a small bowl.

■ Pour the marinade over the baby back ribs and marinate for at least 2 hours at room temperature or 8 to 12 hours refrigerated. Remove the ribs from the refrigerator an hour before cooking.

■ Prepare the fire for indirect grilling and put drip pan in place.

■ Remove the ribs from the marinade and pat dry. Place over medium-high heat and sear and mark the ribs, 3 to 4 minutes per side. Move to the unheated part of the grill, cover, and continue to cook until the meat is tender, another 10 minutes or more. The internal temperature of the meat should be 155°F.

■ Remove from the grill and cover tightly with aluminum foil for 10 minutes before serving.

Oregon's Willamette Valley

There's a pilgrimage every year to the little town of McMinnville in Oregon's Willamette Valley south and west of Portland. Pinot Noir fanatics from France, California, New York's Finger Lakes, and Canada's Okanagan Valley—and even from South Africa and Australia—congregate to taste wines made from this difficult and delicate grape. There's something about Pinot Noir that gets arguments going, and plenty of raised voices and hand-waving go on every year at the McMinnville Pinot Noir Festival. But the attendees don't just attend technical meetings and seminars. They drink plenty of their own products and eat wonderful local foods prepared by West Coast chefs.

Just getting to McMinnville is a pleasant task. The Willamette Valley runs north and south from Eugene to Portland between the Coast Range to the west and the towering Cascades to the east. Carved out by the winding Willamette River and scoured by glaciers, the valley is a fertile land of rolling foothills and sweeping prairies, immensely fertile and green under the Northwest's frequent rains. What brings the Pinot Noir nuts to the valley are the vineyards that blanket the slopes toward its northern end, but most of the valley's floor and gently rolling hills are covered with thriving farms and orchards.

Driving up from California, you enter the valley after bustling Eugene, filled with university students and seemingly endless stretches of pizza parlors, to view fertile fields on every side. It's a green landscape, peaceful and settled, after Northern California's mountains and high deserts. The most pleasant way to traverse the valley is to leave the main interstate and drive up country roads. Here you can see the rich bounty of the valley at close hand. And you can stop at the many roadside stands that dot the landscape.

Summer is berry season in the Willamette Valley, when produce stands are piled high with colorful berries. The cool climate, abundant rain, and fertile soil make Willamette's berries sweet, tart, and firm, bursting with flavor. Strawberries here are among the best in the world, and marionberries (a blackberry developed locally in Marion County), loganberries (a blackberry/raspberry cross), and boysenberries are ripe and sweet. The berries are delicious eaten out of hand or for breakfast with cream, and wonderful in pies and cobblers. Pork is also complemented nicely by other fruit and berry glazes (see Butterflied Pork Tenderloin with Blackberry Glaze and Grilled Fruit, next page).

Mushrooms are another product of the cool, moist climate of the valley and its flanking mountain ranges. In the spring, you can find heaps of morels at local stands; in the fall, brilliant yellow chanterelles; and year-round, if you're lucky, plump and meaty porcini or *Boletus edulis.*

As you drive north in the valley, south-facing hills are covered with grapevines. The valley's many wineries produce fragrant Pinot Gris and luscious Chardonnays, but Pinot Noir is king in this northern climate with its cool summer days and even cooler nights. All through the valley, but especially in Yamhill County near the town of Newberg, Pinot Noir is being made that is truly world-class. Wineries such as Amity, Rex Hill, Sokol Blosser, and Domaine Drouhin (to name but a few) are producing rich and silky Pinot Noirs that rival the best California and Burgundy have to offer.

Pinot Noir is wonderful with beef or lamb and is especially delicious with duck. Michael Wild, a good friend and owner-chef of the Bay Wolf restaurant in Oakland, is featured at the McMinnville festival year after year. Michael's Grilled Duck Breasts with Berry Pinot Noir Glaze (page 150) was inspired by the great wines and local products of the Oregon coastal valleys.

Butterflied Pork Tenderloins with Blackberry Glaze and Grilled Fruit

SERVES 4

Pork's sweet, mild flavor goes beautifully with fruit. The blackberry glaze in this recipe adds a rich taste to the meat, but you could create an Asian feel instead by rubbing the pork with Chinese five-spice powder or Asian Spice Rub (page 110). The fruit goes wonderfully with pork however you prepare it.

Grilling fruit is easy and quick and results in a nicely caramelized crust on the fruit. Use firm, ripe fruit, and dip the cut edge into brown sugar or honey before grilling over a hot fire for a minute or two. We've used peaches or nectarines, figs, and pineapple, but try whatever is in season. Be sure to spray or rub the grill with oil to prevent sticking.

Try drinking a delicate Oregon Pinot Noir along with this.

....

■ Butterfly the tenderloins by cutting lengthwise to about ½ inch of the other side and pounding the meat lightly with the flat of a knife or cleaver. Cut into four uniform pieces and sprinkle with salt and pepper. Cover and let sit for up to 2 hours at room temperature.

■ Prepare the fire for direct grilling. Spray or rub the grill with oil.

To make Blackberry Glaze, stir ingredients together in a small saucepan over medium-high heat for 15 minutes.

■ Grill one side of the pork over medium-high heat for 3 minutes; turn and brush with glaze. Continue grilling, turning often and brushing with glaze until the internal temperature is about 150°F and the meat is slightly pink and very juicy when cut, 8 to 12 minutes total. Remove the tenderloins from the grill, brush generously with glaze, and cover lightly with aluminum foil.

To make Grilled Fruit, cut peaches or nectarines in half and remove the pits; slice the figs in half lengthwise. Sprinkle brown sugar on a platter and place the fruit, cut side down, in the sugar. Spray or rub the grill with oil. Place the peach or nectarine, fig, and pineapple pieces, cut side down, on high heat. Grill for 2 to 3 minutes or more until the fruit is nicely marked and the sugar has caramelized. Be careful not to char or burn the fruit. Check after a minute or so to make sure. Turn and cook for another couple of minutes to heat the fruit through. Do not overcook.

■ Serve the tenderloins on individual plates garnished with equal amounts of fruit and any leftover glaze on the side.

Ingredients

2 pork tenderloins, silverskin and fat removed

Salt and freshly ground black pepper

•

BLACKBERRY GLAZE

1 pint blackberries, puréed and strained

1 tablespoon honey

¼ cup port

•

GRILLED FRUIT

2 ripe peaches or nectarines

8 figs, ripe but still firm

Light brown sugar

4 ripe pineapple slices

SERVES 4

2 pork tenderloins, about 1½ pounds each

•

MISO MARINADE

½ cup miso

¼ cup sake or dry sherry

1 tablespoon sesame oil

2 tablespoons lime juice

3 tablespoons hoisin sauce

4 cloves garlic, finely chopped

2 teaspoons Chinese hot black bean paste or other Asian hot sauce

Pork Tenderloins in Miso Marinade

Miso is a fragrant, pungent, and salty paste made from fermented soybeans. Japanese cooks use it in soups and as a flavoring and marinade in many traditional dishes. Here it is the base for a gingery, slightly spicy marinade for pork tenderloins. The marinade is also delicious on chicken, fish, or vegetables.

Pork tenderloins are ideal for grilling. They are tender, contain little fat, and cook quickly on the grill. The meat takes up flavors easily from marinades, dry rubs, or smoke from the grill. The trick with pork tenderloins is not to overcook them. The lack of fat means that the meat can dry out and become tough at temperatures over 155°F. Use an instant-read thermometer and remove the tenderloin from the grill at 150°F, or cut into the thickest part and make sure that the meat is still slightly pink.

Cook tenderloins whole, or butterfly them (see previous recipe). Whole tenderloins take a little longer to cook and need more time in the marinade to absorb flavors. Butterflied tenderloins cook quite quickly, so be extra careful when grilling them. Another way to prepare tenderloins is to slice them across the grain into small cutlets. As with butterflied loins, these little chops overcook quickly, so test them after they've cooked only a few minutes on either side.

Serve with Asian Noodle and Grilled Baby Bok Choy Salad with Orange Ginger Vinaigrette (page 75) and Grilled Pineapple Relish (page 127).

....

■ Remove excess fat and the silverskin from pork tenderloins. Leave whole, butterfly, or cut into chops across the grain (see above).

To make Miso Marinade, mix the ingredients in a small bowl.

■ Place the pork in a nonreactive dish or zip-lock bag, coat generously with the marinade, and marinate for up to 2 hours at room temperature or 8 to 12 hours in the refrigerator. Turn the meat occasionally.

■ Prepare the fire for direct grilling. Spray or rub the grill with oil.

■ Remove the meat from the marinade and brush off the excess. Place the tenderloins directly on high heat for a few minutes per side to mark and sear the meat. Move to a cooler spot if flare-ups occur. This should be enough cooking time for thinner chops. Move whole or butterflied tenderloins to the cooler part of the grill, cover, and cook to 150°F or until still slightly pink in the middle. Begin checking butterflied tenderloins after 7 minutes total cooking time, whole tenderloins after 12 minutes.

■ Let the meat rest, covered loosely with foil, for a few minutes before serving. Slice whole or butterflied tenderloins or cut them in half for individual servings.

Slow-Smoked Spareribs with Oakland Barbecue Sauce

Look for the heaviest and meatiest slabs of ribs you can find and leave yourself plenty of time for this recipe. Coat the spareribs with spice rub the day before, if you can, and let them marinate overnight in the refrigerator. Or season them early in the morning of the day you're going to cook them. Remove the ribs from the refrigerator an hour or so before putting them on the grill.

The trick for successful ribs is a long, slow fire with plenty of smoke. If you are using charcoal, prepare for indirect grilling with a minimum of coals on each side of the drip pan (follow the manufacturer's directions). With a gas grill, set the heat at low or medium. Ideally, the temperature should stay at or below 300°F during the 2 to 3 hours of cooking. If you don't have a built-in thermometer, try an instant-read thermometer inserted into the top vent. I like to use hickory or oak for the smoke source, but any hardwood will do. Use Oakland Barbecue Sauce or your favorite barbecue sauce for the last few minutes of cooking and as a sauce at the table.

. . . .

■ Rub the spareribs generously with the spice rub and refrigerate, covered, for at least 8 hours. Let the ribs sit for an hour at room temperature before grilling.

■ Prepare the fire for slow indirect grilling (see Indirect Heat, page 19) and put drip pan in place. Fill the smoke box with hickory, oak, or other hardwoods (see Smoke on the Grill, page 21). You will most likely need to add more wood for smoke during the long cooking time. If you have a pan for water in the grill, fill it, and refill it if necessary. If using a charcoal grill, pour water halfway up in the drip pan underneath the ribs and replenish as needed.

■ Place the slabs of rib over the unheated section of the grill and cook at or below 300°F for 2 to 3 hours, until the meat is tender and begins to pull away from the bone. The internal temperature of the meat should be 165°F.

SERVES 4 TO 6

2 slabs of spareribs (2½–3 pounds each)

¼ cup Spice Rub for Pork or Beef (page 38) or Hot Spice Rub for Pork or Chicken (page 40) or Chile Rub (page 143)

•

OAKLAND BARBECUE SAUCE

2 tablespoons vegetable oil

2 cups finely chopped onion

1 cup finely chopped celery

½ cup finely chopped carrot

3 tablespoons chopped garlic

2 teaspoons finely ground black pepper

1 cup red wine

6 cups beef stock

2 cups ketchup

⅓ cup Worcestershire sauce

¼ cup soy sauce

3 tablespoons cider or other vinegar

1–2 teaspoons Liquid Smoke

¼ cup packed dark brown sugar

1 tablespoon dry mustard (preferably Colman's)

2 teaspoons dried thyme

1 teaspoon dried oregano

4 bay leaves

1–2 teaspoons cayenne, or to taste

¼ teaspoon Tabasco or other hot sauce, or to taste

Salt

To make Oakland Barbecue Sauce, while the ribs cook, heat the oil in a heavy pan and cook the onions, celery, carrots, garlic, and pepper, covered, stirring often, until soft, about 10 minutes. Add the wine and boil for 2 to 3 minutes. Stir in the rest of the ingredients except the cayenne, Tabasco, and salt, and simmer, uncovered, for 45 minutes to an hour until the sauce is thickened. Add water if it seems too thick. Taste for heat levels and add salt to taste (canned stock can be salty, so be careful with salt). Remove the bay leaves. The sauce keeps in the refrigerator for up to a month.

■ Brush the ribs generously with heated Oakland Barbecue Sauce or other barbecue sauce before removing from the grill. Cover the ribs tightly with double layers of heavy duty aluminum foil for 10 to 15 minutes before serving.

■ To serve, cut into individual ribs and brush again with barbecue sauce. Serve with heated barbecue sauce on the side.

Source: Oakland Barbecue Sauce adapted from Bruce Aidells and Denis Kelly, *The Complete Meat Cookbook*. Houghton Mifflin, 1998.

Brined Thick Pork Chops with Grilled Apples and Onions

This brine infuses the pork with the flavors of sage and chile, typical Southwest flavors. Smoky apples and onions complement the sweet and aromatic pork. You could also use two whole pork tenderloins in this recipe.

. . . .

■ Trim off excess external fat from the meat. Submerge the pork in brine and place a plate on top to ensure it is completely covered. Refrigerate and let soak 2 to 6 hours. After 2 hours, test the meat; cut a small section off, pat dry, and pan-fry it. If it is flavorful enough, remove the pork from the brine, pat dry, wrap in plastic wrap or foil, and refrigerate until ready to grill. If it needs more flavor, return to the brine and let soak for up to 4 more hours. Let the meat come to room temperature before grilling.

■ Prepare the fire for direct grilling. Fill the smoke box with oak or other hardwood chips (see Smoke on the Grill, page 21). Spray or rub the grill with oil.

■ Sear chops on the hot part of the grill for 2 minutes each side. Transfer to a cooler area of the grill, cover, and cook for 4 to 7 minutes on each side or until the internal temperature reaches 150°F.

■ Spray or rub the apples and onions with oil. Put them over medium-high heat. Cover. Grill each side for 3 to 4 minutes or until nicely marked and starting to soften. Remove from the grill and peel off the onion skins.

■ Serve the pork chops with apples and onions.

SERVES 6

6 double-cut pork loin chops (1½ inches thick)

1 recipe Pork Brine (page 43)

2 apples, cored and quartered

Vegetable oil

2 large onions, skins on, sliced horizontally ½ inch thick

SERVES 6 TO 8

1 pork loin or veal roast (5–7 pounds)

2 tablespoons chopped fresh sage or 1 tablespoon dried

4 cloves garlic, chopped

2 teaspoons salt

1 teaspoon freshly ground black pepper

Smoke-Roasted Pork Loin or Veal Roast

Cooking a large piece of tender pork or veal in a kettle barbecue turns out succulent, smoky meat with great flavor and texture. A boned or bone-in pork loin or a rolled veal roast is a good cut to use on a rotisserie (see Spit-Roasting, page 20). Even without a rotisserie, these roasts are delicious when seasoned well and smoke-roasted using the indirect heat method (see Indirect Heat, page 19). I like the flavor of sage and garlic on these mild-flavored white meats, but you could also use rosemary, thyme, or one of the spice rubs in the Dry Rubs and Marinades chapter (page 35). Hot Spice Rub for Pork or Chicken (page 40) and Spice Rub for Pork or Beef (page 38) are good choices. Serve with Grilled Corn with Cilantro Pesto (page 91) and Tony's Spanish Rice with Smoke-Roasted Tomato Sauce (page 102).

. . . .

■ Trim excess fat from the roast. Mix together the sage, garlic, salt, and pepper, and spread all over the roast, pushing the herb mixture into any crevices. (Or season the roast thoroughly with a spice rub of your choice.) Let the meat sit for an hour or two at room temperature or 8 to 12 hours in the refrigerator. Be sure the meat is at room temperature before cooking.

■ Prepare the fire for indirect grilling and put drip pan in place. Add hickory, oak, apple, or other hardwood chips to the smoke box (see Smoke on the Grill, page 21). Spray or rub the grill with oil.

■ Skewer the roast with a spit and start the rotisserie, or place the meat on the unheated area of the grill. Cover the grill and cook until the internal temperature reaches 150°F for the pork, 135°F for veal. Cut with the tip of a sharp knife, pork and veal should both be lightly pink and still juicy. Cooking times will vary according to the thickness of the meat and the heat of the fire. Start checking after 35 minutes.

■ Once the roast has reached the desired temperature, remove it from the grill and let the meat rest, loosely covered with foil, for 15 minutes before carving.

Beef

When we remember backyard barbecues, with Dad standing by the grill in his apron amid clouds of billowing smoke, beer can in one hand, long-handled tongs in the other, it's usually steak that come to mind. In my house in Southwest Los Angeles, at least—and I suspect in many others along the Pacific Coast and across the country—the weekly ritual on summer Sunday afternoons centered around a substantial sirloin or porterhouse, grilled rare and seasoned with salt and pepper and not much else. Once the steak came off the grill, we all gathered around the picnic table on the patio under the bougainvillea vine and gorged on thick slices of the smoky red meat and Mom's potato salad and a big platter of greens covered with chunks of home-grown tomatoes, red onions, and French dressing. Sometimes the ritual varied, with burgers on toasted buns and occasionally chicken in spicy sauce, but the Real Thing was steak, thick and juicy, charred on the outside, bloodred inside, the symbol of the good life and suburban prosperity.

Lots of things have changed since those childhood barbecues, but the taste for grilled steak remains in most American families. A steak on the grill is still an emblem of the good life, and steakhouses are the most popular restaurants in the country. Steak always tastes better when grilled over a smoky fire. Perhaps it's the memories of ancestral campfires or the nostalgia of childhood feasts, but I suspect that grilled steak appeals just because of its sheer deliciousness: the juicy meat and crisp fat, with the smoke-seared and salty crust satisfies us above all other food.

Steaks are cut from the back of the steer and include tender meat along the loin and ribs. Most steaks (with the exception of round steaks, cut from the rump) are tender enough to grill, although some are more tender than others. Paradoxically, less tender steaks, such as flank or chuck or skirt steak, often have more flavor than tenderer cuts, such as filet mignon and strip loin or New York steaks. Muscles on the flank or shoulder that get more use are tougher but have a "beefier" taste; less-used muscles along the back and loin don't toughen up but can sometimes be a bit bland.

The very tender steaks taste best if they are seasoned lightly with salt and pepper or a spice rub or herb rub before grilling; the slightly tougher steaks are best marinated to enhance flavors and to make them a bit less chewy when cooked. Filet mignon, tournedos, porterhouse, strip loin, and New York steak and top sirloin (see The Perfect Steak: So Cal Style, page 181; Bruce's Extra Thick Porterhouse, page 182) need only a little seasoning before grilling over direct heat (see Direct Heat, page 17). Flank steaks (see Spicy Soy Flank Steak with Grilled Shiitake Onion Relish, page 193), skirt steak (see Skirt Steak Fajitas, page 179; Carne Asada I and II, pages 173 and 174), culotte steaks, or tri-tip steaks (see Guadalupe Skewered Culotte Steaks, page 178) benefit from marinating overnight in an oil-based marinade or dry rub. Most steaks are best cooked by the direct heat method, although very thick steaks are best grilled using the composite method (see Composite Grilling, page 18).

Burgers are a delicious and popular type of grilled beef. For best results, buy freshly ground chuck or ground beef with at least 15 percent fat; 20 percent (the ground chuck level) is best. Ground beef that is too lean will dry out quickly on the grill and become crumbly and unpalatable. Season ground meat before you form it into patties with salt, pepper, and the herbs and spices of your choice (see California Burger with Big Bopper Tomato Topper, page 189; Alvarado Street Chili Burger, page 190). When you grill burgers, for safety's sake, cook them to the medium-well stage (160°F internal temperature).

Larger pieces of tender beef can be roasted very successfully on the grill using the indirect method (see Indirect Heat, page 19) or by spit-roasting (see Spit-Roasting, page 20). Some examples are Santa Maria Tri-Tips (page 176), Smoky Prime Rib, Santa Maria Style (page 177), and Grill-Roasted Beef with Thyme Garlic Crust (page 197). After removing from the grill, be sure to let these roasts sit for 15 minutes, covered loosely with foil, to redistribute the juices and equalize heat levels in the meat before carving and serving.

Beef on the grill is made even more flavorful with smoke. Virtually any type of hardwood works well with beef: I prefer the strong-flavored woods such as oak or hickory, but mesquite, alder, and cherry also work well.

Old Bill and the Cross-Eyed Mule: Carne Asada on the Border

Everybody called him Old Bill, although the name on the sign out front of the grill he presided over read "Sarge's." For years, he made the best burgers and the hottest carne asada tacos on the avenue in Oakland, standing over the smoking grill with spatula in hand, U.S. Army campaign cap on his head, a big white (most times not-so-white) apron wrapped around his ample belly.

After a day in the smoke, serving everybody from flower children to office workers to East Oakland bikers, Old Bill would repair to the local bar, park himself on his favorite stool near the window, and cool off with bottle after bottle of Bohemia, a strong Mexican ale whose virtues he'd extol to all comers. "Hell," Bill would say, "when I was down on the border chasing Pancho Villa, this is all I'd drink. That damn mescal would rot the brain, so I stuck to good Mexican ale. It's kept me alive and kicking all these years."

Now, there were some who might cast doubt on Bill's claims to have fought against Pancho Villa. Never to his face, though. After all, Bill was an old geezer, all right, and definitely a military man, retired, of course. And it was never a good idea to disagree with Bill—there were tales of Bohemia bottles bounced off heads, and he could strip the paint off the side of a house with his cusswords when he got going, which was often.

I hung around Bill for the stories and because I was always trying to wheedle his carne asada recipe out of him. He'd say that he got his secret carne asada rub from an ancient *asadero*, or Mexican grill master, in a cantina in Nogales one long night, and he swore he'd never reveal it. At least that was one story. Other times it was an old *bruja* or wise woman in Tucson with a wooden leg and an Aztec curse. You never knew with Old Bill, but one thing was for sure: he made the best damn carne asada I ever ate. So I'd buy him Bohemias and prod him for stories and occasionally drop in a question about the carne asada. Over the years, I heard plenty of stories and got a pretty good idea of what went into the rub. D Alexander and I worked it up into a recipe (see Carne Asada I, next page).

One of Bill's stories had to do with barbecuing (or, as Bill called it, *barbacoa*) in the Old West. It's a story Bill loved to tell again and again about his favorite mule, the highly intelligent, cross-eyed, and endlessly cantankerous Sam.

When Bill was driving mules and cooking for the Army down near the border one hot summer day, Sam was leading the mule train. Bill had packed all the important items onto Sam as usual: the barbacoa— a contraption of rods and grills for cooking carne asada over mesquite coals—along with Bill's all-important sack of chiles and seasonings, beans, and other necessaries. As Bill described it, they were inching along a mountain trail about a foot wide with "a wall of rock on one side and the mouth of Hell on the other." As they rounded a blind curve in the trail, Sam stopped suddenly. Bill thought that one of the mule's many moods had come over him or that Sam had stopped just to be ornery. So he leaned around the mule to see what was ahead on the trail, and, as Bill put it, "I was staring into the calm, yellow eyes of the biggest cougar I'd ever seen. We had a dilemma here. If anybody got excited, the whole damn mule train, including Sam, the barbacoa, and my carne asada rub, and most probably me, would be 10 feet out and 400 feet up with nothing but air underneath. It was all up to Sam. He turned his head and looked me in the eye.

Now, I know that mules can't speak, but I swear that Sam said to me, 'Don't panic, you damn fool, let's give this here lion a chance to save face.' And Sam began to back up very carefully, and so did I and all the rest of the mules in the whole damn train. I peeked around the mule, and there was the lion, backing up himself, also very carefully. It was clear that he and Sam had come to some sort of understanding. We continued until we couldn't see the lion and he couldn't see us. And then we waited until Sam deemed it advisable for us to get a move on again.

That night, we all celebrated with carne asada and plenty of cold Bohemias. I even offered a drink of my ale to Sam, but he gave me a long look and refused to let me buy him a drink. There was no bribing that damn mule, he had a mind of his own. So I had to go all the way back to the cantina to get Sam his favorite beer, Carta Blanca. Sam always preferred lager, never could abide a strong ale like Bohemia. Slowed his brain down, I guess."

Carne Asada I

The *asadero*, or grill master, is an important person in Mexican and Southwest cooking. The grill master knows the secrets of creating and maintaining a grill fire and, as importantly, has special recipes for rubs and marinades. That's why there are as many recipes for Mexican grilled steak or carne asada as there are *asaderos*. This recipe was put together from Old Bill's stories by D Alexander (see D Alexander and the World's Most Expensive Chicken, page 136) and myself.

Lots of chile, garlic, and jalapeños and plenty of lemon and lemon pepper are the secrets to great carne asada. Hanger steaks or butcher's steaks (thin steaks that hang from the diaphragm of the steer and that butchers take home for themselves) make the best carne asada. Thin-cut rib steaks or flank steaks are also delicious. Carne Asada Paste is also very good on chicken breasts or pork tenderloins.

Serve with Grilled Corn Tortillas (page 52) with Salsa Verde (page 50) or Pico de Gallo (page 51).

· · · · · · · · · · · · · · · · ·

■ Trim excess fat from the steaks and pierce all over with a fork or skewer.

To make Carne Asada Paste, mix the chile powder, garlic powder, paprika, lemon pepper, cumin, and salt in a small bowl. Stir in the lemon juice and chopped jalapeños and enough jalapeño juice to make a thin paste.

■ Rub the paste all over the steaks and marinate them in a ziplock bag or nonreactive bowl for 2 hours at room temperature or 8 to 12 hours in the refrigerator. Remove the steaks from the refrigerator about an hour before cooking.

■ Prepare the fire for direct grilling. Put mesquite or other hardwoods in the smoke box (see Smoke on the Grill, page 21). Spray or rub the grill with oil.

■ Grill the steaks over high heat, turning once or twice, to rare or medium-rare (125°F to 130°F, or until red and juicy in the center). This won't take long for thin-cut steaks, perhaps 3 to 4 minutes per side. Move the steaks to a cooler part of the grill if flare-ups occur. Let the steaks rest for 5 minutes, loosely covered with foil, before slicing into strips.

4 thinly cut (1 inch or less) rib steaks, bone in or boneless, or 4 hanger steaks or 1 flank steak—about 2 pounds of meat total

•

CARNE ASADA PASTE

1 tablespoon chile powder

2 tablespoons garlic powder or granulated garlic

1 tablespoon paprika

1 tablespoon lemon pepper

1 teaspoon ground cumin

1 teaspoon salt

Juice of 1 lemon

2 or more canned jalapeños en escabeche, seeded and finely chopped, juice reserved

SERVES 4

1 flank steak (2–2½ pounds) or skirt steak (2–3 pounds)

•

CARNE ASADA RUB

1 tablespoon chile powder

1 teaspoon lemon pepper

1 teaspoon ground cumin

1 teaspoon salt

½ teaspoon cayenne

•

CARNE ASADA MARINADE

2 tablespoons red wine vinegar

2 tablespoons olive oil

2 tablespoons finely chopped garlic

Juice of 2 lemons

2 jalapeño or other hot chiles, seeded and finely chopped

1 bunch cilantro (10 ounces), finely chopped

1 bunch green onions (10 ounces), finely chopped

2 very ripe tomatoes, finely chopped, with juice

Carne Asada II

This spicy marinade for Mexican-style grilled steak, or carne asada, comes from John Neudecker, a talented Bay Area grill cook. The recipe is a popular one at cookouts and festival barbecues in John's native town of Fresno and is used by local asaderos, Latino grill masters, to flavor flank steak or skirt steaks. Substitute Chile Rub (page 143) for the Carne Asada Rub if you wish. Serve the steak sliced and wrapped in Grilled Corn Tortillas (page 52) along with some Pico de Gallo (page 51) or Salsa Cruda (page 50).

· · · · · · · · · · · · · · · · · ·

■ Trim the steak of any external fat and pierce all over with a fork or skewer.

To make Carne Asada Rub, mix ingredients in a small bowl.

■ Coat the meat with Carne Asada Rub. Let is sit for an hour at room temperature.

To make Carne Asada Marinade, mix all ingredients in a zip-lock bag or nonreactive bowl.

■ Marinate the steak 8 to 24 hours in the refrigerator, turning occasionally. Let the meat sit at room temperature for an hour or so before cooking.

■ Prepare the fire for direct grilling. Put mesquite or other hardwood in the smoke box (see Smoke on the Grill, page 21). Spray or rub the grill with oil.

■ Remove the steak from the marinade and pat dry. Reserve the marinade, and use it to baste the steak occasionally as it cooks.

■ Grill over direct heat, turning once or twice, until rare to medium-rare (125°F to 130°F internal temperature, or red and juicy when cut). This should take 7 to 10 minutes total, depending on the thickness of the meat and the heat of the fire. Move the steak to a cooler area of the grill if flare-ups occur.

■ Remove the steak from the grill and let sit, loosely covered with foil, for 5 minutes before slicing it on the bias against the grain.

Santa Maria Barbecue

The town of Santa Maria on California's Central Coast north of Santa Barbara claims to be the Barbecue Capital of the World. Now, some folk in Texas or Tennessee or Kansas City might argue that point, but for grilled prime beef, Santa Maria–style barbecue is hard to beat. Grilling tender locally grown beef over red oak coals has long been a tradition along California's coast. In rancho days, vaqueros would thread pieces of beef loin on green willow stakes and grill them over oak fires. By the 1900s, this tradition had taken hold in the cattle town of Santa Maria, and local ranchers and businessmen founded the Santa Maria Club as a place to hold barbecues, drink copiously, play poker, and promote local causes.

The original Santa Maria barbecue style featured 3-inch–thick slabs of boneless prime rib, seasoned simply with salt, pepper, and garlic salt, and spitted on long metal rods. The meat was suspended over red oak coals, grilled until done, and then sliced into big galvanized washtubs for serving to crowds (often in the hundreds) of hungry folk. Accompaniments were (and are) always the same: split loaves of French bread, grilled and slathered with butter and garlic; cooked pinquito beans—small, pale pink beans grown locally; and Pico de Gallo (page 51) or Salsa Cruda (page 50). You put slices of bread on your plate, arranged thick slices of juicy beef on top, ladled on some beans, and spread around as much salsa as you could stand.

In recent years, tri-tips—triangular pieces of tender sirloin—have largely taken the place of the thick rib steaks in Santa Maria, although you can still find these luscious steaks in local restaurants. The tri-tip is a by-product of the modern practice of breaking down the beef carcass into primal cuts before shipping. If you bone out the sirloin for steaks, a small triangular muscle is left over. You can think of the tri-tip as a very thick steak or a small roast—it works both ways. It is also cut along the grain into long, thick culotte steaks. It's a wonderful cut for grilling, compact and tender and full of beefy flavor.

Santa Maria Tri-Tips

SERVES 4 TO 6

2 whole tri-tips (about 1½–2½ pounds each)

•

SEASONINGS

2 teaspoons salt

½ teaspoon freshly ground black pepper

1 tablespoon garlic salt

OR

2 tablespoons Chile Rub (page 143)

OR

2 tablespoons Chipotle Spice Rub (page 145)

The tri-tip is one of the tastiest cuts of beef around and is very easy to cook on the grill. I usually grill two or three tri-tips together for family parties, hoping to have some leftovers for sandwiches. That doesn't often happen, though, because the savory meat is a big hit with young and old.

Classic Santa Maria barbecue masters tend to keep the seasonings simple; they combine salt, pepper, and garlic salt and roll thick pieces of beef loin in the mixture before grilling. I prefer to add a spice rub, such as Chile Rub or Chipotle Spice Rub.

To cook tri-tips over oak coals, see Building a Charcoal or Hardwood Fire (page 12). If you prefer to cook with charcoal or gas, use plenty of oak chips (see Smoke on the Grill, page 21) for a smoky flavor.

Santa Maria Tri-Tips are delicious served with cooked pinquito or other cooked beans, Pico de Gallo (page 51) or Salsa Cruda (page 50). Full-bodied California wine such as Syrah or Zinfandel, or a powerful ale such as Mexico's Bohemia or California's Sierra Nevada Pale Ale, would make a nice accompaniment.

••••••••••••••••••

■ Trim the tri-tips of extra external fat, leaving about ¼ inch. Slash across the grain in a few places to prevent curling. Sprinkle generously with salt, pepper, and garlic salt (or rub with a spice rub). Let the meat sit at room temperature for about an hour.

■ Prepare the fire for direct grilling. Spray or rub the grill with oil.

■ When the fire is hot and smoky, place the tri-tips directly over the fire to sear and mark them. Watch for flare-ups; move to a cooler spot if needed. Cover and cook for about 3 to 5 minutes. Turn to sear and mark the other side, cooking another 3 to 5 minutes.

■ Move the tri-tips to the unheated area of the grill and test with an instant-read meat thermometer. If you want rare meat, remove the tri-tips from the grill at 125°F; for medium-rare, at about 130°F. Or you can cut into a thick part to check the meat. Cover and cook until the meat reaches the desired doneness—anywhere from 5 more minutes to half an hour, depending on the thickness of the meat and the heat of the fire. After removing from the grill, let tri-tips rest, covered loosely with foil, for 10 minutes before slicing against the grain.

Smoky Prime Rib, Santa Maria Style

SERVES 4 TO 6

1 piece prime rib, 3 inches thick

1 recipe Rosemary Garlic Paste (page 207) or 2 tablespoons spice rub of your choice

This is my version of the original Santa Maria–style grilled rib steak. Ranchers on California's central coast would select their finest beefs and have them butchered especially for Santa Maria festivals and barbecues. Prime ribs were aged for weeks in the cooler and then cut into huge 3-inch-thick steaks or blocks that were then strung on metal rods to be roasted over red oak coals.

The trick here is in finding the beef. I buy a lot of my meat at a local discount warehouse store that sells choice beef in primal and subprimal cuts. The advantages? I get choice meat from one of the best American meat packers, cheaper prices than in most supermarkets, and big pieces of meat that I can cut any way I want and freeze for later use.

To make this dish, I buy a whole boned prime rib and cut a 3-inch steak out of the small end, about two or three ribs worth. The rest makes a great roast for a special occasion. More simply, ask your favorite butcher to cut you a piece of boneless prime rib at least 3 inches thick from the small end. The advantage of the small end is that you get a compact piece of very tender meat; the large end of the prime rib nearer the chuck is a bit chewier and tends to separate into individual muscles. Trim off the exterior fat.

Serve with traditional Santa Maria fare (see Santa Maria Barbecue, page 175) or with Grill-Roasted New Potatoes (page 101) and Grilled Asparagus with Roasted Garlic Oil (page 97). California Cabernet Sauvignon is the wine of choice.

· · · · · · · · · · · · · · · · · · ·

■ Rub the meat all over with herb paste or rub. Try to get some inside any crevices in the meat. Skewer the meat on a long metal skewer into a solid block, rolling the tail up into the center. Let the meat sit for up to an hour at room temperature before cooking.

■ Prepare the fire for direct grilling. Add oak chips to your smoke box or fire (see Smoke on the Grill, page 21). Spray or rub the grill with oil.

■ Cook the meat to sear and mark over high heat, covered, for 3 to 4 minutes, being careful to avoid flare-ups. Move to a cooler spot if necessary. Turn to the other side for 3 to 4 minutes to sear and mark. Move the meat to the cooler area of the grill, and cook, covered, until you reach the desired internal temperature, 120°F for rare, 130°F for medium-rare. If you have a thermometer, regulate the heat inside the covered barbecue to about 350°F. The meat will take anywhere from 15 minutes to half an hour more to cook, possibly even longer, depending on the thickness of the meat and the heat of the fire.

■ Let the steak sit, covered loosely with foil, for 10 to 15 minutes. Cut the meat into thick slices and serve.

Guadalupe Skewered Culotte Steaks

SERVES 4

4–6 culotte steaks (about 2 pounds total)

2 tablespoons chile powder

1 tablespoon dried oregano

1 teaspoon salt

½ teaspoon freshly ground black pepper

In the little town of Guadalupe on Highway 1 on the coast west of Santa Maria, you'll find tasty grilled tri-tip served in roadside restaurants. You can usually get classic Santa Maria tri-tip and rib steaks along with Mexican-accented versions of the central coast's favorite cut of beef.

Culotte steaks are cut along the grain of the tri-tip. They are inexpensive but tender and full of beef flavor. The steaks are usually oblong in shape with varying degrees of thickness, so they can be a little tricky to grill whole. But cut up into uniform-size chunks, tossed in a spicy rub, skewered, and grilled over a smoky fire, culotte steaks can make the finest meat you'd ever want for tacos or burritos, especially when paired with Rajas: Grilled Chile and Pepper Strips (page 101), Pico de Gallo or other salsa of your choice (see Salsas Frescas, page 50). Instead of the chile powder and oregano suggested here, you could use 2 tablespoons Chile Rub (page 143) or Chipotle Spice Rub (page 145).

. . . .

■ Trim culotte steaks of most fat and cut into 1½-inch cubes. Toss with chile powder, oregano, salt, and pepper (or spice rub). Thread onto small metal or bamboo skewers. Let sit for 15 minutes to an hour before cooking.

■ Prepare the fire for direct grilling. Spray or rub the grill with oil.

■ Place the skewers over high heat, close the cover, and grill, turning often for 7 to 10 minutes total until medium rare. (Cut into a chunk to test.)

Skirt Steak Fajitas

Skirt steak is a lean and flavorful steak that was a favorite with Mexican vaqueros, who called it the "little belt," or *fajita* in Spanish. Marinate and grill the steaks and serve in Grilled Corn Tortillas (page 52) with Rajas: Grilled Chile and Pepper Strips (page 101) and garnished with Salsa Cruda (page 50).

SERVES 4

1 skirt steak (2–3 pounds)

Double recipe Lime Tequila Marinade (page 141)

Chile powder

Salt and freshly ground black pepper

· · · · · · · · · · · · · · · · · ·

■ Marinate the steak in Lime Tequila Marinade for up to 2 hours at room temperature or 8 to 12 hours in the refrigerator. Remove and pat dry; sprinkle with chile powder, salt, and pepper.

■ Prepare the fire for direct grilling. Spray or rub the grill with oil.

■ Grill or broil over high heat for 2 to 3 minutes per side to medium-rare (130°F). Slice into bite-size pieces and serve.

Korean Barbecue

On-the-table grills are a popular feature of West Coast Korean restaurants. Beef and poultry are marinated in a sweet and spicy sauce before grilling and served with rice.

SERVES 4

2½ pounds thin rib-eye steak

1 recipe Kalbi (page 140)

· · · · · · · · · · · · · · · · · ·

■ Place the meat in a zip-lock bag or shallow dish. Pour half of the marinade on the meat. Shake or turn to coat the meat thoroughly. Marinate for 2 hours at room temperature or 8 to 12 hours refrigerated. Return to room temperature before grilling.

■ Prepare the fire for direct grilling. Spray or rub the grill with oil.

■ Grill the meat for 3 minutes on each side, basting with marinade. Heat the remaining sauce in a microwave or in a saucepan. Serve with the cooked beef.

SERVES 4

SATAY MARINADE

2 teaspoons minced fresh ginger

2 tablespoons minced
lemon zest

1 tablespoon lime juice

2 tablespoons soy sauce

4 cloves garlic, chopped

1 tablespoon Asian fish sauce
(*nuoc cham* or *nam pla*)

1 tablespoon packed light
brown sugar

1 teaspoon turmeric

1 teaspoon cumin

1 teaspoon coriander

1 teaspoon Sriracha or other
Asian hot sauce

•

2–3 pounds skirt steak or flank
steak, cut into 4-inch-long strips
1 inch wide and ½ inch thick

•

PEANUT SAUCE

1 tablespoon peanut or
vegetable oil

½ cup finely chopped onion

1 clove garlic, finely chopped

½ teaspoon dried red
pepper flakes

¼ cup unsweetened coconut
milk

3 tablespoons crunchy
peanut butter

2 tablespoons soy sauce

1½ tablespoons lime juice

1 teaspoon lime zest

Salt and freshly ground
black pepper

Sriracha or other Asian hot
sauce to taste

Beef Satay

**Spicy skewers of tender meat or chicken, Southeast Asian
satays are favorites at summer fire pits and barbecues along
Southern California beaches. Serve with this spicy Peanut
Sauce and a cold Mexican lager; Dos Equis is a good choice.**

....

To make Satay Marinade, combine all ingredients in a food
processor. Blend until smooth.

■ Place the meat in a zip-lock bag or shallow bowl. Pour in the
marinade and shake the bag or turn the meat to coat. Refrigerate
for 4 to 12 hours.

To make Peanut Sauce, combine the oil, onion, garlic, and
pepper flakes in a medium-size saucepan. Sauté over medium heat
for 5 minutes or until the onions are soft. Turn the heat to low and
add the remaining ingredients, stirring often. Heat through. If too
thick, add a bit of water. Correct the seasoning for salt and pepper,
spiciness, and lime juice. Keep warm until ready to serve.

■ Prepare the fire for direct grilling. Spray or rub the grill with oil.

■ Skewer the meat slices lengthwise on wooden skewers. Grill for
about 2 minutes on each side. Serve with Peanut Sauce for dipping.

Joel and Polly's Backyard Steaks

Good friends Joel Herman and Polly Rose, some years back, lived in a stark white concrete designer house in the middle of the hippest part of Venice, just west of Los Angeles. Venice was indeed lively in those days, with uzis sputtering and L.A.P.D. helicopters clattering all night long, punk rock bands practicing across the alley, the fast Hollywood set whooping it up over by the canal, and the local motorcycle gang revving up in the garage next door.

Joel was a TV editor and Polly worked in movie PR, and we were, like many people then, living in the fast lane. We spent a lot of time out in their garden Sunday afternoons, drinking cold Chardonnay and discussing serious topics such as The Perfect Steak. We all had opinions, and the argument went on for many Sundays, until one day we thought we had found it: a whole beef fillet, rubbed with olive oil and covered with fresh herbs and garlic from their flourishing garden. We got the barbecue good and hot and stoked it with plenty of hickory chips and grilled the fillet to perfection. Was it The Perfect Steak? Who knows! We'll just have to keep trying again and again!

The Perfect Steak: So Cal Style

SERVES 4

Here's what we call **The Perfect Steak**, though you could also call it a roast fillet or chateaubriand if you want. Get a whole fillet and trim it yourself (many warehouse clubs sell whole fillets in cryovac), or have your butcher prepare it for you. Use USDA choice or prime beef if you can find it, because the marbling will ensure juicy and succulent meat.

The flavor of great beef can stand alone with just the hint of smoke the grill gives to it. But the fresh herbs and garlic in this recipe will have the neighbors jealously peeking over the fence. Just tell them you are cooking The Perfect Steak—and give them a taste to ensure friendly relations. Serve with **Miso-Marinated Grilled Eggplant (page 99)** and a platter of **Rajas: Grilled Chile and Pepper Strips (page 101)**. For wine, try Pinot Noir from California's southern coast.

• • • • • • • • • • • • • • • •

To make Herb Paste, mix the oregano, rosemary, garlic, salt, and pepper, and moisten with enough olive oil to make a paste, or mash all ingredients together with a mortar and pestle.

■ Rub Herb Paste all over the fillet, poking paste in crevices and under any fat, and let sit 1 to 2 hours at room temperature or 8 to 12 hours, covered, in the refrigerator. Make sure the meat sits at room temperature for at least an hour before cooking.

HERB PASTE

1 tablespoon chopped fresh oregano or 1½ teaspoons dried

1 tablespoon chopped fresh rosemary or 1½ teaspoons dried

2 cloves garlic, finely chopped

1 teaspoon salt

½ teaspoon freshly ground black pepper

Extra-virgin olive oil

•

1 piece of beef fillet (3–4 pounds), preferably from the thinner end, trimmed of fat and silverskin

■ Prepare the fire for direct grilling. Add hickory, oak, mesquite, or other hardwood chips to the smoke box or fire (see Smoke on the Grill, page 21). Spray or rub the grill with oil.

■ Sear the fillet over high heat on all sides for 7 to 8 minutes total. Take care to avoid flare ups; if necessary, move to a cooler part of the grill.

■ Move the fillet to the cooler part of the grill and test for doneness: 125°F for rare, 130°F for medium-rare—or cut into a thick part of the meat with the point of a sharp knife to check (rare meat will be reddish; medium-rare red to pink). If done, remove the meat and cover loosely with foil. If not, cover the grill and cook over low heat until done, turning the fillet from time to time. This might take another 10 to 15 minutes, depending on the thickness of the fillet and the heat of the fire. If the outside is charring and the inside of the meat is still not done, move the fillet to the unheated part of the grill, and cook in the covered grill until done.

■ Let the fillet rest, covered loosely with foil, for 5 to 10 minutes. Cut into thick slices.

Bruce's Extra Thick Porterhouse

SERVES 4 TO 6

1 tablespoon extra-virgin olive oil

2 teaspoons kosher salt

1 teaspoon freshly ground black pepper

1 tablespoon minced garlic

1 porterhouse steak (2½–3 inches thick)

They call Bruce Aidells the Sausage King because of the unbelievably delicious sausages he creates for his company, Aidells Sausage Company. To his friends, though, Bruce is King of the Grill. People just love to invite Bruce and his wife, Nancy Oakes, owner-chef of the award-winning San Francisco restaurant Boulevard, for a weekend in the country. Not only are they charming companions, full of good cheer and wonderful stories, but you know you are going to eat well with them, to say the least.

Bruce tells a story of flying to an island in the middle of Puget Sound in a raging storm for one of these weekend visits with friends. He and Nancy were in a tiny plane, the wind and rain howling about them, tossing to and fro and hanging on for dear life. Bruce held onto the plane with one hand, and in the other he clutched a huge 3-inch-thick porterhouse steak he was bringing to grill that night for dinner. He knew he didn't want to fall out of the plane, but he also knew he damn well wasn't going to let go of that steak. Bruce swears that they found his finger marks etched deeply into the tender meat when they grilled it.

Grilling a steak this thick can give you a wonderful dining experience and some succulent meat, but it does present problems. The idea is to end up with rare or medium-rare meat inside, with a beautifully browned surface. How to keep the surface from charring while the meat inside cooks is a bit tricky. Here's how Bruce has figured out this tasty problem.

Serve with Grill-Roasted New Potatoes (page 101) and Sweet Onions on the Grill (page 100).

．．．．．．．．．．．．．．．．．

■ Mix the oil, salt, pepper, and garlic and rub all over the steak. Marinate at room temperature for 1 to 2 hours or in the refrigerator for 8 to 12 hours. Turn the meat occasionally. Make sure the meat sits at room temperature for at least an hour before grilling.

■ Prepare the fire for direct grilling Fill the smoke box with hickory, oak, or other hardwood chips (see Smoke on the Grill, page 21). Spray or rub the grill with oil.

■ Sear the steak on the hottest portion of the grill for 3 to 4 minutes per side. Move to a cooler area if flare-ups occur. When it is nicely marked and seared by the grill, move the steak to the cooler area and cook, covered, over low heat for 3 to 4 more minutes per side. Check with an instant-read meat thermometer or with the point of a sharp knife near the bone. If the interior of the meat has reached 120°F for rare or 125°F to 130°F for medium-rare, or if the meat is blood red but cooked, remove it from the grill and cover it loosely with foil. If not, move the steak to the unheated part of the grill and place the base of the bone toward the heat. This will help conduct heat and cook the inside of the meat. Cover the grill and let the steak cook, turning occasionally, until the desired temperature is reached.

■ Let the steak rest for 10 minutes, loosely covered with foil, before carving.

Ten Grilling Tips from Bruce Aidells

Bruce Aidells, the founder and creative force behind the Aidells Sausage Company, is a great meat cook. He and I wrote the *The Complete Meat Cookbook* (Houghton Mifflin, 1998) together and had a very tasty time testing recipes, many on the barbecue. Here are Bruce's tips on grilling, excerpted from the book and published widely in newspapers all over the country.

▪ Best bets for grilling are 1½-inch- to 2-inch-thick steaks, lamb or veal chops, or burgers, kebabs, or sausages.

▪ Salt beef, pork, and lamb *before* grilling, not after. The meat will be much more flavorful and juicy.

▪ Sauces made with sugar or honey burn easily. Use caution when grilling meats that have been soaked in a sweet marinade. Brush on sugary barbecue sauces after cooking or during the last few minutes on the grill.

▪ Don't parboil spareribs before grilling. That only toughens the meat and drains it of flavor.

▪ Prepare three temperature zones on your barbecue. High heat (two to three layers of coals), medium (one layer), and an area with no coals around the edges. Sear meat over the high area, then move to the medium area to finish cooking or to the no-coal zone to keep fully cooked pieces warm while the others finish. Food kept in this area will continue to cook, so don't leave it too long.

▪ Use the "hand test" to check for coal readiness: Hold the palm of your hand an inch from the grill over the high-heat zone. If your hand becomes too hot by the time you count to 3, it's time to grill.

▪ Cover kettle grills during cooking, and use the vents to regulate heat and control the flare-ups. Open vents to raise the temperature; close vents to reduce it.

▪ Use a digital instant-read meat thermometer to test for doneness. See our Temperature Chart (next page) for a guide to doneness temperatures for various meats. With the exception of hamburgers, which should be cooked to medium-well, grilled beef and lamb are at their best when cooked to no more than medium-rare.

▪ Remove meat from the heat when the thermometer reads 5°F less than the desired temperature. Keep loosely covered on a warm plate. Carry-over heat will continue to cook the meat.

▪ To allow the juices to absorb balance the internal temperature, let the meat to rest for 5 to 10 minutes before carving or serving.

Temperature Chart

I don't think much of recipes that only tell you how long to grill a piece of meat or poultry, and cooking times in my recipes are usually approximate. There are just too many variables—the thickness of the meat, the heat of the fire, even the weather—to give exact times. Unless you get skilled at the grill cook's touch test (see D Alexander and the World's Most Expensive Chicken, page 136), the way to find out what the inside of grilled meat or poultry is like is either to cut into it and take a look or to check the interior temperature with an instant-read meat thermometer. Cutting and looking will work, and I'll tell you what to look for, but for best results, I recommend the instant-read thermometer, preferably digital. These are inexpensive and easy to use. You'll find them at suppliers of grilling accessories or specialty food stores (see Sources, page 225).

For best results you should remove food from the grill and let it rest, loosely covered with aluminum foil, for 5 minutes for smaller pieces to up to a half hour for larger roasts or birds. This allows the juices in the meat to settle and the temperature to equalize throughout. While meat or poultry rests, the interior temperature will rise from 5°F to 10°F or more, so take this into account when checking meat on the grill. If you prefer it rarer, take it off when it's 5°F under the suggested temperature; if you like it a little more well done, take it off at the suggested temperature and the meat will cook slightly as it rests.

Meat and Poultry

■ Very Rare—115°F to 120°F: For beef steaks and roasts only. Called *bleu* by French grill cooks from the color of virtually raw meat. Not to my taste.

■ Rare—125°F to 130°F: For beef steaks and roasts, lamb chops and roasts. Red and juicy meat. Best level for tender steaks, in my opinion.

■ Medium-Rare—130°F to 135°F: For beef steaks and roasts, lamb chops and roasts. Red to pink meat, still quite juicy. My favorite for beef roasts, lamb.

■ Medium—140°F to 150°F: For beef, lamb, veal steaks, chops, and roasts. Meat pink at center, gray at edges. Good for fattier cuts.

■ Medium-Well—150°F to 165°F: Pork chops and tenderloin should come off the fire at the lower temperature; pork roasts and most poultry at the higher.

■ Well Done—165°F+: Most meat is overcooked here. Poultry and fattier cuts of pork such as spare ribs should be cooked to this temperature.

Fish and Seafood

I go by appearance here and do not rely on the thermometer. Shellfish is done when it is opaque and firm; fish when it can be flaked with the tip of a knife. Some fish is cooked quite rare: tuna, for example. The trick is not to overcook fish or seafood. Take it off the grill early and check.

Los Angeles: The Trends Start Here

They say that Los Angeles is trendy, and they're right. In fact, some observers of American culture feel that most trends in fashion, art, music, and food start here among glitterati and the punks, the grifters and the deal makers, the *vatos locos,* teeny boppers, Valley girls, boyz in the hood—Angelenos all—and then the trends spread out across the country and ultimately the world. Think of Japanese teenagers or French models on their night off or really rich English kids who want to blow Mum's mind—who do they want to look like? Whether it's pink hair or torn jeans, pierced navels or retro footwear, hot rods with pinstripes or pizzas with caviar, graffiti as high art or gangsta rap as low, if it's happening, it most likely started happening in L.A.

This is certainly true of food, that trendiest of substances. Whether you're breathing the rarefied air of Bel Air or Beverly Hills or getting down with the folk downtown, Los Angeles's food manias have been on the cutting edge of America's food scene for quite some time now.

Creative artists are drawn by money, and there's plenty of that in Hollywood and the surrounding communities. Chefs from all over the world have migrated to the boulevards and hilly streets of the capital of the world's most popular and lucrative art form, and they have created trends that have revolutionized restaurant food in America. Artists love audiences, and the chefs of trendy L.A. restaurants perform nightly before an appreciative clientele that is hungry for novelty, excellence, and opulence. Caviar pizzas, foie gras salads, and sashimi ice cream cones become common fare here, and the quest for the new sensation seems endless. The search for the perfect meal is the Holy Grail of Southern California's endlessly creative chefs and home cooks (see The Perfect Steak: So Cal Style, page 181). Many of America's favorite dishes, sophisticated and humble, fancy shmancy or everyday, got their start here in a world of constant innovation and changing fashions.

Take that ultimate symbol of American food, the hamburger. The burger didn't originate in L.A. (nothing really *originates* in L.A.), but here it got gussied up and showcased and turned into a new sensation, then a national trend, finally a franchise, and ultimately a cliché. If that sounds just like the movies, it's no accident.

I grew up in L.A. in the hot-rodding days of the 1950s when car clubs cruised the drive-ins and standard Saturday-night fare was a malt and a big burger topped with tomatoes, onions, lettuce, cheese, and pink goop. When I left So Cal and tasted what the folk back East called a hamburger, it came as a shock: this piece of gristly meat on a soggy bun was nothing like the Big Boppers I remembered. The California burger spread out from a tiny drive-in in San Berdoo and became the great McEmpire that defines our culture today. And L.A.'s still got the best burgers, whether the classic California Burger with Big Bopper Tomato Topper (page 189) or the gooey, greasy, spicy, wonderfully messy Alvarado Street Chili Burger (page 190).

Whenever I get back to L.A., I head for my favorite burger joints. For classic hamburgers, I seek out a drive-in in that seedy section of Hollywood where the Boulevard meets the barrio. This venerable establishment still has plenty of bright pink neon and orange velvet banquettes and bleached-blonde waitresses who call you "honey" and old guys with tans and gold chains in Hawaiian shirts who are working on their next deal and wear aviator shades at two in the morning. A burger there is the real thing: thick and juicy from the grill, with plenty of salt and pepper, served on a toasted bun brushed with butter, topped with ripe tomato, a piece of raw onion, and slices of real kosher half-sour pickles, with that wonderful pink goop we remember so well anointing everything.

For chili burgers, I head to East L.A. and a place I know that is packed with hungry burger aficionados from noon to four A.M. You line up outside the window with people dressed in everything from Rodeo Drive Armani suits to *Baywatch* hot pants to LAPD blues. You tell the harried counterman inside whether you want a single, double, or triple burger, with or without cheese, with chili con carne, chili beans, salsa, or nada. Hardly anybody orders nada. There is no thought of ever picking up one of these chili burgers with your fingers and taking a bite. Maybe some macho types with really big hands can do this, but I've never seen it. You're served the burger in a small cardboard box on a big sheet of butcher paper and with a small plastic fork. You sit at big concrete tables with everybody else and do the best you can. These burgers call for plenty of napkins. And quantities of cold beer supplied by the all-night convenience store very conveniently located next door.

Salsa is another trend these days, and I don't just mean the music. Mexican-style salsa recently surpassed ketchup as the most popular condiment in America, and the love of salsa and Mexican food started with Los Angeles's vibrant tradition of Latino cooking. Nowadays, chile- and tomato-based salsas, tacos, and burritos are as much a part of American cooking as pizza, French fries, and apple pie. Street food in Southern California means Mexican (or, increasingly, Honduran or other Latino) handheld snacks. Taco trucks are found everywhere from East L.A. to Santa Monica and serve some of the best food in the city. You can get *tacos al pastor* made from marinated, grilled, and very spicy pork, or burritos made from lemon- and chile-laced carne asada (see Carne Asada I and II, pages 173 and 174) or paper plates piled up with crisp and juicy pork carnitas. For the more adventurous, there's *lengua* (tongue) or *seso* (brains) or *cabeza* (head), the meat stuffed into tortillas with salsas based on all kinds of chiles from mild to very hot. You'll also find fish tacos (see Fish Tacos with Three Salsas, page 51) and *mariscos*—grilled shrimp or scallops—or grilled corn with chile butter (see Grilled Corn, page 91) and grilled chile strips (see Rajas: Grilled Chile and Pepper Strips, page 101). Deep-fried taquitos are filled with shredded beef, crisp chimichangas with beef or chicken, quesadillas with cheese or chicken or seafood (see Grilled Seafood Quesadillas, page 55). All this delicious stuff is sold right on the street, or you can go inside restaurants and eat Mexican regional foods such as moles, spicy nut-based sauces from Oaxaca, or banana leaf tamales from Yucatan, red snapper Vera Cruz style, or Baja's special grilled lobsters (see Baja Lobster or Prawns with Lime Ancho Chile Butter and Salsa Roja, page 107).

California Burger with Big Bopper Tomato Topper

This is the traditional hamburger, including Pink Goop to spread on the bun. Serve with Out-of-the-Garden Grilled Salad (page 71), Summer Vegetable Skewers (page 95), or Grill-Roasted New Potatoes (page 101).

• • • • • • • • • • • • • • • • • •

■ Prepare the fire for medium-hot direct grilling. Spray or rub the grill with oil.

To make California Burger, in a large bowl, combine the meat, salt, and pepper. Mix thoroughly with hands. Form four equal patties, about ¾ inch thick. Grill each side for 4 to 6 minutes or until medium-well, with no pink (see Temperature Chart, page 185).

To make Pink Goop, combine all ingredients and mix well.

■ Toast rolls on the grill for 2 minutes each side just to warm. Layer on burgers, Pink Goop, tomatoes, lettuce, and pickles.

CALIFORNIA BURGER

1 pound freshly ground beef chuck

1 teaspoon salt

½ teaspoon freshly ground black pepper

•

PINK GOOP

½ cup mayonnaise

¼ cup Heinz Chile Sauce or ketchup

½ teaspoon Worcestershire sauce

A couple of dashes Tabasco

•

4 large hamburger rolls

•

GARNISH

4 large tomatoes, thinly sliced

Shredded lettuce

Sour dill pickles, thinly sliced

SERVES 4

L.A. CHILI

½ pound ground beef or cooked steak chopped into small pieces

½ medium onion, coarsely chopped

1 cup chopped tomatoes, fresh or canned, with juice

2 tablespoons chile powder, or more to taste

1 clove garlic, chopped

1 teaspoon cumin

1 teaspoon dried oregano

1 teaspoon salt

1 teaspoon freshly ground pepper

2 cups cooked pinto beans, homemade or canned

•

CHILI BURGER

1 pound freshly ground beef chuck

1 teaspoon chile powder

1 teaspoon salt

½ teaspoon freshly ground black pepper

1 tablespoon Worcestershire sauce or A-1 steak sauce

½ onion, minced

4 slices cheddar cheese

•

4 hamburger buns or French rolls, split

•

GARNISH

Tomatoes, thickly sliced

Onion slices

Pickles

Jalapeños en escabeche, sliced

Alvarado Street Chili Burger

Los Angeles is a city of small hamburger joints. These tasty, greasy burgers are a world apart from the cardboard-in-a-bun offered by the franchises that seem to rule other towns. L.A. has independently run stands that attract families on Friday nights, cheerleaders and football players from the nearby high schools, and late-night party-goers (most stands are open *late*). If you aren't familiar with these menus and you innocently order a burger and fries at one of these stands, you might get a surprise: chili. And the chili is great! It adds to the flavor and contrasts with fresh tomatoes and crunchy raw onions. Classic L.A. chili is made with hamburger meat, but you can also use leftover grilled steak chopped into little pieces and mixed into the beans instead.

••••••••••••••••••

To make L.A. Chili, sauté the meat and onion over medium-high heat. When the onion begins to soften and the meat is brown, add all the remaining ingredients except the beans. Sauté for another 3 minutes. Add the beans, reduce the temperature, cover, and simmer for 20 minutes.

■ Prepare the fire for direct grilling. Spray or rub the grill with oil.

To make Chili Burger, thoroughly mix the burger ingredients by hand in a large bowl. Form four equal patties, about ¾ inch thick. Grill for 3 to 5 minutes on each side over high heat. When almost done, put a cheese slice on each patty and cover the grill to melt. Burgers should be cooked medium-well, not pink (see Temperature Chart, page 185).

■ Toast the buns for a few minutes, if you wish.

■ Serve burgers on buns with chili ladled on top. Garnish with toppings. Eat as best you can.

Burger Variations

Burgers can carry any of your favorite tastes. Just add the designated ingredients to a pound of hamburger meat, mix thoroughly, and make patties. Follow the grilling instructions for California Burger (page 189) and try these different toppings.

Asian Burger

1 tablespoon chopped fresh ginger

2 cloves garlic, minced

2 tablespoons chopped green onions

■ Serve with Spicy Ketchup (page 93).

Garlic Burger

1 tablespoon chopped garlic

■ Top with Roasted Garlic Aioli (page 95).

Berkeley Burger

2 tablespoons chopped fresh basil or oregano

1 tablespoon chopped garlic

■ Top with Cilantro Pesto (page 91).

Southwest Burger

2 tablespoons chopped red onion

1 tablespoon chile powder

■ Top with Chipotle Mayonnaise (page 94).

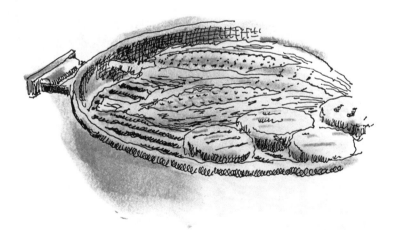

Thai Beef Salad with Lime Basil Vinaigrette

SERVES 4

1 flank steak (2–2½ pounds)

Thai Cilantro Sauce (page 67)

•

LIME BASIL VINAIGRETTE

½ cup peanut, sesame, or vegetable oil

2 tablespoons lime juice

1 tablespoon fish sauce (*nuoc cham* or *nam pla*)

2 tablespoons soy sauce

¼ cup chopped fresh basil

Salt and freshly ground black pepper

•

2 bunches watercress, tough stems removed (about 2 cups)

4 baby bok choy, chopped into bite-size pieces

¼ cup chopped fresh mint leaves

5 radishes, thinly sliced

1 head butter lettuce

•

GARNISH

8 whole basil leaves

Thai-accented beef is wonderful grilled and sliced over a tangy salad. A cold Sierra Nevada Pale Ale will cool the palate.

• • • • • • • • • • • • • • • • • •

■ In a zip-lock bag or a shallow dish, coat the meat with Thai Cilantro Sauce. Marinate for 2 hours at room temperature or 8 to 12 hours refrigerated. Let the steak come to room temperature before cooking. Remove from the marinade and pat dry.

■ Prepare the fire for direct grilling. Spray or rub the grill with oil.

■ Grill flank steak for 3 minutes, turn, brush on marinade, and grill for another 3 to 5 minutes, turning once or twice. The internal temperature should be 120°F to 135°F; meat should be red and juicy when cut. Cover the steak with foil and let it rest for at least 5 minutes before slicing thinly on the bias across the grain.

To make Lime Basil Vinaigrette, whisk together the ingredients.

■ Put watercress, bok choy, mint, and radishes into a bowl and toss with the vinaigrette. Separate, clean, and dry the butter lettuce leaves and arrange into cups on separate plates. Put the watercress mix into lettuce cups and lay the slices of beef on top of the salad. Garnish with whole basil leaves.

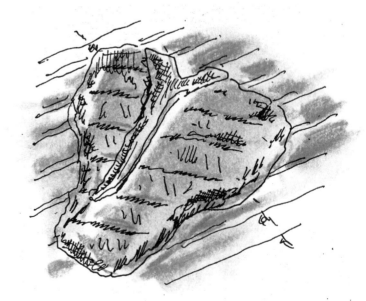

Spicy Soy Flank Steak with Grilled Shiitake Onion Relish

SERVES 4

Flank steak is delicious when marinated in a soy-based sauce. The firm-textured and flavorful meat should be cut on the bias into thin slices for maximum tenderness. Serve with Asian Noodle and Grilled Baby Bok Choy Salad with Orange Ginger Vinaigrette (page 75).

. . . .

To make Spicy Soy Marinade, mix all the ingredients in a small bowl.

■ In a zip-lock bag or nonreactive bowl, combine the flank steak and Spicy Soy Marinade. Let marinate, refrigerated, 8 to 12 hours.

■ Prepare the fire for direct grilling. Spray or rub the grill with oil.

■ Remove the beef from the marinade and pat dry. Grill over high for 3 to 4 minutes per side or until the internal temperature is 125°F to 130°F. Remove the steaks and cover loosely with foil.

To make Grilled Shiitake Onion Relish, grill the mushrooms and onion over high heat for 3 minutes on each side. Remove from the grill. Remove the skin from the onion and chop finely. Finely chop the mushrooms and stir in hoisin sauce. Add a little water if the relish seems too thick.

■ Slice the steak on the bias into thin slices. Top the flank steak with relish and serve.

SPICY SOY MARINADE

4 cloves garlic, chopped

½ cup soy sauce

2 tablespoons chopped fresh ginger

1 teaspoon dried red pepper flakes

2 teaspoons hot chile oil or other hot sauce, or more to taste

•

1 flank steak (2–2½ pounds)

•

GRILLED SHIITAKE ONION RELISH

1 pound fresh shiitake or portobello mushrooms, cleaned, caps only

1 medium onion, skin on, sliced horizontally in 2-inch rounds

2 tablespoons hoisin sauce

SERVES 6

1 teaspoon cinnamon

1 teaspoon ground cumin

½ teaspoon freshly ground black pepper

1 teaspoon salt

½ teaspoon dried thyme

½ teaspoon paprika

3 pounds boneless beef chuck steak or rib steak, cut into 1-inch pieces

2 bay leaves

4 cloves garlic, chopped

2 tablespoons olive oil

¾ cup red wine

2 onions, peeled and quartered

2 bell peppers, cut into 1-inch pieces

Balsamic vinegar

Grilled Beef Brochettes

This recipe comes from *Rhone Appétit*, by Jane O'Riordan, a California writer who created recipes to go with California's hearty Rhone-style wines. Margaret Smith, founder of Toyon Press, which published the book, is an old friend and wine-lover who worked for *Sunset* magazine for years and has done much to promote fine California wine.

You could use cut-up leg of lamb in this recipe as well. The author suggests a full bodied Rhone-style red made from Mourvèdre or even a spicy white Viognier with this aromatic dish. I think a hearty Zinfandel would also do well.

....

■ Mix the cinnamon, cumin, pepper, salt, thyme, and paprika in a large bowl. Add the meat and toss to coat all pieces. Add the bay leaves, garlic, olive oil, and wine. Mix well. Cover and refrigerate 6 to 12 hours.

■ Prepare the fire for direct grilling. Spray or rub the grill with oil.

■ Place the meat on skewers, alternating with onion and pepper sections, about four pieces of meat per skewer. Grill over a hot fire, turning frequently to brown all sides, about 10 minutes total. The meat should be rare to medium-rare or red and juicy when cut. Sprinkle with balsamic vinegar just before serving.

Northwest Cow Country: Côte de Boeuf au Cowboy

As you head east from the coastal valleys of the Northwest, you get into harder country—what the folk up there call the great desert. You'll still find patches of land near the rivers that grow vegetables and fruits, and some intense and delicious Cabernet Sauvignon is being made in hillside vineyards near the Snake and Columbia Rivers. Once you are away from a source of water, though, the countryside gets very dry and pretty rugged.

The land, with irrigated exceptions, is fit only for grazing sheep and cattle. This is the cow country of the Great Basin, where 10 inches of rain is considered a good year. The main crops out here are sagebrush and manzanita and cattle, if you can find enough water to keep them alive.

Ranchers and homesteaders led rough lives in this desert country. Some made it big, creating cattle empires that took days to ride across. Others, in the words of one old-timer, "just up and blowed away with the dust and tumbleweeds." Ranch-house cooking was pretty basic, and still is for that matter. You cooked up pinto or other dried beans with chiles and onions, you "burned a steak" on a wood stove or over the campfire coals, you had vegetables and fruit when you could get them fresh, or you served whatever you had put up or canned at harvest time.

My old friend Tom Moran comes from this hard land. His family settled in eastern Washington early on and still owns many acres in this hardscrabble country. Most of the land is leased to local herders these days, but Tom has plenty of stories of cowboy uncles and tough-minded women who grew up on the ranch.

Tom lives in Paris now and teaches math and philosophy at the University of Paris. We were students in the Latin Quarter together quite a few years back. In those days, we would all gather 'round Tom's tiny grill on the balcony of his minuscule apartment near the Sorbonne to cook what came to be called Côte de Boeuf au Cowboy. We'd chip in for the biggest steak we could afford at the butcher shop in the Rue Mouffetard and bring it back in triumph to the fifteenth-century building Tom lived in. He was up on the top floor, of course, and we would lug up the stairs the steak, bread, charcoal, and cheap red wine we had bought from the Vins et Charbons merchant in the Place de la Contrescarpe.

Tom would tell stories of life on the range as he rubbed the steak with crushed garlic, chile powder, oregano, and pepper. The French students couldn't get enough of these tales, like the one about his uncle trapped in a canyon filled with rattlesnakes or *les serpents à sonnettes*. They hung on Tom's every word while I got the fire going in a big steel wastebasket we had "borrowed" from the Sorbonne, poked a few holes in it for draft, and fitted it with a steel grill bought at the Marché aux Puces, the huge flea market on the outskirts of Paris. Once the fire was going, Tom would tell us all how cowboys cooked their steaks over the campfire—thus the origin of Côte de Boeuf au Cowboy. As the fragrant smoke of beefsteak, garlic, and chile wafted from the balcony, neighbors would poke their heads out the windows and shout imprecations or encouragements, depending on whether they were honest citizens or bohemian ne'er-do-wells like ourselves. We would ignore the shouts, devour the smoky, luscious steak, and drink plenty of vin rouge while Tom and I gave lessons in authentic cowboy yodeling, whoops, and hollers to our fellow students in their brand-new *le jeans* and *chapeaux aux cowboys*.

Grill-Roasted Beef with Thyme Garlic Crust

SERVES 6 TO 8

1 cross rib or other beef roast (4–6 pounds)

Olive oil

3 cloves garlic, minced

3 tablespoons chopped fresh thyme or 1½ tablespoons dried

1 teaspoon salt

½ teaspoon freshly ground black pepper

Roasting a tender piece of beef in a covered barbecue over indirect heat or on a spit is one of the best ways to create a succulent centerpiece for a special meal or holiday feast. The mixture of smoke, herbs, and spices creates a beautifully caramelized surface, and if you use an instant-read thermometer to check internal temperatures, the meat will be juicy and perfectly done. I feature a cross rib roast here, but a boned strip loin or rib-eye or top sirloin roast would also be delicious. If you have a rotisserie and spit attachment, this is a good time to use it. If using a spit, purchase a symmetrical, cylindrical roast such as a cross rib or boned loin (see Spit-Roasting, page 20). For indirect roasting, bone-in prime rib or other roasts work fine. Instead of the garlic, thyme, salt, and pepper, you could use 2 tablespoons of Herb Rub for Beef or Lamb (page 37) or your choice of spice rubs suitable for beef (see Dry Rubs and Marinades, page 35). Serve with Grill-Roasted New Potatoes (page 101) and Grilled Asparagus with Roasted Garlic Oil (page 97).

••••••••••••••••••

■ Prepare the fire for indirect grilling and put drip pan in place. Fill the smoke box with oak, hickory, or the hardwood of your choice (see Smoke on the Grill, page 21).

■ Rub the roast with olive oil. Mix the garlic, thyme, salt, and pepper in a small bowl (or use a spice rub of your choice) and rub all over the meat.

■ Place the roast in the unheated middle of the grill over the drip pan (see Indirect Heat, page 19) or place on a spit (see Spit-Roasting, page 20). Cover and roast at 350°F or moderate heat until you reach the desired internal temperature: for rare, 125°F, medium-rare, 130°F. Times on the grill will vary according to the thickness of the meat and the heat of the fire. Start checking the meat after 35 minutes, and check every 15 minutes or so after that. Remove the meat from the grill at or before the suggested temperature and let the roast rest for at least 15 minutes, covered loosely with aluminum foil. The temperature will rise 5°F or more during that time.

Brisket on the Grill

1 tablespoon dried oregano

1 teaspoon salt

½ teaspoon freshly ground black pepper

1 beef brisket or chuck (4–5 pounds)

½ cup Smoke-Roasted Tomato Sauce (page 98) or other tomato sauce

4 cloves garlic, chopped

1 large onion, thinly sliced

1 or more chipotles en adobo, seeded (optional)

Pot roast on the grill: the no-mess way to achieve "pull-apart" beef. It's so easy and tender we may never go back to the classic oven roast. This brisket would be great with Grill-Roasted New Potatoes (page 101) and a bottle of Amador County Zinfandel from California's Gold Rush country.

••••••••••••••••••

■ Mix the oregano, salt, and pepper. Rub the meat with the herb mixture and let sit for up to an hour.

■ Prepare the fire for indirect grilling.

■ Cut a large (1-by-2-foot) piece of heavy-duty aluminum foil. Place the meat on the center of the foil. Spread the tomato sauce, garlic, and onion on the meat, and top with a chipotle or two if you wish. Seal the foil around the meat, making a large packet. Place in a dish to prevent spillovers. Put the brisket on the unheated part of the grill and cook, covered, at low heat (about 325°F) for 2½ to 3 hours. Rotate to ensure even cooking. The meat should be very tender when pierced with a fork. If the brisket needs more time, wrap it back up and return it to the covered grill. You can open up the foil to brown the meat and onions for the last 15 minutes or so of cooking, if you wish.

Grilled Veal Chops with Garlic-Sage Butter

SERVES 4

Old-time Italian cooks in San Francisco's North Beach have long recognized that veal and sage make a great combination. Recently, many of the city's trendy young chefs have come around to the same view, grilling chops and roasting veal loin with garlic and fresh sage. Just about every new restaurant has a wood-burning or charcoal-fired grill in an open kitchen, often equipped with rotisseries for spit-roasting.

I am not a great fan of white, milk, or formula-fed veal, for a number of reasons. I think there is an ethical question with the way some calves are raised, although the claims of the more extreme animal activists seem exaggerated. Actually, I find white veal a bit bland. I much prefer range- or grass-fed veal, often called red veal, which has a robust, meaty flavor. Ask your butcher for it and look for large pieces of veal with a pinkish tint. This used to be called baby beef, a term you still see occasionally.

You could use the same seasonings for a small veal roast or a roast pork loin on the spit (see **Smoke-Roasted Pork Loin or Veal Roast, page 169**). Serve with Penne with Grill-Roasted Vegetables (page 100) and Pinot Noir from Oregon.

8 veal loin chops, at least 1½ inches thick

Olive oil

2 tablespoons chopped fresh sage or 1½ teaspoons dried

Salt and freshly ground black pepper

•

GARLIC-SAGE BUTTER

2 tablespoons chopped fresh sage or 1 teaspoon dried

3 cloves garlic, finely chopped

¼ pound salted butter (1 stick), melted

¼ teaspoon freshly ground black pepper

....

■ Trim the chops of any excess fat, rub with oil, and pat sage on both sides. Sprinkle with salt and pepper.

To make Garlic-Sage Butter, combine the sage with the garlic, butter, and pepper.

■ Prepare the fire for direct grilling. Spray or rub the grill with oil.

■ Place the chops over high heat and grill for 2 to 3 minutes until seared and marked. Turn and baste the chops with Garlic-Sage Butter. (Move to a cooler spot if flare-ups occur.) Sear for 2 to 3 more minutes; and then turn the chops and move them to a cooler part of the grill. Cover. Baste the chops with the butter, turning occasionally, for 5 to 6 minutes more, depending on the thickness of the chops, until they reach 135°F internal temperature or are lightly pink and still juicy when cut. Serve.

Grilled lamb is an ancient Near Eastern tradition and today's best lamb dishes originated in the Fertile Crescent, where civilized living began. Greek, Armenian, and Middle Eastern cooks know that lamb and aromatic herbs and spices such as garlic, oregano, mint, cumin, paprika, and pepper go together. These chefs know the secret to grilling lamb: use plenty of seasonings in rubs, pastes, and marinades, and don't overcook the delicate meat—no more than medium-rare.

Shish kebab (see Fresno Shish Kebab, page 206) is one of the oldest and best ways of grilling lamb. Chunks of tender leg or shoulder are marinated in oil, garlic, lemon, parsley, and other flavorful herbs and spices, skewered, often with vegetables such as onions and peppers; and then grilled directly over medium-high heat. As with all lamb dishes, use plenty of spices, and cook the tender lamb rare to medium-rare (125°F to 135°F).

Lamb chops from the rib or loin are delicious on the grill. Highly seasoned and briefly grilled, tiny rib chops can serve as magnificent hors d'oeuvres (see Grilled Lamb Chops with Mint Cilantro Relish, page 208), while large chops or steaks make a substantial and elegant main course (see Basque Sheepherder Lamb Steaks, page 209).

Leg of lamb, butterflied and smeared with an aromatic paste, makes a wonderful centerpiece for an outdoor party (see Butterflied Leg of Lamb with Oregano Mint Paste, below). Boned leg of lamb can also be stuffed and cooked by indirect heat or spit roasted for an unforgettable pièce de résistance for an elegant dinner party (see Boned Leg of Lamb with Wild Mushroom and Fresh Herb Stuffing, page 205).

Butterflied Leg of Lamb with Oregano Mint Paste

SERVES 6 TO 8

OREGANO MINT PASTE

¼ cup chopped fresh oregano or 2 tablespoons dried

¼ cup chopped fresh mint

6 cloves garlic, finely chopped

Juice of 2 lemons

¼ cup olive oil

1 tablespoon salt

1 tablespoon paprika

1 teaspoon freshly ground black pepper

1 leg of lamb (3–5 pounds), boned and butterflied

Butterflied leg of lamb marinated with a savory herb paste makes a dramatic centerpiece for a summer dinner. Use fresh herbs from the garden or a farmers' market if you can. I like oregano and mint with lamb, but any combination of mint, rosemary, thyme, or basil would also be delicious. The herb paste can be used for Grilled Lamb or Venison Chops in place of Rosemary Garlic Paste (page 207) and in Boned Leg of Lamb with Wild Mushroom and Fresh Herb Stuffing (page 205).

Serve the lamb with Grilled Asparagus with Roasted Garlic Oil (page 97) and Grill-Roasted New Potatoes (page 101). For the wine, choose a Lemberger or Merlot from the Yakima Valley.

To make Oregano Mint Paste, mix the ingredients in a small bowl to make a paste.

■ To butterfly the lamb leg, cut along the bone using a sharp, thin knife, and remove it. Flatten the meat and trim off excess fat. Or have the butcher butterfly the lamb leg for you. Rub the herb paste all over the lamb, pushing it into any crevices left by the removed bone. Put the lamb into a zip-lock bag or nonreactive dish and refrigerate, covered, for 8 to 24 hours. Remove from the refrigerator an hour before you are going to cook.

■ Just before grilling, remove from the marinade and run two long skewers crosswise through the lamb to stabilize the piece of meat and make it easier to handle on the grill.

■ Prepare the fire for indirect grilling and put drip pan in place. Add apple, alder, or other hardwood to the smoke box (see Smoke on the Grill, page 21). Spray or rub the grill with oil.

■ Sear and mark the lamb over medium-high heat for 3 to 4 minutes per side and then place on the unheated part of the grill. Cover the grill and roast the lamb for 20 minutes, turning the meat occasionally and repositioning it on the grill so that it cooks evenly. Test the thickest part of the lamb with an instant-read thermometer, or cut into it. Medium-rare, the way that I like lamb, is 125°F to 130°F or reddish and juicy inside and firm to the touch. Cook longer if desired.

■ Remove the lamb from the grill and cover loosely with foil for 5 to 10 minutes. Cut into thick slices against the grain and serve.

California: Wine Country

The Coastal Range protects California's river valleys from the fog and cold air that flows in from the Pacific. Almost. And it's the *almost* that makes the wine so delicious. The coastal valleys (Napa, Santa Maria, Russian River, Livermore, Sonoma Dry Creek) and other prime grape-growing areas in the state let some of the Pacific's coolness in through natural breaks in the mountain range but are far enough inland to be warm enough to ripen grapes.

Wine from these valleys has gained a worldwide reputation in recent years. Cabernet Sauvignon from Napa's Rutherford Bench or Stag's Leap area, Chardonnay from the Santa Maria Valley, Pinot Noir from the Russian River Valley, Sauvignon Blanc from the Livermore Valley, and Zinfandel from the Dry Creek Valley (to name but a few) compare to the best wines of Europe and Australia.

In keeping with the Pacific Coast tradition of outdoor living, winemakers love to grill food to go with their products. In the late winter, California's vintners prune their vineyards, ending up with vine cuttings that they use to create aromatic, smoky fires in their barbecues. The cuttings can also be added to a charcoal fire to create a spicy and flavorful smoke (see Smoke on the Grill, page 21). Another trick often used by California grill masters is to tie up a bunch of fresh herbs—fresh rosemary is most often used, but oregano, marjoram, and thyme are also delicious—and toss the herbs right on the charcoal to create intensely perfumed smoke.

Zinfandel is one of my favorite wines with just about anything from the grill: beef, lamb, pork, or chicken. Try it with Grilled Lamb or Venison Chops with Rosemary Garlic Paste (page 207) or Smoke-Roasted Pork Loin or Veal Roast (page 169).

Here are a few more wine and food pairing recommendations:

Cabernet Sauvignon Smoky Prime Rib, Santa Maria Style (page 177); The Perfect Steak: So Cal Style (page 181); Bruce's Extra Thick Porterhouse (page 182).

Chardonnay Grilled Lobster or Monkfish Salad with Blood Orange Vinaigrette (page 78); Gene's Prawn's on the Grill (page 104); Brined Salmon Steaks (page 131).

Gewürztraminer Tea-Smoked Scallops with Hoisin Vinaigrette (page 113); Ahi Skewers with Miso-Sesame Crust (page 119); Butterflied Pork Tenderloins with Blackberry Glaze and Grilled Fruit (page 163).

Merlot Smoke-Roasted Turkey or Chickens with Three-Pepper Rub (page 146); Santa Maria Tri-Tips (page 176); Butterflied Leg of Lamb with Oregano Mint Paste (page 202).

Pinot Noir Grilled Lamb or Venison Chops with Rosemary Garlic Paste (page 207); Boned Leg of Lamb with Wild Mushroom and Fresh Herb Stuffing (page 205); Grill-Roasted Beef with Thyme Garlic Crust (page 197); Michael Wild's Grilled Duck Breast with Berry Pinot Noir Glaze (page 150).

Riesling Chinatown Prawn and Baby Bok Choy Skewers (page 112); L.A. Seafood Mixed Grill with Mango Vinaigrette (page 110); Ono with Grilled Pineapple Relish (page 127).

Sauvignon Blanc Grilled Seafood Quesadillas (page 55); Grilled Prawns or Scallops with Thai Cilantro Sauce (page 67).

Boned Leg of Lamb with Wild Mushroom and Fresh Herb Stuffing

SERVES 6 TO 8

WILD MUSHROOM AND FRESH HERB STUFFING

1 pound wild mushrooms, such as porcini, chanterelles, morels, fresh shiitakes, or crimini

2 tablespoons olive oil

4 cloves garlic, minced

2 tablespoons chopped fresh thyme or marjoram or 1 tablespoon dried

1 teaspoon salt

½ teaspoon freshly ground black pepper

•

1 leg of lamb (5–7 pounds), boned

Salt and freshly ground black pepper

1 tablespoon chopped fresh thyme or marjoram or ½ tablespoon dried

Have your butcher bone a leg of lamb for you, or do it yourself following the directions for Butterflied Leg of Lamb with Oregano Mint Paste (page 202). You now have a nice pocket to fill with savory stuffing. I use wild mushrooms and herbs here, but you could also stuff the boned leg with chopped and lightly steamed chard or spinach with garlic and lemon juice, with whole roasted garlic cloves (see Smoke-Roasted Garlic, page 59) and pitted kalamata olives, or with Rosemary Garlic Paste (page 207). After you've stuffed the center pocket, roll the lamb into a cylindrical shape and tie with butchers' twine. I don't remove the fell, or skin, from the lamb leg when I barbecue it. If left on, it protects the meat and keeps the juices in.

Pinot Noir and lamb seem made for each other. Serve a rich and silky Pinot Noir from California's Carneros district with this delectable roast. Ratatouille from the Grill (page 96) and Grill-Roasted New Potatoes (page 101) would be good accompaniments.

· · · · · · · · · · · · · · · · · ·

To make Wild Mushroom and Fresh Herb Stuffing, wipe the mushrooms clean, removing any dirt from the gills. Remove and discard tough stems from shiitakes, if using. Chop the mushrooms coarsely. Heat the olive oil in a skillet over medium-high heat and sauté the mushrooms for 3 or 4 minutes. Stir in the garlic, herb, salt, and pepper and sauté for another minute or two. Cool.

▪ Lay the lamb out skin side down and spread the inside with the mushroom mixture. Roll the lamb leg up into a cylindrical shape and tie in three or four places. Sprinkle the outside of the lamb with salt and pepper and whatever herb you used in the stuffing.

▪ Prepare the fire for indirect grilling and put drip pan in place. I don't usually use hardwood smoke for lamb, but if you do, pick a mild wood such as alder, cherry, or mesquite. If you have a rotisserie, thread the lamb on the spit and put it over the drip pan between the two heat sources (see Spit-Roasting, page 20). To cook by indirect heat (see Indirect Heat, page 19), center the roast on the grill between the two heat sources with the drip pan underneath. Keep the temperature of the covered grill in the moderate range, about 350°F. For medium-rare lamb, remove the roast from the grill when the internal temperature reaches 125°F to 130°F or when the meat is red and juicy near the center. Start checking after 30 to 40 minutes; times will vary depending on the thickness of the meat and the heat of the fire.

■ Let the lamb sit for 10 minutes, loosely covered with foil, before serving.

Fresno Shish Kebab

SERVES 4

2 pounds leg or shoulder of lamb, cut into 1½-inch cubes

•

SPICY LAMB RUB

1 teaspoon paprika

1 teaspoon cayenne

1 teaspoon salt

1 teaspoon freshly ground black pepper

•

LAMB MARINADE

2 tablespoons red wine vinegar

2 tablespoons olive oil

2 tablespoons finely chopped garlic

Juice of 2 lemons

1 green bell pepper, finely chopped

1 bunch green onions (10 ounces), finely chopped

1½ bunches fresh mint (10 ounces), finely chopped

1 bunch cilantro (10 ounces), finely chopped

2 very ripe tomatoes, finely chopped, with juice

•

1 red bell pepper, cut into 1-inch pieces

1 green bell pepper, cut into 1-inch pieces

1 large red onion, cut into 1-inch wedges

Salt and freshly ground black pepper

When one thinks of great cooking, the dusty San Joaquin Valley town of Fresno doesn't leap to mind. But up and down California's Central Valley, Armenian fruit growers and farmers and Basque sheep raisers have created a style of grill cookery based on spicy lamb that is truly delicious. You can find the Armenian specialty shish kebab on roadhouse, tavern, and truck stop menus all up and down the Valley, and Basque Sheepherder Lamb Steaks (page 209) appear in Basque hotels and boardinghouse restaurants from Bakersfield to San Francisco. This recipe comes from John Neudecker, a Bay Area resident and accomplished griller who hails from Fresno and still attends Armenian and Basque barbecues and festivals in his hometown whenever he can. Serve with rice pilaf or Greek salad, sourdough French bread, and California Zinfandel.

....

■ Cut away most of the fat from the lamb and puncture the pieces all over with a fork.

To make Spicy Lamb Rub, combine all ingredients.

■ Sprinkle all over the lamb pieces, or coat by shaking a few pieces at a time in a paper bag containing the rub. Let sit for an hour at room temperature.

To make Lamb Marinade, mix all ingredients in a large ziplock bag or nonreactive bowl.

■ Soak the lamb pieces in the marinade in the refrigerator for at least 24 hours, turning the ingredients from time to time.

■ Prepare the fire for direct grilling. Add mesquite or other hardwood to the smoke box (see Smoke on the Grill, page 21). Spray or rub the grill with oil.

■ Remove the lamb from the refrigerator and take it out of the marinade. Reserve the marinade. Skewer pieces of lamb alternately with red and green bell pepper pieces and onion wedges. Brush the skewers with marinade on the grill over medium-high heat, turning frequently, until the lamb is medium-rare (130°F, or reddish pink when cut), about 10 to 12 minutes total. Baste occasionally with the reserved marinade; move the skewers to a cooler spot on the grill if flare-ups occur.

Grilled Lamb or Venison Chops with Rosemary Garlic Paste

Rosemary's intense flavor goes beautifully with lamb or venison. If you have tiny rib chops you can skewer them on rosemary branches before grilling. It's best to use fresh rosemary here, although the dried herb will do.

....

■ Trim the chops of most external fat.

■ Prepare the fire for direct grilling. Spray or rub the grill with oil.

To make Rosemary Garlic Paste, combine the garlic and rosemary, using enough olive oil to blend them well. Stir in the salt and pepper.

■ Spread the paste on both sides of the chops. Grill or broil for 3 or more minutes per side to desired doneness.

SERVES 4

12 rib lamb chops or 8 loin lamb chops or 8 venison chops (about 2 pounds total)

•

ROSEMARY GARLIC PASTE

4 cloves garlic, finely chopped

1 tablespoon chopped fresh rosemary or 1½ teaspoons dried

Olive oil

½ teaspoon salt

¼ teaspoon freshly ground black pepper

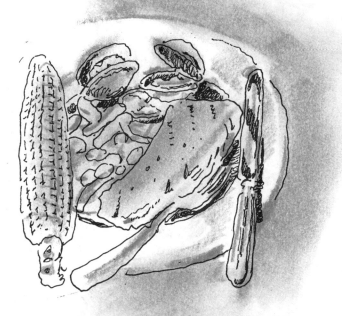

Grilled Lamb Chops with Mint Cilantro Relish

SERVES 4

MINT CILANTRO RELISH

1 white onion, chopped

1 cup chopped fresh mint

1 cup chopped fresh cilantro

2 yellow tomatoes, coarsely chopped

¼ cup extra-virgin olive oil

Juice of 1 lime

1 teaspoon salt

1 teaspoon lemon pepper

½ teaspoon ground allspice

•

12 small lamb rib chops or 8 lamb loin chops (about 2 pounds total)

1 teaspoon Chinese five-spice powder

Salt and freshly ground black pepper

I like to use small lamb rib chops here, but the bigger and tenderer loin chops are also delicious with this tangy relish. Little rib chops make unusual and very tasty appetizers with Bruschetta (page 56), especially if served with a Pinot Noir vin gris or rosé from California's southern coast or with a light Oregon Pinot Noir. Larger chops make a more substantial main course when paired with Grilled Polenta with Smoke-Roasted Tomato Sauce (page 98) and Summer Vegetable Skewers (page 95).

. . . .

To make Mint Cilantro Relish, mix the ingredients in a small bowl.

■ Prepare the fire for direct grilling. Spray or rub the grill with oil.

■ Trim any excess fat from the lamb chops and sprinkle lightly with five-spice powder, salt, and pepper. Grill over medium-high heat, covered, for 3 to 5 minutes per side, turning once or twice, until medium rare (130°F to 135°F, or reddish and juicy when cut). Place the chops on a platter, and put a generous spoonful of Mint Cilantro Relish on each chop. Serve with extra relish on the side.

Basque Sheepherder Lamb Steaks

Basque sheepherders have been the mainstay of western lamb raising for generations. These hardy folk have braved wind, rain, drought, coyotes, and other tribulations of the wild life to get luscious and tender lamb on our tables. Basque hotels and boardinghouses throughout the west serve up some of the best lamb you'll ever eat. Elko, Reno, Fresno, San Francisco, and other western cities have large Basque populations who love food and wine and life. If you ever have a chance to attend a local Basque festival, be sure to show up with plenty of appetite.

Lamb steaks are big chops cut from the sirloin part of the leg. Use these or loin or rib chops here. Tony's Spanish Rice with Smoke-Roasted Tomato Sauce (page 102) and Rajas: Grilled Chile and Pepper Strips (page 101) go well with this aromatic lamb.

••••••••••••••••••

■ Trim any excess fat from the steaks or chops.

To make Basque Marinade, mix the ingredients in a small bowl.

■ Pour the marinade over the lamb in a zip-lock bag or nonreactive bowl. Marinate the steaks or chops for 1 to 2 hours at room temperature or 8 to 12 hours in the refrigerator. Remove the steaks or chops from the marinade and pat dry. Reserve the marinade. Make sure the chops are at room temperature before cooking.

■ Prepare the fire for direct grilling. One section of the grill should be hot, one cooler, and one without any heat beneath it. Hardwood chips are optional; use a mild wood such as alder, cherry, or mesquite. Spray or rub the grill with oil.

■ Sear the chops over high heat for 2 to 3 minutes per side. Move to a cooler side of the grill if flare-ups occur. Move the chops to the cooler portion of the grill, cover, and cook until done, turning occasionally. Start checking after 5 minutes. Medium-rare lamb should be 125°F to 130°F internal temperature when removed from the grill, or red and juicy near the bone. Let the chops sit, covered loosely with foil, for at least 5 minutes before serving.

■ Put the reserved marinade in a skillet and reduce over high heat until it thickens slightly. Pour over steaks or chops and serve.

4 large lamb steaks or 8 to 12 lamb chops, depending on size (about 2 pounds total)

•

BASQUE MARINADE FOR LAMB OR CHICKEN

¼ cup olive oil

1 tablespoon red wine vinegar

8 cloves garlic, chopped

1 onion, chopped

1 red bell pepper or pimiento, chopped

2 plum (roma) or other tomatoes, chopped

1 tablespoon chopped fresh rosemary or 1½ teaspoons dried

1 tablespoon chopped fresh oregano or 1½ teaspoons dried

1 tablespoon paprika

1 teaspoon salt

½ teaspoon freshly ground black pepper

Desserts

My daughter, Meghan, has been a tremendous help with this book. Not only has she done research, tested recipes, and kept everything organized on the computer, but she created most of the recipes in this section. Here are her thoughts on desserts on the grill:

"Think back to a time when you've been camping—singing, talking, laughing around the fire until it was only a glowing mass of coals and everyone headed to their tents for warmth. The campfire is the social and culinary center when you're in the woods.

"The grill is our modern substitute, our mobile campfire. Now, while camping, would you cook your whole meal on the fire—your burgers, corn, and potatoes—and then pull out some store-bought cookies? I don't think so. You would linger by the fire, tell ghost stories and sing songs, and grill marshmallows and make gooey s'mores over the coals (see Sierra S'mores, page 216). Many other delicious desserts can be made over the coals or on the backyard barbecue as well.

"I know what you're thinking: we've lost it here and taken the concept of grilling where it was never meant to go. But while exploring the options of the grill, I found it was really a wonderful place to make quick, no-mess desserts. And like other grill courses, desserts convey the best aspects of the outdoors—fresh flavors, smoky tastes, and the feeling that comes of being outside with people you love.

"Smoky desserts? This sounds like a mistake rather than a goal. But surprisingly, the grill adds complexity to fruit's natural sweetness, and as the sun goes down in the backyard and the temperature begins to drop, the warmed fruit is a pleasant surprise.

"Every area on the West Coast offers its own distinct fruit flavors that work beautifully on the grill. On the beaches of Baja and Southern California, the parties last long into the night; people don't just pack up and head to Ben and Jerry's. Instead, friends and family come in out of the water and begin to form a circle around the fire. The eating starts after sunset, with people clustering near the grill, snacking and talking. After devouring Fish Tacos with Three Salsas (page 51) and Rajas: Grilled Chile and Pepper Strips (page 101), try a Grilled Sweet Summer Wrap (page 222) topped with Raspberry Mint Salsa and grated Mexican chocolate. These warm fruit burritos are so tasty that they'll be a topic of conversation on their own and really keep the party going.

"In the valleys along the coast of Northern California, huge old fig trees flourish. The figs, small sweet treats, are a real surprise on the grill. Figs are very tender, but they do not fall apart on the fire. Brushed with a honey and Pernod sauce, Grilled Figs (page 221) combine many smells and tastes in one bite. The figs inspired me to get creative on the grill: if these fragile morsels worked, what else would?

"How about cobblers and crisps? Smoky flavors mix well with berries, and the cobbler is perfect for grilling them (otherwise, those juicy berries would slip right through the grates). The cobbler dish allows the berry juices and the crust to soak up the smoke. You could make the cobbler with berries you picked that day, while camping in the Northwest. If you don't happen to be exploring bald eagle country and are in your backyard at home, though, don't fret. Fire up the grill and make our Alaskan Campfire Berry Cobbler (page 214). Just put on that dream cap and try to listen for the bears charging toward the camp when they smell the berries baking.

"One of the easiest and most dramatic desserts I found was Grilled Peaches with Amaretto Mascarpone (page 218). Firm peaches seem made for the grill; they caramelize beautifully, and fresh, ripe peaches are incredible when warm (as those of us who love peach pie know well). Right after testing this recipe for the first time, I went out to dinner at a fancy East Bay restaurant where my roommate waits tables, and lo and behold, grilled peaches were being served for dessert. I felt very stylish and trend-setting.

"Grilled fruits were a wonderful surprise for me and helped build my confidence to try new things on the grill. So explore your own sweet ideas and combine different fruits and toppings to match your style. If by chance your creative adventure slips through the grates and into the fire, you can always fall back on the traditional dessert for the campfire: Sierra S'mores (page 216). Every kid I know would just love this mishap and step up to the grill for more and more s'mores."

Meghan's Tips on Grilling Desserts

■ Because most desserts created on the grill feature fruit, I'll start here. Choose slightly unripe, firm fruit. If too ripe, the fruit will be difficult to turn and the juices may cause flare-ups. Also, you can leave firm fruit on the grill longer, producing caramelized score marks and a smoky flavor. Overly ripe fruit may fall apart and slip through the grates or become too mushy to turn.

■ Before grilling desserts, clean the grill thoroughly. Desserts have unique flavors that do not mix well with leftover garlic or fish stuck to the grill.

■ After scraping the grill completely, spray well with oil to prevent sticking. Fruits are delicate and may fall apart if you have to pry them off the grill.

■ For desserts grilled directly on the grates (not in foil or in a pan), use a very hot grill that will score the fruit and caramelize the natural sugars.

■ Watch desserts carefully, and make sure you test them. Fruits should be warmed through, scored and tender but still intact. If they need more time, return them to the grill and cook some more.

■ Grilled desserts are dramatic and beautiful. When serving, show off the score marks and the burned edges in your presentation.

■ Be creative! For me, these sweet treats were an exciting discovery. Try different fruit, use different flavorings or toppings, and have fun.

Alaskan Campfire Berry Cobbler

SERVES 4

¾ cup plus 3 tablespoons packed brown sugar

1 tablespoon cornstarch

5 cups mixed berries (strawberries, blackberries, blueberries, raspberries)

2 cups flour

1 teaspoon baking powder

½ teaspoon salt

4 tablespoons cold unsalted butter, plus 2 tablespoons to melt

½ cup milk

½ teaspoon vanilla

Vanilla ice cream (optional)

Up in Alaska, you can pick all the berries you want in late summer, but you've got to keep an eye out for other, furry berry lovers. Bears love berries, too, so I'd just as soon go to the local farmers' market for my fruit. In fact, the whole Northwest is berry country, and in season, you can get a huge variety of juicy, sweet berries at markets and roadside stands.

We cook this cobbler on the grill, but its ancestor was campfire cobbler or berry crisp topped with biscuit dough and baked in a Dutch oven set into the coals. If you're really going for the camping feeling, you can use Bisquick and leave in a few lumps.

• • • • • • • • • • • • • • • • • •

■ Prepare the fire for indirect grilling.

■ Combine ¾ cup of the brown sugar and the cornstarch. If using strawberries, slice them. Add all the berries to the brown sugar mixture. Pour into an 8-by-10-inch baking pan (a disposable aluminum foil pan works fine here; you can also divide the cobbler into two 5-by-8-inch aluminum pans that Weber sells for catching grease from its gas grills).

■ Mix the flour, baking powder, and the salt in a large bowl. Add 2 tablespoons of the brown sugar and the 4 tablespoons of cold butter, cut into cubes, to the dry mix. Mix with a pastry knife, fork, or fingers until crumbly and the butter is in small pieces. Add milk and vanilla and mix with your hands until the dough will hold together as a ball. If too sticky, add a bit more flour. Do not overmix; once you have a cohesive ball, stop mixing. You can either roll the dough to fit the top of the pan you're using or stretch it with your hands. It does not have to be a perfect fit and does not have to touch the edges.

■ Melt the remaining 2 tablespoons of the butter and combine with the remaining tablespoon of brown sugar. Brush the top of the cobbler with this mixture.

■ Place on an indirect hot grill (about 400°F), cover, and cook for 30 to 45 minutes. When done, the top should be browned, the dough cooked, and the berries bubbling. Serve warm with vanilla ice cream.

Yakima Valley Bounty

When you drive through the Cascades east of Seattle, you cross from one distinct climatic zone to another. The western slopes rise quickly above Puget Sound, and clouds off the Pacific dump their accumulated water, providing the rain and lush vegetation that the Seattle region is known for. Once you cross the summit and begin to travel down the eastern side of the mountains, the landscape changes dramatically. The dense green forest gives way to a brown, dry vista of sagebrush and scrub trees, the sparse vegetation of high desert country.

The Yakima Valley east of the Cascades is a part of this desertlike environment that was transformed by irrigation in the early years of the century into one of the richest farming regions in the country. The fertile volcanic soil and warm sunlight of the valley produce a great variety of wonderful fruits, vegetables, hops, and grapes. Driving to Yakima to buy fresh produce is a tradition with Seattle home cooks. While you can find a good selection of whatever's ripe in the valley at Pike Place Market and other farmers' markets, there is nothing like making a family excursion into the sunny valley for a picnic, some wine tasting, and the chance to buy the freshest and ripest fruits and vegetables at bargain prices from roadside stands.

The Yakima Valley is apple country, and during the late summer harvest you can see virtually every variety of apple, modern or heirloom, heaped up on counters and in bins at farmers' markets and local fruit stands. Along with sweet and juicy Red and Golden Delicious, you'll also see old-fashioned Gravensteins, green and streaked with red, alongside traditional favorites such as Northern Spy, pippins, and Jonathans. You can also find new varieties bred in New Zealand, Washington state, and Japan, such as the tart and tasty Granny Smith, Jonagolds (a cross between Jonathan and Golden Delicious), Galas, and Fujis. These crisp and luscious varieties are perfect for grilling, as in our Grilled Apple and Goat Cheese Salad with Walnut Oil Vinaigrette (page 79). Many valley stands sell freshly squeezed cider, which can be frozen for later use or fermented naturally into delicious hard cider.

Pears are another fruit that brings families into the valley at harvest time. Bartletts, red and green, are abundant, but you can also find firm-fleshed winter pears such as Bosc, Anjou, Comice, and Seckel at local stands. The firmer pears grill well and can be used in our recipes for Grilled Fruit Pizza (page 220) or Pear Ginger Crisp with Ginger Cream (page 219). Crunchy Asian pears, also Yakima Valley specialties, are found at stands and markets in great numbers and variety in late summer and early fall.

Among the most dramatic sights in the Yakima Valley are the hop plants that are trained to grow up to 18 feet high on trellises at harvest time. The pungent yellow flowers are used to flavor much of America's beer, and the perfume of ripe hops fills the air on hot days in early fall. The valley is the country's premium supplier of this bitter herb, and local beer and ales emphasize hop flavors and aromas. Bert Grant founded his Yakima Valley Brewing Company in 1982 and quickly established Grant's Scottish Ale, India Pale Ale, and Russian Imperial Stout as some of the finest ales in the region. The hoppy, full-bodied Northwest style is also found at Seattle's Redhook Brewery, which produces rich, tangy ales using Yakima Valley hops.

The Yakima Valley is Washington state's most important grape-growing area, and wines from the valley, especially Cabernet Sauvignon, Merlot, Sauvignon Blanc, and Semillon, have done much to establish the state's reputation as a premium wine producer. Many think that because of Washington's northern latitude, the state would concentrate on grape varieties such as Pinot Noir that do well in cool weather. While Oregon's Willamette Valley, west of the Cascades, specializes in this cool-weather variety, the Yakima Valley's location in the eastern rain shadow of the mountain range means that grapes that do better in warmer climates thrive here. Yakima Valley Merlot, a fruity and lightly tannic red grape that originated in France's Bordeaux region, is especially prized by local wine-lovers. It is an excellent accompaniment to the valley's delicious lamb raised around the town of Ellensburg and often found on Seattle restaurant menus and in local markets.

Sierra S'mores

SERVES 4

8 marshmallows

8 graham crackers

2 semisweet chocolate bars (8 ounces each)

California's Sierra Nevada mountains are full of great hiking trails and campsites. You hike through Sequoia groves, discover new streams and vistas, pause to view deer in a meadow, and finally end your day around the campfire. S'mores are the ultimate kids' comfort food, the end to a long day's trek. You don't really need a recipe here; you know the ingredients—roasted marshmallows, graham crackers, and chocolate bars. Children have fun making them, and everybody has a great time with mushy marshmallows all over their fingers. Roast marshmallows on the grill, over a campfire, or in the fireplace in the city. Make the yummy sandwiches and then wrap them in foil and put them on the grill to melt the chocolate and heat all the ingredients.

■ Prepare the fire for direct grilling. Spray or rub the grill with oil.

■ Skewer marshmallows, two per skewer. Lay them directly on the grill. Turn often, so all areas get a bit browned. If they begin to stick, move to a cooler part of the grill. Grill for 2 to 5 minutes, depending on the heat of the grill.

■ Cut four 1-foot-long pieces of aluminum foil. Layer one graham cracker, half a chocolate bar, two roasted marshmallow, and another graham cracker. Wrap tin foil and seal. Return to the grill for 2 minutes, covered. Turn and grill for another 2 minutes. Remove. Unwrap, and serve hot.

Grilled Banana Split

This tasty dessert adds a new, warm twist to the traditional ice cream treat. Depending on your mood or the type of ice cream you're craving, you can vary the mixture that coats the bananas. Try adding 1 tablespoon of rum to the sugar-butter mixture and topping with Coconut Rum Ice Cream (page 223). Or, if you're serving a fruit sorbet, try rolling the bananas in ¼ cup granulated sugar, 3 tablespoons melted butter, and 1 tablespoon lime juice before grilling.

....

■ Prepare the fire for direct grilling. Clean the grill very well and spray or rub with oil.

■ Combine the brown sugar and 3 tablespoons butter. Carefully toss bananas in the mixture. Grill cut side down for 2 to 3 minutes. When lightly browned, carefully turn the bananas and grill for another 3 minutes.

To make Chocolate Sauce, combine the chocolate, milk, and butter in a saucepan. Warm over medium heat, stirring constantly, until thickened. Remove from the heat.

To make Whipped Cream, whip the cream with an electric mixer, gradually adding the sugar. Beat until soft peaks form.

■ Serve the bananas warm, two halves per dish, topped with ice cream, whipped cream, chocolate sauce, and any other garnishes.

SERVES 4

¼ cup packed brown sugar

3 tablespoons unsalted butter, melted

4 slightly unripe bananas, peeled and split lengthwise

•

CHOCOLATE SAUCE

4 ounces semisweet chocolate

2 tablespoons whole milk

1 tablespoon unsalted butter

•

WHIPPED CREAM

1 half pint heavy cream

1 tablespoon sugar

•

Ice cream

•

GARNISH

Cherries

Chopped nuts

SERVES 4

AMARETTO MASCARPONE

½ cup mascarpone cheese

2 tablespoons packed brown sugar

2 teaspoons amaretto

•

4 peaches, peeled, halved, and pitted

½ cup brown sugar

•

GARNISH

4 amaretti Italian cookies, crushed

½ basket raspberries

Grilled Peaches with Amaretto Mascarpone

Nothing beats fresh peaches at the height of the season, and the Northwest provides every variety you can think of at farmers markets and roadside stands. Serve Grilled Peaches for dessert with a cool, fruity Gewürztraminer from Washington's Yakima Valley or from the Anderson Valley of Northern California.

. . . .

To make Amaretto Mascarpone, mix the mascarpone, brown sugar, and amaretto.

■ Prepare fire for direct grilling. Clean the grill very well and spray or rub with oil.

■ Dip the cut side of the peaches into ½ cup brown sugar. Grill cut side down for 2 minutes, covered. Flip and grill for another 3 to 4 minutes. Remove from the heat. Top each peach with a dollop of mascarpone mixture in the hole where the pit was. Sprinkle with crushed cookies and garnish with raspberries.

Pear Ginger Crisp with Ginger Cream

SERVES 4

One of my favorite combinations is pears and ginger. For a simpler version of this dish, just grill halved pears for 2 minutes on each side on a medium-hot grill and top with the delicious cream. Clear Creek Distillery in Oregon makes delicious eaux de vie, clear and aromatic brandies, from local fruits and berries. Use their pear eau de vie or another fruit brandy in this dessert.

. . . .

To make Ginger Cream, combine cornstarch, sugar, and milk in a medium saucepan. Heat over medium heat, until the milk is warm. Remove from the heat, add eggs and vanilla, and whisk. Return to medium-low heat, stirring constantly until the cream thickens, about 4 minutes. Remove from the heat and add the ginger. Stir thoroughly. Cool the mixture in the refrigerator until it sets, about 2 hours.

■ Prepare the fire for indirect grilling.

To make Ginger Crisp Topping, mix the flour, brown sugar, and ground ginger. Cut the butter into cubes and add to the flour mixture, mixing until crumbly in texture.

■ Place pear slices in a 8-by-10-inch baking dish or two 5-by-8-inch pans. You can use the disposable aluminum pans normally used for catching drippings, if you wish. Toss in the pear eau de vie and ginger and spread evenly. Crumble Ginger Crisp Topping over the top. Bake on the unheated part of a covered grill for 20 to 30 minutes at 350°F. Rotate occasionally to ensure even baking. When done, the pears should be tender and the top brown.

■ Serve warm with scoop of Ginger Cream.

GINGER CREAM

2 tablespoons cornstarch

¼ cup sugar

3 cups milk

2 eggs, lightly beaten

1 teaspoon vanilla

3 tablespoons grated fresh ginger

•

GINGER CRISP TOPPING

1 cup all-purpose flour

¾ cup packed brown sugar

1 teaspoon ground ginger

⅓ cup unsalted butter

•

4 cups sliced pears (about 5 pears)

1 tablespoon pear eau de vie or other fruit brandy (optional)

2 tablespoons grated fresh ginger

SERVES 6

1 recipe Pizza on the Grill (page 60) or 2 ten-inch precooked pizza crusts

2 tablespoons unsalted butter, melted

1 cup strawberries, stems removed and halved

1 cup blueberries

2 kiwi fruits, sliced

2 peaches, sliced

⅓ cup firmly packed light brown sugar

1 pint heavy cream

2 tablespoons amaretto

Grilled Fruit Pizza

You can make one big tart or smaller individual ones. Grilling time will vary; bake pizza crust until it is firm to the touch and golden brown on the bottom. If you prefer, you can purchase a precooked pizza round, heat through, and add toppings. You can use any summer fruit in this tart; just be careful that it is not too juicy or the pizza will be soggy. After removing the pizza from the grill, top with flavored whipped cream, or try Ginger Cream (page 219), Coconut Rum Ice Cream (page 223), Amaretto Mascarpone (page 218), or your favorite ice cream.

• • • • • • • • • • • • • • • • • •

■ Follow the instructions for Pizza on the Grill, with the following exceptions: when you have formed your pizza circles and crimped the sides to form edges, brush each side with butter instead of olive oil, and do not use the cornmeal.

■ Toss the fruits with brown sugar and let sit.

■ Prepare the fire for indirect grilling. Spray or rub the grill with oil.

■ Grill each side of the dough on high heat for 5 minutes or until it is firm to the touch and browned. Move to the unheated area of the grill to cook through for another 5 to 10 minutes. Or grill precooked pizza crusts over high heat for 1 to 2 minutes per side.

■ Pile the sliced fruit onto the crust. Cover and grill on the cooler part of the grill for another 4 minutes. Remove and slice.

■ Whip the cream with an electric mixer, gradually adding amaretto. Whip until soft peaks form. Dollop cream on each slice of warm pizza.

Grilled Figs with Honey Pernod Sauce

SERVES 4

4 tablespoons honey

3 tablespoons Pernod or anise liqueur

12 figs, sliced lengthwise

½ pint heavy cream

Figs are a wonderful, often overlooked fruit. They work surprisingly well on the grill. They need to be slightly firm; if too ripe and mushy, they'll fall apart on the grill. This unusual dessert is a real treat when served with a fruit brandy from Oregon or California.

....

■ Combine the honey and Pernod. Marinate the figs for up to 2 hours at room temperature.

■ Prepare the fire for direct grilling. Clean the grill very well and spray or rub with oil.

■ Remove the figs from the marinade and pat dry. Reserve the marinade. Grill the figs over medium heat for 3 minutes each side, starting with the cut side. They should caramelize and brown nicely. Remove the figs to a platter, cut side up, and spoon on a bit of the reserved marinade.

■ Whip the cream with an electric mixer; add a bit of marinade to taste for sweetness. Whip to soft peaks. Spoon the whipped cream around the figs and dribble on the remaining marinade.

Grilled Sweet Summer Wrap with Raspberry Mint Salsa

SERVES 4

½ cup packed brown sugar

2 teaspoons cornstarch

4 cups sliced bananas and peaches or other summer fruit

1 teaspoon lime juice

•

RASPBERRY MINT SALSA

½ pint raspberries

1 tablespoon sugar

1 tablespoon chopped mint leaves

1 teaspoon lime juice

•

4 flour tortillas

4 ounces chopped Mexican chocolate or semisweet chocolate chips

1 pint heavy cream

Sugar

•

GARNISH

Grated Mexican chocolate or semisweet chocolate chips

These fruity treats are quick and easy to make. Thick 10-inch flour tortillas work best. I use the Mexican hard chocolate that contains cinnamon and sugar, but you could also use chocolate chips. You can vary this dish by trying different fruit combinations. Try a berry, kiwi, and nectarine combo with rum and brown sugar in the whipped cream. Or try apples and cinnamon in the tortilla. Or how about strawberries, bananas, and Nutella (hazelnut-chocolate spread) for a crêpelike treat?

● ● ● ● ● ● ● ● ● ● ● ● ● ● ● ● ● ●

■ Prepare fire for direct grilling.

■ Mix together the brown sugar and cornstarch in a large bowl. Add sliced fruit and 1 teaspoon lime juice. Mix thoroughly. This mixture can sit for up to 2 hours.

To make Raspberry Mint Salsa, combine in a separate bowl raspberries, sugar, chopped mint, and lime juice. Let sit until needed.

■ Spread four 18-inch pieces of heavy-duty aluminum foil on a work surface. Spray one side of each with vegetable oil. Put a tortilla in the center of each. Put one-quarter of the chocolate into the center of each tortilla. Using a slotted spoon, put one-quarter of the fruit mixture down the center of each tortilla. Don't add juice from the fruit or your wrap will be soggy. Save the juices to add to the whipped cream.

■ Fold the tortilla like a burrito: fold the sides in over the middle, and then fold the top and bottom under to make a neat bundle. Wrap the foil around the tortilla and seal tightly.

■ Place each bundle directly on a hot grill (about 400°F). The cooking time will vary based on the heat of your grill. Grill for about 5 minutes, covered, then turn the bundles over. Grill for another 5 to 8 minutes. Check to see if the tortilla is lightly browned and crisp and the fruit is warm. If not done, wrap it up and put it back on.

■ Whip the cream to soft peaks. Whip in the leftover juices from the fruit mixture and add sugar to taste. Unwrap and serve the wraps warm with a dollop of whipped cream and a spoonful of Raspberry Mint Salsa. Sprinkle with chocolate. Serve immediately.

Grilled Pineapple with Coconut Rum Ice Cream

SERVES 4

If you want a Hawaiian dessert, you don't have to look much further than the natural flavors of delicious tropical fruit. Grilling pineapple adds a smoky taste that is perfectly complemented by coconut ice cream. This ice cream recipe is easy to make and low in fat. With this dessert, you'll be dreaming of white sands, warm breezes, and piña coladas.

· · · · · · · · · · · · · · · · · ·

To make Coconut Rum Ice Cream, combine in a stainless steel bowl the coconut, milk, cream, and sugar. Mix to dissolve the sugar. In a separate bowl, beat the egg white until stiff, and fold it into the cream mixture. Fold in the rum if desired. Freeze in the metal bowl (it conducts the cold better). If using a food processor, freeze the cream until solid, 2 to 3 hours. Scrape it into a food processor and blend until smooth. Refreeze for about 15 minutes and serve. If using a whisk, whisk the frozen cream every hour to fill it with air and make it smooth.

■ Prepare the fire for hot direct grilling. Spray or rub the grill with oil.

■ Dip the pineapple slices in brown sugar. Grill each side for 4 to 5 minutes or until the sugar caramelizes.

■ Serve the pineapple warm with a scoop of ice cream and sprinkled with macadamia nuts.

COCONUT RUM ICE CREAM

½ cup unsweetened shredded coconut

½ cup milk

¼ cup heavy cream

2 tablespoons sugar

1 egg white

1 tablespoon rum (optional)

•

4 slices pineapple

½ cup packed brown sugar

2 tablespoons macadamia nuts, chopped

Sources

GRILLS AND ACCESSORIES

Char-Broil
PO Box 1240
Columbus, GA 31902
(800) 241-7548

Williams-Sonoma
3250 Van Ness Avenue
San Francisco, CA 94109
(800) 541-2233

CHARCOALS, HARDWOODS, AND CHIPS

Barbecue Wood Flavors Co.
Route 1, Box 51 A
Ennis, TX 75119
(972) 875-8391

Kingsford Charcoal
www.kingsford.com
(800) 232-4745

Nature's Own/People's Woods
55 Mill Street
Cumberland, RI 02864
(800) 729-5800

W.W. Wood, Inc.
PO Box 244
Pleasanton, TX 78064
(830) 569-2501

SPECIALTY FOODS: HERBS, SPICES, SAUCES

Dean & Deluca
Catalog Department
560 Broadway
New York, NY 10012
(800) 221-7714

Foodalicious
2055 NE 151st Street
North Miami, FL 33162
(305) 945-0502

Frieda's, Inc.
4465 Corporate Center Drive
Los Alamitos, CA 90720
(800) 241-1771
(714) 826-6100

G.B. Ratto, International Grocers
821 Washington Street
Oakland, CA 94607
(800) 325-3483
In California: (800) 228-3515

Zingermans
422 Detroit Street
Ann Arbor, MI 48104
(313) 663-3354
(888) 636-8162

ASIAN INGREDIENTS

Kim Man Food
200 Canal Street
New York, NY 10013
(212) 571-0330

Oriental Pantry
423 Great Road
Acton, MA 01720
(800) 828-0368

Tokyo Fish Market
122 San Pablo Avenue
Berkeley, CA 94706
(510) 524-7243

Uwajimaya Market
6th Avenue and South King Street
Seattle, WA 98104
(206) 624-6248

MEXICAN/SOUTHWEST INGREDIENTS

Carmen's of New Mexico
PO Box 7310
Albuquerque, NM 87194
(800) 851-4852

The Chile Shop
109 East Water Street
Santa Fe, NM 87501
(505) 983-6080

The Kitchen Food Shop
218 Eighth Avenue
New York, NY 10011
(212) 243-4433
Mail order: (888) 468-4433

Texas Spice Company
PO Box 3769
Austin, TX 78764
(800) 880-8007
(512) 444-2223

BRINES AND CURES

Sikes Enterprises
Scott's Brine Mixes
PO Box 1208
Klamath Falls, OR 97601
(503) 882-3336

Index